Applications and Developments in Semantic Process Mining

Kingsley Okoye
University of East London, UK

A volume in the Advances in Data
Mining and Database Management
(ADMDM) Book Series

Published in the United States of America by
    IGI Global
    Engineering Science Reference (an imprint of IGI Global)
    701 E. Chocolate Avenue
    Hershey PA, USA 17033
    Tel: 717-533-8845
    Fax: 717-533-8661
    E-mail: cust@igi-global.com
    Web site: http://www.igi-global.com

Library of Congress Cataloging-in-Publication Data

Names: Okoye, Kingsley, 1983- author.
Title: Applications and developments in semantic process mining / by
  Kingsley Okoye.
Description: Hershey, PA : Engineering Science Reference, an imprint of IGI
  Global, [2020] | Includes bibliographical references and index. |
  Summary: "This book explores the need for the effective management of
  data across different process domains and the need for the enhancement
  of process mining results and analysis"-- Provided by publisher.
Identifiers: LCCN 2019042217 (print) | LCCN 2019042218 (ebook) | ISBN
  9781799826682 (hardcover) | ISBN 9781799826699 (paperback) | ISBN
  9781799826705 (ebook)
Subjects: LCSH: Process mining.
Classification: LCC T57.67 .O46 2020 (print) | LCC T57.67 (ebook) | DDC
  622.0285/6332--dc23
LC record available at https://lccn.loc.gov/2019042217
LC ebook record available at https://lccn.loc.gov/2019042218

This book is published in the IGI Global book series Advances in Data Mining and Database Management (ADMDM) (ISSN: 2327-1981; eISSN: 2327-199X)

British Cataloguing in Publication Data
A Cataloguing in Publication record for this book is available from the British Library.

All work contributed to this book is new, previously-unpublished material.
The views expressed in this book are those of the authors, but not necessarily of the publisher.

For electronic access to this publication, please contact: eresources@igi-global.com.

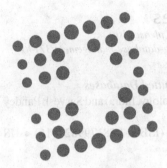

Advances in Data Mining and Database Management (ADMDM) Book Series

ISSN:2327-1981
EISSN:2327-199X

Editor-in-Chief: *David Taniar* Monash University, Australia

MISSION

With the large amounts of information available to organizations in today's digital world, there is a need for continual research surrounding emerging methods and tools for collecting, analyzing, and storing data.

The **Advances in Data Mining & Database Management (ADMDM)** series aims to bring together research in information retrieval, data analysis, data warehousing, and related areas in order to become an ideal resource for those working and studying in these fields. IT professionals, software engineers, academicians and upper-level students will find titles within the ADMDM book series particularly useful for staying up-to-date on emerging research, theories, and applications in the fields of data mining and database management.

COVERAGE

- Web-based information systems
- Association Rule Learning
- Predictive Analysis
- Data Analysis
- Text Mining
- Cluster Analysis
- Educational Data Mining
- Profiling Practices
- Data Warehousing
- Enterprise Systems

IGI Global is currently accepting manuscripts for publication within this series. To submit a proposal for a volume in this series, please contact our Acquisition Editors at Acquisitions@igi-global.com or visit: http://www.igi-global.com/publish/.

Titles in this Series

For a list of additional titles in this series, please visit:
http://www.igi-global.com/book-series/advances-data-mining-database-management/37146

Handling Priority Inversion in Time-Constrained Distributed Databases
Udai Shanker (Madan Mohan Malaviya University of Technology, India) and Sarvesh Pandey (Madan Mohan Malaviya University of Technology, ndia)
Engineering Science Reference • © 2020 • 338pp • H/C (ISBN: 9781799824916) • US $225.00

Feature Extraction and Classification Techniques for Text Recognition
Munish Kumar (Maharaja Ranjit Singh Punjab Technical University, India) Manish Kumar Jindal (Panjab University Regional Centre, Muktsar, India) Simpel Rani Jindal (Yadavindera College of Engineering, India) R. K. Sharma (Thapar Institute of Engineering & Technology, India) and Anupam Garg (Bhai Gurdas Institute of Engineering and Technology, India)
Engineering Science Reference • © 2020 • 300pp • H/C (ISBN: 9781799824060) • US $225.00

Neutrosophic Graph Theory and Algorithms
Florentin Smarandache (University of New Mexico, USA) and Said Broumi (Faculty of Science Ben M'Sik, University Hassan II, Morocco)
Engineering Science Reference • © 2020 • 406pp • H/C (ISBN: 9781799813132) • US $245.00

Handbook of Research on Big Data Clustering and Machine Learning
Fausto Pedro Garcia Marquez (Universidad Castilla-La Mancha, Spain)
Engineering Science Reference • © 2020 • 478pp • H/C (ISBN: 9781799801061) • US $285.00

Big Data Analytics for Sustainable Computing
Anandakumar Haldorai (Sri Eshwar College of Engineering, India) and Arulmurugan Ramu (Presidency University, India)
Engineering Science Reference • © 2020 • 263pp • H/C (ISBN: 9781522597506) • US $245.00

For an entire list of titles in this series, please visit:
http://www.igi-global.com/book-series/advances-data-mining-database-management/37146

701 East Chocolate Avenue, Hershey, PA 17033, USA
Tel: 717-533-8845 x100 • Fax: 717-533-8661
E-Mail: cust@igi-global.com • www.igi-global.com

Table of Contents

Preface

Today, most of the existing business models and information technologies have become smarter and tend to not only produce data about the different activities that underlie the said processes or models but has also become increasingly important for the process scientists/analysts to take advantage of more powerful machines or techniques in managing the resultant models. Theoretically, the speedy shift from the big data notion to big (data) analysis and processing targeted at providing a value-added understanding or perspective of the different organizational processes; means that it has become ever more indispensable to develop and apply intelligent (automated) methods for the recorded data analysis and further steps of discovery of worthwhile models. For example, *data science* discipline which encompasses the *process mining* techniques and the many other overlapping terms (not to mention but a few; semantic web (SW), data analytics and business process modelling, machine learning, natural language processing (NLP), artificial intelligence (AI), semantic annotation and reasoning, etc.) all have one common goal or features. The characteristic goal is that existing methods that supports the different fields are all focused on how to make use of the new (information) technologies to provide solutions which are capable not just for representing the information (data) in formats that can be easily understood by humans or computer, but also for building applications (systems) that tend to inclusively process the information that they contain or support.

THE MOTIVATION AND MAIN CHALLENGE

There are a number of factors that spans the motivation of this book that includes the need for development and application of computerized (automated) intelligent methods for data and/or process analysis both in theory and in practice.

On the one hand, modern tools for collection of data and analysis of the existing processes in all fields of Science and Technology (e.g. business process management) are providing more and more data with increasing complexity in their structure. Those growing complexities are evidenced by the need for a richer and more precise description of automated (intelligent) methods and/or applications that allows for flexible exploration of the different events (data) type and derived models (such as the semantic-based method introduced in this book, see Chapters 3 and 4).

On the other hand, the challenge has been on how to create (machine-understandable) systems capable of providing platforms for the recorded events (data) exploration by deriving understandable patterns or information as well as making the discovered patterns explicable in reality.

According to report by National Academies of Sciences, Engineering, and Medicine (2017); emerging methods (opportunities) for digitalization and automation of tasks and/or business processes are far from exhausted. Besides, information technologies have already transformed society, and more changes are inevitable. Interestingly, those transformation has been experienced in different areas of computing and business process management fields; ranging from digitalization of business operations to improved processing speed and capabilities of the IT tools, access to the world wide web or everyday application of internet of things (IoT). Moreover, the new and existing IT tools have been steadily used to augment the traditional methods for education, research, and training purposes leading to the emergence of modern learning analytical platforms that are used to support (educational) process innovations (National Academies of Sciences, Engineering, and Medicine, 2017). Although, a massive chunk of those progress is made possible, thanks to advances in artificial intelligence (AI) to the field of augmented intelligence (AI's) and the overlapping areas of Data Science, or yet, the later Process Science. No doubt, computers and humans are becoming aware of the different operations, activities and/or events that make up the underlying information systems and/or processes.

Indeed, such process-related methods or technologies, often allied to *process mining*, means that there is not only the need for techniques that are capable of extracting valuable information from the events logs (which makes up the various processes) but also requirement for novel methods that can be used to analyse and provide abstract (conceptual) knowledge about the processes in question. In other words, the process mining has become a very useful technique for the pattern recognition (workflows) and information exploration (analysis) that is successfully applied for classical mining of any given real-time process (whereby each process execution is recorded in terms of the events log sequences, and as a result, useful information about how activities depend on each other in a process domain has been made possible). Besides, the process mining technique has proven to be essential for extracting models capable of creating new knowledge.

However, a common challenge with most of the existing process mining techniques is that they depend on tags (labels) in event logs information about the processes to produce the models (process mappings) and therefore to a certain extent are limited, because they lack the abstraction level required from real-world perspectives. In short, a majority of the process mining techniques in literature are purely syntactic in nature, and to this effect, appears to be vague or limited when confronted with unstructured data. This means that the existing techniques do not technically gain from the real-world knowledge (semantics) that describe the tags or labels in event logs of the domain processes.

Therefore, the main challenge and motivation of this book which are summarised as follows:

- the need for effective management of data across the different process domains, and
- the need for enhancement of the process mining results and analysis from the syntactic to a more abstraction level.

THE SEARCH FOR A SOLUTION

Given the aforementioned challenges, this book shows that analysis provided by current process mining techniques can be improved by adding semantic information (see: Chapter 2) to the event logs and resultant models about the different domain processes.

Most organization's processes are complex because the amount of data available today has outgrown human expectations and the processing capabilities of the existing IT tools or methods. Although, the good news as represented in this book is that there is a solution. If we can understand those increasing data and models with an advanced level of Intelligence, then we will start to realize the power of the *semantic-based process mining* method and its associated technologies described in this book.

Accordingly, in order to provide solutions to the noted challenges especially as it concerns the process mining techniques, this book introduces a method that integrates the process mining with semantic technologies (otherwise referred to as *semantic data engineering*). The semantic-based approach is introduced as a means towards discovering and enhancement of the set of recurrent behaviors (patterns) that can be found within any given process domain for improved analysis and/or understanding of the different elements that make up the process. In essence, to tackle the identified challenges - this book looks at the current tools, applications, and methods that are suitable for the development of the semantic process mining technique. Consequently, the series of experiments (Chapter 6), algorithms (Chapter 4), proposed methodology (Chapter 3), and results of the analysis (Chapters 7 and 8) in this book, are carried out in order to solve some of the didactic issues and to answer some common questions with regards to how to effectively apply the process mining technique (e.g. process models discovery, pattern recognition, conformance checking, model enhancement, and reasoning aptitudes) to resolve real-time problems.

In theory, the semantic-based process mining method of this book is put forward to help address the problem of determining the presence of different patterns or traces that can be found within the discovered process models, as well as, provide an understanding of how the different process instances are related or rely on each other within the process execution environment. Moreover, one of the main standpoints of this book is based on the probe:

"to what extent can references to the semantic information and effective raising of the process models and analysis from the syntactic to conceptual level enable real-time insights or understanding about the process domains in view".

Clearly, the aforementioned viewpoint is intended to help provide a solution to the problem of analyzing the different set(s) of data captured about the existing (business) processes, perhaps, based on concepts rather than just the events tags or labels about the processes in question.

In fact, the semantic perspectives are captured by structuring the different components (chapters) in this book; by taking into account two main types of analysis:

- How to make use of the semantics that describes the readily available datasets? and
- How to mine the semantic information from the resultant models?

For all intents and purposes, this book focuses on ascertaining through the series of experiments and case studies; how the results of the process mining techniques and proposed algorithms can be improved through semantic representation of the deployed models. In consequence, this book focuses on how the semantic technologies (e.g. ontologies) with effective (semantic) reasoning can be used to lift process mining analysis from the syntactic to a more conceptual level. Technically, as one of the main contributions of this book, the proposed semantic-based process mining and analysis framework (SPMaAF) takes advantage of the rich semantics described in events logs about the different processes by linking them to concepts in an well-defined ontology in order to allow for extraction of useful patterns (or information) by means of the semantic reasoning aptitudes. Besides, the semantic reasoning aptitude is supported due to formal definition of ontological concepts and assertion of the different relationships that exist between the process instances (entities) that make up the said processes. Practically, we say that this book presents a framework that uses information (semantics) about the different sets of activities (in any given process domain) to generate rules (or metadata description relating to the different tasks) to automatically discover and enhance the resultant process models. This is done through a combination of the main building blocks, i.e, *semantic annotation*, *representation,* and *reasoning* about the different elements that can be found within the knowledge-base. Thus, in summary, this book proves and ends with the supposition that "a system which is formally encoded with semantic labelling (annotation), semantic representation (ontology) and semantic reasoning (reasoner) has the capacity to lift the process mining results and analysis from the syntactic level to a more conceptual level".

To the best of my knowledge and existing works of literature, this is the first book that entirely focuses on the semantic process mining and its enabling technologies. Although, a number of researchers and authors have written articles, conferences and workshops papers related to the topic. Likewise, other books in exception of the wider area covered by this book only look at the current trends in big data analysis with little attention being paid to the semantic information or metadata details that are hidden within the underlying datasets and/or information systems at large. Therefore, the main advantage of this book (Applications and Developments in Semantic Process Mining) in comparison to other existing books in the current literature is the *semantic aspects it considers for its analysis, proposed algorithms, methods,* and *general discussion.* Moreover, this book takes into account the different stages of process mining (or yet, big data analysis and its application in real-time) from the initial phase of collecting and transformation of the captured event data logs to discovering of worthwhile process models, and then expounds the classical process mining techniques to semantical preparation of the extracted models for further analysis and querying at a more abstraction level. In addition, although other related books include the recent technologies such as advances in areas of big data, they have not looked in-depth at the motivation and rapid shift from the *big data* to *big analysis* paradigm. Henceforth, this book (including the different chapters or contents) tend to be a more robust and valuable intellectual property, industry, and academic (resource) material due to the fact that not only does it present state of the art method for (big) data analysis, but also it takes into account the semantics perspectives (or information) about the readily available event logs and derived process models. Thus, this book supports *big (data) analysis* using formal (core) *methods for information analysis (semantics)*. Theoretically, this book is self-contained whilst covering the entire spectrum and idea of combining the process mining techniques with semantic technologies.

The intended audience and readership of this book is quite broad and encompassing. The book provides a wide range of ideas (application and development of semantic process mining) that is expected to be beneficial and used by Information Technology (IT) researchers and practice community (workforce); ranging from IT experts and professionals to Software developers and Data scientist/engineers, including Business owners and Entrepreneurs, Process analysts and Data architects, etc. Indeed, the aim of this book is to provide the readers with an in-depth understanding of their different everyday processes particularly as it concerns the need for effective (state-of-the-art) methods that can be used to adequately carry out big (data) analysis, or better still, process mining tasks. Thus, one of the main reasons the author refers to the method and outcome of this book as semantic data engineering in general. For the educational higher institutions and scientific community, this book is considered useful for teaching/learning especially for conducting research and other academic purposes it may serve. In fact, this book will inform and guide the work of the students, academics, and the research community in general about the latest development, theories, and technical application of the semantic process mining technique.

In summary, the Semantic-based Process Mining and Analysis Framework (SPMaAF), sets of semantically motivated Algorithms, and the resultant methods and application (Semantic Fuzzy Mining) that is presented in this book can be applied by:

- The Process Owners in understanding the basic contents and organizational structuring of their existing processes, as well as, how the different activities that make up the processes relate or are being performed in real-time settings.

- Process Analyst to analyse any given process domain as long as there is available data from the said process in question.
- Software Developers and Vendors to facilitate the development of process mining algorithms and tools that exhibit a high level of intelligence and reasoning capabilities.
- IT experts and professional, Academics and the Research community in diaspora in understanding the basic principles and theories surrounding the newly advanced topic and enactment of the semantic-based process mining technique. Perhaps, this includes guiding the work/curriculum for the undergraduate as well as post graduate and doctorate level students and practitioners alike. For example, the post-graduate students carrying research in the areas of data science, machine learning and analytics, knowledge engineering, artificial intelligence, process modelling and semantic web search, as well as, practitioners/entrepreneurs involved in business process management and process-related decision-making or innovative practices will find many aspects in Chapters 1 to 8 of this book quite useful.

Besides, the noted readers of this book can immediately put the semantic-based process mining into practice due to the step by step guide and description of its enabling technologies and applicability of the proposed method in real-world settings.

Finally, this book is self-explanatory and consists of an intuitive outline of information (including the latest trends in development and application of the process mining and semantic technologies) for the different categories of audience and readership both in terms of industry and academic hemisphere.

STRUCTURE AND ORGANISATION

This book is organized into eight chapters. The following are a brief description of each of the chapters:

The introduction outlines and discusses the motivation behind the semantic-based process mining method of this book. It sets out by looking at the need for novel approaches in design, integration, and implementation of technologies such as the semantic-based process mining into everyday (e.g. business) processes. This includes a description of how the method sprouts new insights and unceasing research investigations - particularly looking on how to exploit such tools for use in improving the various domain processes. The chapter also introduces the idea of the Process Mining with Semantic Technologies – which are core modules (concepts) upon which the method of this book is grounded.

Chapter 1 emphasizes the idea of embracing the process mining and applying its methods for real-time processing or tasks. The chapter also looks at the related fields and background information that are essential for understanding the method, and largely describes the tools and approaches that can be applied for the semantic-based process mining to follow.

Chapter 2 establishes the key components and mechanisms behind the process mining and semantic modelling method by describing the state-of-the-art tools that enable the practice and application of the technique.

Chapter 3 introduces the Semantic-based Process Mining and Analysis Framework (SPMaAF) design, and subsequently, illustrates how the proposed framework is applied for ample implementation of the proposed algorithms and method.

Chapter 4 provides the different sets of semantically motivated process mining algorithms and its formalizations.

Chapter 5 presents the technique for annotation and modelling of the domain processes using the ontological schema/vocabularies.

Chapter 6 introduces the experimental setup and case studies examples this book uses to demonstrate how the SPMaAF framework is applied to answer real-time questions about any given process domain, as well as the method for population and classification of the individual process instances or entities.

Chapter 7 demonstrates the real-time application of the process mining method with semantics.

Chapter 8 measures the extent to which the semantic-based approach allows for an abstract analysis of the events logs and discovered models. Essentially, the chapter looks at the sophistication of the proposed method in terms of the discovered models, validation of the classification results and their influence compared to other existing benchmark techniques and algorithms used for process mining.

The conclusion presents the epilogue and conclusions of this book. It highlights some of the limitations and threats to the validity of the work carried out in this book and then point out the direction for future works.

In summary, the layout (structure) and presented chapters of this book are all aimed at providing answers to how:

- Process mining is applied to improve the informative value of any given process domain data.
- Describe how improved process models can be derived from the large volume of event (data) logs.
- Use of semantic technologies to enrich the results of the process mining technique through the semantic representation of the derived models.
- Use of the semantic schema/vocabularies (e.g. ontologies) with effective semantic reasoning to lift the process mining analysis from the syntactic level to a much more conceptual level.

In turn, by tackling the stated scope of this book, the work delivers knowledge on how the said semantic data engineering method (a combination of the process mining and semantic technologies) and its application in real-time contributes to the body of knowledge in current literature. Thus, the main purpose for writing and integrating all the chapters of this book to support:

- Semantically motivated synchronization of event log formats (e.g. big data) formats for real-time processing and analysis.
- Semantic-based driven search for explorative analysis of big data analysis and process executions.
- Technique for annotation of unlabelled activity sequences using business process model notations and ontology schema/vocabularies.
- Use of semantics tools (technologies) to manage perspectives of process mining and definition of (automated) methods for discovery and enhancement of process model and analysis.
- Useful strategies towards the development of process mining algorithms that are intelligent with higher levels of semantic reasoning capabilities.
- Importance of semantic process mining to augment the information value of data and models about any given process domain.

Kingsley Okoye
University of East London, UK

REFERENCES

National Academies of Sciences, Engineering, and Medicine. (2017). *Information Technology and the U.S. Workforce: Where Are We and Where Do We Go from Here?* Washington, DC: The National Academies Press. doi:10.17226/24649

Acknowledgment

A lot of people contributed to the authenticity and successful completion of this book. Therefore, it's my pleasure to acknowledge their hard work, supports and contribution.

First of all, I will like to thank my PhD Supervisors; Dr. Syed Islam and Dr. Usman Naeem for their relentless encouragement and precise support and advice throughout the course of my research and consequently the production of this book. They both assisted me a lot in clarifying the research issues, and even more, make it become a successfully completed project. Indeed, their professionalism influenced me academically from which I have also gained the benefit of how to discipline and manage my workload especially for my future careers and engagements.

I will also like to express my special thanks to Dr Abdel-Rahman H. Tawil and Dr Elyes Lamine for their immeasurable input to the success of this book. I am very grateful to them for their insightful guidance and valuable advice when this research idea all started.

Thank you also to the Graduate School and all the staffs at the School of Architecture Computing and Engineering, College of Arts Technology and Innovation, University of East London, UK for providing me with the necessary programs, materials, facilities, and enjoyable and productive environment that allowed me to conduct and finish the writing of this book and ideas therein.

I would also like to extend my gratitude to the Director of Writing Lab, TecLabs, Tecnologico de Monterrey; Dr. Samira Hosseini and colleagues at the department for their immense technical support in ensuring the completion of this book. Thank you all for the wonderful support and most importantly for the understanding that "writing is indeed its own reward".

My tremendous and most important thanks and gratefulness goes to my beloved family, friends, and relatives who have stood behind me, both through my academic endeavours and time of writing this book. I have received from them overwhelming encouragement, support both financially and in kind, and even solace at times of difficulty. I must say thank you all for your continued belief in my education and academic engagements, and I will forever be indebted to each and every one of you. You have all been wonderful, a great inspiration, and pillar to me. Of course, my thanks would not be complete without expressing my ever-deep thankfulness to all of your support. Indeed, not only have I gained your support in every step of my education and career, but also, I have a great joy that I have developed into the person that you can all count on.

Introduction

This book sets out by looking at the need for novel approaches in design and integration of the different tools such as the semantic technologies into everyday (e.g. business) processes, and how the method sprouts/supports new insights and unceasing scientific research and real-life process modelling. In short definition, this chapter introduces the aim and scope of this book particularly focused on how to exploit the semantic technologies for use in improving the various domain processes. Principally, this introduction introduces the notion of the Process Mining with Semantics that forms the core mechanism upon which the method of this book is developed.

SEMANTIC DATA ENGINEERING? PROCESS MINING AND SEMANTIC TECHNOLOGIES

Nowadays, many of the existing organizations' method for data collection and/or procedures for analysing the captured datasets is proving to be more and more complex in nature. The unprecedented rate or growing complexities is a result of the need for a richer and more precise description of real-time processes (e.g. the business process) that allows for a more flexible exploration and/or abstract analysis of various activities that make up the said processes. Indeed, the value of data has become a central focus for most big data analysis tasks. This is due to the fact that *value* in comparison to the other big v's (volume, velocity, variety, and veracity) has spanned a set of additional measurements or standards for an effective big data analysis which includes; validity, variability, venue, vocabulary, and vagueness. In turn, whereas:

Volume: determines the size of the recorded or stored data sets.
Velocity: calculates the speed at which data is generated.
Variety: represents the different types of data.

Veracity: measures the data accuracy.

Validity: measures the data quality, governance, or massive management.

Variability: considers the dynamic or evolving behaviour of the different data sources.

Venue: manages the distribution and heterogeneity of the data from multiple platforms

Vocabulary: represents the data models and semantics that describes the different data structures, and

Vagueness: resolves the confusion over the meaning of big data and/or technologies used to perform the analysis

Value: actually means control over all of the other v's.

According to Marr (2016), it is all well and good having access to big data but unless we can turn it into *value* it is meaningless. Therefore, one can safely argue that *value* is the most important of the big v's especially as it concerns the increasingly rapid shift from big data to big (data) analysis.

Likewise, handling the large volumes of datasets extracted from the operational (business) processes or IT systems have raised intense debate within the academic and industrialized community in diaspora. For instance, one of the many areas in which such research and search for insightful process analysis have been applied is within the field of process mining (PM) (Van der Aalst, 2016), and those investigations/research are mostly championed by IT experts, business process managers, data scientists, and artificial intelligence (AI) companies, etc.

More or less, a majority of the said organizations have invested in projects aimed at modelling or managing the various operational processes. However, most of the derived process models are often unfitting, non-operational, or represents a form of reality that is pointed towards comprehensibility rather than covering the entire actual business process and data values or analysis. Moreover, in recent years, a common challenge with many of the business processes and the underlying operations have been on how to create techniques capable of providing platforms for exploring the additional, and most often, the monotonous tasks of managing the entire processes and/or quality of the information systems. Perhaps, this book notes that this could be done by providing understandable and useful insights on the best possible ways to make the envisioned information explicable in reality.

Besides, some of the existing researches (Dou, et al., 2015; de Medeiros & Van der Aalst, 2009; Van der Aalst, 2016; Okoye, et al., 2019) have shown that a better way of attaining a closer look at any of the given organization's operational process is to consider the event logs that are readily available in its process base or database systems. Apparently, an effective and accurate exploration (analysis) of the events log is capable of providing vital (valuable) knowledge or insightful information with regards to the quality of support being offered for the so-called organizations and the information systems at large. For example, by revealing the underlying relations the process elements (instances) share amongst themselves within the knowledge-base (Okoye et al, 2019 & 2020; Calvanese et al, 2017).

To this end, this book shows that a method such as the *semantic-based approach (semantic data engineering)* which integrates the process mining techniques with semantic technologies - has the capacity of not just discovering meaningful and valuable patterns/models from the readily available events logs, but also supports an abstract analysis (through the conceptualization method) of the discovered models. Moreover, the semantic data engineering approach benefits from *semantics-aware* methods that exploit knowledge kept in (big) data to better the process of reasoning (process automation) on data beyond the possibilities offered by most traditional data mining techniques. Although, process mining has proved itself to be the missing link between the model-based process analysis and data-oriented analysis techniques. Perhaps, when it comes to process modelling of the different datasets extracted from the several process domains, the semantic-aware methods, or yet still, semantic data engineering stands as a plethora of tools that help to manage and formally process the (big) data or events logs based on the semantics they express. Thus, semantic data engineering is said to combine methods ranging from big data indexing to big data design models, the big data querying to big stream data processing, and big data mining to big data analytics, and in consequence, supports the semantic-based process mining. Obviously, the semantic process mining encompasses the idea of leveraging the semantic data engineering tools and technologies to manage any said business process.

Accordingly, the structuring and integration of the different chapters of this book and contents shows both the theoretical and practical application/development of the state of the art tools and methods that support semantic-based process mining particularly applied for real-time data processing and model/pattern recognition.

Therefore, for the remainder of this chapter, the work looks at the concept of process mining and semantic technologies as it concerns the work done in this book. This chapter explains the main reasons it has applied the combination of the process mining with semantics (otherwise referred to as a hybrid intelligent system) to solve real-world data and process modelling problems.

Indeed, the process mining (PM) (Van der Aalst, 2016) has of late become a valuable technique used to discover non-trivial or meaningful information from the recorded events data logs. In theory, the process mining field combines techniques from *computational intelligence* which has been lately considered to encompass artificial intelligence (AI) and even the latter, augmented intelligence (AI's) systems, and data mining (DM) to *process modelling* in order to analyse recorded event logs. In actual sense by definition, the process mining algorithms use event logs to learn and reason about processes by technically coupling events history *data* and the deployed *process models*. Thus, the process mining serves as the bridge between the data-centric and process-related (model) analysis.

Nevertheless, a common challenge with most of the existing process mining techniques is that they depend on tags (i.e. labels) in event logs (information) about the processes they represent, and therefore, to a certain extent are limited because they lack the abstraction level required from real-world perspectives. This means that most of the existing techniques used for process mining do not technically gain from the real knowledge (*semantics*) that describe the tags in the events log of the domain processes. For example, a greater number of the derived models and/or methods tends to support just *machine-readable* systems rather than *machine-understandable* systems at large. Considerably, by machine-understandable systems, we refer to methods that are developed not just for representing information in formats that can be easily understood by humans, but also for creating applications or systems that trails to inclusively process the information that they contain or supports. Perhaps, this book notes that an adequate knowledge-base or information processing system is one which is considered to be;

- understandable by humans, and
- understandable by machines.

Technically, this means that the captured event logs or derived process models are either semantically labelled (annotated) to ease the analysis process, or represented in a formal structure (e.g. ontology) which allows a computer (e.g. the reasoner) to infer new facts by making use of the underlying relations or axioms.

For this purpose, this book explores the technological potentials and prospects of using the semantic-based approach to manage perspectives of the process mining. In turn, it addresses the challenges posed by the traditional process mining techniques by providing a method that focuses on analysing the readily available events log based on *concepts* rather than the *tags* or *labels* in events log of the different processes. Thus, the application and development of the semantic-based process mining method of this book which is totally constructed on the combined idea of integrating the *Process Mining* with *Semantic Modelling* techniques.

On the one hand, for all intent and purposes, this book refers to the *process mining* as a method used to pilot the structure of event logs by defining useful formats (insightful viewpoints) on the level of the systems and/or activities executions and performance in relation to how a process has been previously performed, and to determine the real process workflows (Van der Aalst, 2004; Ingvaldsen, 2011). Essentially, different types of process mining and areas in which they are applied to solve the real-time problem are discussed in detail in Chapters 1 and 7 of this book.

On the other hand, the *semantic modelling* method used to provide a conceptual analysis of the different datasets and models provides the readers of this book (e.g. the process analysts and software developers) with the basic knowledge and opportunity to design and develop tools or algorithms that exhibits a high level of (intelligent) reasoning capable for enhancing the models through explicit specifications (i.e. conceptualization) (Balcan, et al., 2013; Montani, et al., 2017; Polyvyanyy, et al., 2017) of the derived process models or mappings. Consequently, the resulting algorithms or method as described in this book helps in the identification of appropriate domain semantics and association of related attributes amidst the different process elements that can be found within the underlying knowledge-base(s).

Overall, the concept (integration) of the process mining and semantic modelling approach proves to be important because, indeed, it involves a real-time (e.g. ontology-based) descriptions or reformulation of the meanings of the process elements (labels or attributes). Also, the method is presented in comparison with (significance/influence) other standard procedures for analyzing data or models (particularly as it concerns the information retrieval and/or extraction to processing modelling and analysis approaches).

Despite the fact that the common problem with process mining has been the technical focus of the event logs (where most of the existing process mining techniques depend on labels in the events log information about the captured process to discover process models); the technical and intellectual understanding or interpretation of this book is that the discovered models are aligned with the available event logs (at an abstraction level). As noted earlier in this chapter, the majority of the process mining techniques in literature are purely *syntactic* in nature, and to this effect are somewhat vague when confronted with unstructured data. As part of its solution to resolving the unstructured data problems; this book (see chapter 2) looks at the different formats for storing the events logs, and how to overcome some of the data quality problems, structuring, or processing challenges.

In other words, this book mainly addresses the following challenges:

- lack of process mining tools that supports semantic information retrieval, extraction and analysis, and
- mining of event logs and models at a more conceptual level as opposed to the syntactic nature or method of analysis exhibited by the classical process mining technique.

The purpose of covering the aforementioned key areas is mainly as a way of providing formal structures for the datasets used for process mining as well as enhancement of the analysis/interpretation of the derived process models. Thus, the term semantic data engineering. Furthermore, for the rest of chapters 3 through to chapter 7 of this book; the work applies the proposed semantic-based process mining and analysis framework (SPMaAF) (see: chapter 3) on a series of case study experiments (expanded in chapter 6) in order to demonstrate the usefulness of the method. This includes the sets of semantically motivated algorithms and its formalization (chapter 4) which was introduced for ample implementation of the proposed framework (SPMaAF). In addition, the technique for semantic annotation and description of the process models (see: chapter 5) is also covered in this book and a practical application of the resulting semantic fuzzy mining approach discussed in chapter 7.

Nonetheless, it is important to note that the proposed SPMaAF framework and its main application for real-time processing takes into account the different stages of the process mining and analysis. This includes the initial phase of collecting and transformation of the readily available events data logs, to discovering of useful (insightful) process models, and then, expounds the standard process mining method to semantical preparation of the extracted datasets or models for further analysis and querying at a more abstraction level. In terms of abstraction (i.e. the conceptual method of analysis) the book shows that the SPMaAF framework and the formalization of the different algorithms are able to provide an easy, and yet, effective way to analyze the datasets (event logs and models). Moreover, the method allows the meaning of the process elements to be enhanced through the use of the semantic schema/vocabularies (metadata or property descriptions) such as the Web

Ontology Language (OWL) (Bechhofer, et al, 2004; W3C, 2012), Semantic Web Rule Language (SWRL) (Horrocks, et al., 2004), Description Logic (DL) queries (Baader, et al., 2003), etc. The stated (semantic) technologies were used to make available the inference knowledge (assertions) which are then utilized to determine (useful) patterns from the models by means of the semantic reasoning aptitudes. Henceforth, the proposed semantic-based approach involves augmentation of the informative value of the events log and resultant models by semantically annotating the process elements with concepts they represent in real-time settings, and then linking them to an ontology in order to allow for analysis of the extracted data (event logs) and models at a more conceptual level.

In theory, one of the main benefit of the method described in this book is that it shows how it makes use of the real-world case studies and series of experiments to demonstrate the capability of the SPMaAF framework, the different sets of algorithms, and resulting semantic fuzzy mining approach. This is shown by analysing the available input datasets and models based on *concepts* rather than the *tags* (i.e. labels) in the event logs about the process domains. The case study experiments are based on the example of a Learning Process and data about a Business Process used for the purpose of this work.

In summary, this book implements the SPMaAF framework, the different sets of semantically motivated algorithms, and the semantic fuzzy mining approach to find out patterns or behaviours that define or distinguish certain entities (instances) within the process knowledge-base(s). The purpose is not only to answer the identified questions and objectives of this book (see: next section – main objectives) by using the process mining and semantic-based approach but to show (i) how by referring to the attributes (e.g. within the ontological model) in a conceptual manner and (ii) application of the semantic reasoning (reasoner); it becomes easy to refer to particular concepts or individual trace for an enhanced process analysis. For example, such a process could insinuate automatically computing (infer) of a certain group of learners or help determine the cause of bottlenecks (or frequent patterns) in a business transaction model. In other words, this book shows how the semantic process mining technique is applied to represent and answer real-time questions about the different domain processes in question.

SCOPE AND CONTEXT

This section outlines the scope and target problems which the book addresses. It looks at the motivation behind the proposal and development of the semantic-based process mining method, and how it can be applied in the wider context of the business process management, or better still, real-world application.

Primarily, this book covers and presents the start-of-the-art or suitable ways towards the:

1. Use of process mining techniques to discover, monitor and analyse events log about any given process domain by discovering useful and worthwhile process models? and

    Secondly, the book looks at:

2. How effective semantic modelling and reasoning methods can be used to enhance the process mining results and analysis from the syntactic to a more conceptual level?

Specifically, the aforementioned scope and/or context of this book are covered comprehensively in chapter 3 through to chapter 7. Thus, in order to illustrate the importance of the first scope of context, the work proposes and applies the SPMaAF framework (chapter 3) and uses some case studies (chapters 6 and 7) to show how one can effectively mine and analyse the various set(s) of unobserved behaviours/patterns (about the process instances) that can be found within the process knowledge-base. For the second part of analysis, the book shows through provision of formal structures for the derived models (semantic representation) (chapters 3 to 5) how the semantic technologies or schema can be applied to support an abstraction method of process mining.

Therefore, the scope and context of this book are summarised as follows:

I. At first, the book adopts the *process mining* technique to extract useful models from the events log about the domain processes. Perhaps, it is important to note that for all intents and purposes, the work in this book refers to the *process domains* as specific class of problems which are identified and pursued to be resolved within any given particular process in question (e.g. case study of the Learning Process and Business Process presented in this book) (see: chapters 6 and 7). Moreover, the extracted models from the different process domains allow for the opportunity or capacity to explore the processes into multiple directions (process maps or workflow-nets) and to answer real-time questions about the process maps/workflows (e.g. to determine how the activities have been performed in reality). More importantly, the method allows us to further model and perform inference reasoning (automatic computation) to generate process improvement ideas along the way.

II. Second, through the *semantic modelling* technique (ontology-based approach), the book provides data inputs and models that are enriched with semantic annotations and then links them to concepts defined in ontologies in order to extract useful patterns by means of the semantic reasoning. Moreover, the technique applied for the semantic modelling focuses on providing useful information (semantics) about the different sets of activities within the domain processes. Besides. this is done in order to generate rules and/or semantic assertions in relation to the different activities that have been performed or are associated with the process elements, and in turn, enhances the informative values of the resulting process models or domain ontologies. Again, this is achieved due to the rich semantic annotations and/or reasoning capabilities of the method.

In fact, the two main analysis (scope) of this study forms the core components used for validation or integration of the different chapters of this book. Grounded on those core validation components or context (i.e. process mining and semantic modelling); different other areas evolve and were also discussed during the course of writing this book. Although, those areas and the identified components which are also discussed in detail accordingly are directed towards achieving the primary aim and objectives of this book as outlined in the next lines or paragraph of this chapter. Basically, for the stated aim and objectives, the book focuses on ways towards accomplishing the main goal of application and development of the semantic-based process mining approach by taking advantage of the rich semantics that describes the input logs and models. Thus, the method is proposed and carried out in order to extract useful (abstraction) knowledge that allows for analysis of the event logs and models based on *concepts* rather than the event *tags* or *labels* about the process.

Main aim: the overall goal of the work carried out in this book is to:

extract streams of event logs from any given process domain and describe formats that allow for mining and improved analysis of the captured datasets.

In other words, the focus of the different chapters of this book is to:

- apply process mining techniques to any given process domain (for example, the case studies in chapters 6 and 7)
- provide real-time analysis (semantic knowledge) and understanding about the different process domains, and
- Useful strategies towards the development of process mining algorithms that are intelligent with a high level of conceptual (or abstract) reasoning capabilities.

Main objectives: practically, this book shows *how* to do the following:

1) Extract data from real-time processes to show how one can semantically synchronize the events log formats for the various process domains (Chapters 2 and 5)
2) Semantical preparation of the input data through an ontology-driven search for explorative analysis of the process executions or activities (Chapter 3 to 5)
3) Transform the extracted datasets into mining executable formats to support the discovery of valuable process models through the proposed technique for annotation of unlabelled activity sequences using semantic schema/vocabularies (Chapter 5 and 6)
4) Provide a method for accurate classification of unseen process instances or traces within the discovered process models (Chapter 7)
5) Monitor and/or enhance the said real-time processes through further semantic analysis of the discovered models. (Chapter 7 and 8)
6) Importance of the application and development of the semantic-based process mining approach to augment information values or data captured about any given process domain: using some case studies example and scenarios (Chapter 6 to 8)

ACHIEVEMENTS

The achievements/contributions of this book are centered around the scope and stated objectives Accordingly, the achievements are rooted on the following two main components;

- process mining, and
- semantic modelling

Clearly, the aforementioned components are characteristically developed and applied based on the following implementation aspects, namely:

(i) *Process Discovery:* to discover new process models based on the events data or logs about any given process domain without any prior information on how those activities have been performed. For example, the case studies scenario of a *learning process* (Chapter 5, section 7.1) and *business process* data (Chapter 7 and 8) described in this book.

(ii) *Conformance Checking:* checks how much the data as contained in the event logs matches the presented behaviours or patterns in the deployed models?

(iii) *Model Extension:* the need for both the process model and its logs to discover information that will enhance this model.

(iv) *Semantics:* although the different events data logs are captured and modelled with an acceptable level of performance to accurately reflect the process executions, they are still limited for some real-time process mining or analysis task because they lack the abstraction level required from a real-world perspective. To this effect, this book shows that analysis provided by using the classical process mining techniques can be improved by adding semantic information to the derived models or input data logs.

Based on the listed application aspects, particularly as it concerns semantics; the *semantic process modelling* is shown to form a key part of this book. This is exclusively discussed and illustrated in details in this book to help elaborate and in achieving the main aim and focus - which is on extracting the streams of event logs from the various process domains and then describe formats that allow for mining and improved process analysis of the captured datasets.

Perhaps, driven by such an effort and application aspects; this book consequently studies suitable techniques for process mining, and then provide resolutions on *how* best to design and develop process mining algorithms that highly influence and support the semantic-based process mining as well as its application in real-time. Clearly, in the effort to achieve the stated objectives; the work has made the assumption that *ontologies* can help in harmonizing the different sets of input data or models especially in alignment with the pre-defined *concepts* or unobserved behaviours. Moreover, this work believes that the *adoption and application of semantic annotations* and *reasoning* aptitudes will help provide (add) useful *knowledge (information) discovery* and conceptual *process querying* capabilities to support the process mining outcomes. To this end, this book proves that through ontological modelling of the different process elements, or yet, application of the semantic rule-based approach - that it is possible to make inferences over a process knowledge-base (e.g. case study of the learning process and business process domain) that leads to automated discovery of useful (valuable) patterns or behaviours. Besides, this claim is demonstrated in details in chapters 6 to 8 of this book. Indeed, the aforementioned affirmations are the main motivation for writing this book. Although, there are existing books on data mining to business process management and artificial intelligence, there cease to exist a book that solely discusses or integrates the basic and/or rudimentary tools for applying semantic process mining (i.e. annotation of events logs/models, ontologies, and semantic reasoner) covered in this book. Thus far, this book is considered the first book to cover the whole spectrum of the semantic process mining and its supporting/enabling technologies.

Furthermore, it is important to note that at the core of the proposed method of this book is the Semantic Process Mining and Analysis Framework (SPMaAF) presented in chapter 3, the sets of semantically motivated algorithms and its formalizations (chapter 4), and the resulting Semantic Fuzzy Mining application described in chapter 7. Apparently, those main components/ achievements of this book were all developed to help find answers to the identified challenges in the current literature and to realize the stated aim and objectives as discussed earlier in this introduction.

Therefore, the overall purpose and main components realized as a result of implementing the proposed SPMaAF framework, the sets of semantically motivated algorithms, and the semantic fuzzy mining approach in this book are summarised as follows:

- **Event Logs**: To show how process mining is applied to improve the informative value of any given data captured about an actual (executed) process.

- **Process Modelling:** Describe how improved process models can be derived from the large volumes of events data logs recorded about the process domains.
- **Semantic Annotation**: Describe how semantic descriptions (metadata assertions or data labelling) of the deployed model can help enrich the results of the process mining and outcomes through provision (or inference) of new knowledge about the process elements.
- **Ontology:** Use of semantic technologies/schema with effective reasoning to lift process mining analysis from the syntactic level to a more abstraction level.
- **Semantic Process Mining Algorithms and Application (e.g. Semantic Fuzzy Mining approach)**: Demonstrates how references to ontologies and effective raising of process mining and analysis from the syntactic to abstraction level, enables real-time viewpoints on the different process domains. Henceforth, the semantic viewpoints, in turn, help to address the problem of analyzing the available input datasets at a conceptual level (i.e. based on concepts) and to answer questions about relationships the process instances share amongst themselves within the knowledge-base.

Contribution to Knowledge: the main contributions of this book are summarised as follows:

1. Definition of a semantic-based process mining approach that exhibits a high level of semantic reasoning and capabilities (entire chapters in this book)
2. Design framework (SPMaAF) that highly influence and support the development of the semantic process mining algorithms (chapter 3).
3. Sets of semantically motivated process mining algorithms that prove useful towards extraction, semantical preparation, and transformation of events log about any given process domain (chapter 4).
4. Method which provides formal structures on how to perform and present process mining results in a more intuitive, effective and contextual manner (chapter 5)
5. A process mining technique that is able to accurately classify and induce new knowledge based on previously unobserved behaviours (chapter 6 and 7)
6. An ontology-based system that is able to perform information retrieval and query answering in a more abstraction way compared to other standard

logical procedures for process analysis and/or information management (see: chapter 6 and 7)

7. A series of case studies showing that semantic-based process modelling approach can be used to enhance process mining results and analysis from the syntactic level to a more conceptual level (Chapters 6 to 8)

8. Empirical evaluation of the impact of the resultant semantic fuzzy mining approach and its outcomes compared to other benchmark algorithms/ techniques used for process mining (Chapter 8)

Outlook

This book is utterly built on process mining and semantic modelling techniques. Thus, the main reason for the design and application of the combined approach is as follows: the *process mining* techniques prove to offer a significant bridge between the data mining and process modelling to business process management at large. Whereas, *semantic modelling* is supported due to need for novel methods that trails to address the challenges with process mining or who have to interpret the results of the process mining, especially from a real-world or business process perspectives. Indeed, the semantic process mining represents as a method that unifies the process mining techniques with semantic modelling approaches or technologies. Therefore, for the audience and readers of this book, the work done in this book (if not the only book currently in literature) serves as an introduction to the concepts and applications development in both fields. Besides, the work provides a comprehensive overview of the process mining and semantic modelling methods in terms of its application for real-time process (data) analysis.

Theoretically, this book makes use of both the *qualitative* and *quantitative* research methods to carry out the proposals and experimentations/analysis. Moreover, the proposed semantic-based process mining method of this book can be regarded as a fusion theory that is devoted to represent and analyse information in a qualitative and yet quantitative manner.

The SPMaAF design framework (see: chapter 3) sits at the central focus and foundation of this work upon which other chapters are written. The work *qualitatively* carries out a series of case studies to show how data from various domain processes are extracted, semantically prepared, and transformed into mining executable formats to support the discovery, monitoring and enhancement of the real-time processes through further semantic analysis of the discovered models. Moreover, this work also *quantitatively* assesses the precision and recall (level of accuracy) of the proposed semantic-based approach and classification results being able to predict unobserved behaviours or traces (e.g. attributes the process instances share amongst themselves) within the process knowledge-base. This is done by determining, for example, which individual traces are fitting or not fitting in the discovered models. Typically, this work makes use of a training set and test log from the real-time business process data (see: chapter 7) to implement and perform the experiments and evaluations.

In general, this book employs both methods (qualitative and quantitative) for the purpose of validation and comparison by evaluating the level of impact and usefulness of the proposed semantic-based process mining method and framework, validity of the classification results, and their influence compared to other existing benchmark algorithms/techniques that are closely relevant and used for process mining.

Based on the content of each of the chapters of this book as outlined in the preface section, the rest of this book is structured as follows:

This book discusses in *chapter 1*, adequate background information in areas related to the process mining and semantic modelling techniques. It discusses and analyses the relevant theories in alignment with existing technologies or tools (within the field of process mining and the semantic modelling) that are fundamental for the readers to have a comprehensive understanding of the contents and contributions of this book. Thus far, the chapter (chapter 1) provides the preliminaries necessary for grasping the remainder of this book. In addition, the chapter also constructively critique existing works and identifies the gaps that are addressed in this book. *Chapter 2* covers the state-of-the-art and main components of the proposed method in this book. It presents the different types of process mining, and its supporting tools, especially when applying the technique to any given process domain and tasks. Essentially, the chapter starts by describing what is the *events log* and the different source of the data for process mining. It also looks at some of the common problems with data quality for process mining. And then continues by describing the relevant state-of-the-art (tools, techniques, and algorithms) that are used to support the discovery and analysis of the events log and process models. In the end, the chapter (chapter 2) points out some of the existing challenges and planned (proposed) methods for managing the complications with the learned models or input data. Consequently, it looks at the semantic technologies and the ontological concepts/schema, and how they can be applied to represent the various information hidden in the datasets or discovered models in a formal way. Given the identified challenges, the work presents in *chapter 3* the proposed SPMaAF framework and its main components which this book has proposed for ample implementation and application of the semantic-based process mining approach. The chapter starts by describing in details the architectural design (specifications) of the SPMaAF framework, and specifically, illustrates the main tools that are used to support the development and application of the framework. In addition, the chapter (chapter 3) highlights the main functionalities offered by the SPMaAF framework and the different substantial areas of its implementation and benefits. *Chapter 4* continues with a description of the semantically motivated process mining algorithms and its formalizations. It starts by explaining the main phases of the SPMaAF framework including the incremental requirements (procedures) for implementing each of the phases, and then finalize by discussing the resultant algorithms in detail. In other words, the chapter (chapter 4) describes in detail the procedures for ample implementation of the semantic-based process mining framework. Equally, the technique for semantical annotation of the process models and its underlying properties (particularly the OWL schema), and the key functions that allows for definition of the different domain classes, objects and data types, including the semantic reasoner (which are used to classify and query the resulting model) - is discussed in *chapter 5*. *Chapters 6 and 7* guides the readers on how to effectively apply the semantic-based process mining in practice by introducing the case studies and series of experimentations. It demonstrates the proposed semantic-based method using the use case scenario of the learning process and data about a business process to show how to effectively mine the said processes and events data at a more conceptual level.

Finally, the book evaluates and cross-validates the method against other existing benchmark algorithms/techniques used for process mining (chapter 8) and then present the epilogue and a summary of the chapters as well as highlight the limitations and direction for future work in the conclusion. In short definition, *Chapter 8* presents the analysis and validation of the developed method of this book. It qualitatively and yet quantitatively evaluates and discusses to what extent the book has achieved the stated aim and objectives, as well as, addressed the identified questions. Fundamentally, the chapter compares the outcome of the proposed method of this book to the other relevant benchmark (state-of-the-art) approaches used for process mining as a way of indicating the impact and contributions of this book to knowledge. The conclusion revisits and provides a bird's eye view on the contents presented in the preceding chapters, and then concludes the book by summarizing the main achievements and novelty of the findings and impact particularly in terms of opportunities offered by the semantic-based process mining technique. Last but not least, a general discussion on the limitations and threats to validity of the work done in this book including a road map on topics that could be investigated as future work is discussed in the conclusion.

REFERENCES

W3C. (2012). *Web Ontology Language (OWL)*. Oxford, UK: OWL Working Group.

Baader, F. (2003). *Description Logic Handbook: theory, implementation, and applications* (1st ed.). New York, NY: Cambridge University Press.

Balcan, N., Blum, A., & Mansour, Y. (2013). Exploiting ontology structures and unlabeled data for learning. *Proceedings of the 30th Int. Conference on Machine Learning 2013*, 1112-1120.

Bechhofer, S. (2004). *OWL Web Ontology Language Reference*. Manchester, UK: Technical report W3C Proposed Recommendation.

Calvanese, D., Kalayci, T. E., Montali, M., & Tinella, S. (2017). Ontology-based Data Access for Extracting Event Logs from Legacy Data: The onprom Tool and Methodology. *Proceedings of 20th International Conference on Business Information Systems 2017*, 220-236. 10.1007/978-3-319-59336-4_16

de Medeiros, A. K. A., & Van der Aalst, W. M. P. (2009). Process Mining towards Semantics. In T. Dillon, E. Chang, R. Meersman, & K. Sycara (Eds.), Lecture Notes in Computer Science: Vol. 4891. *Advances in Web Semantics I* (pp. 35–80). Berlin: Springer. doi:10.1007/978-3-540-89784-2_3

Dou, D., Wang, H., & Liu, H. (2015). Semantic Data Mining: A Survey of Ontology-based Approaches. *9th IEEE Int. Conference on Semantic Computing*, 244 – 251. 10.1109/ICOSC.2015.7050814

Horrocks, I. (2004). *SWRL: A Semantic Web Rule Language Combining OWL and RuleML*. Network Inference, Canada and Stanford University: W3C Member Submission - 2004 National Research Council of Canada, Network Inference, and Stanford University.

Ingvaldsen, J. E. (2011). *Semantic process mining of enterprise transaction data* (PhD thesis). Norwegian University of Science and Technology.

Marr, B. (2016). Big Data in Practice: How 45 Successful Companies Used Big Data Analytics to Deliver Extraordinary Results. In *Business & Management Special Topics*. Wiley Publishers. doi:10.1002/9781119278825

Montani, S. (2017). Knowledge-Based Trace Abstraction for Semantic Process Mining. In A. ten Teije, C. Popow, J. Holmes, & L. Sacchi (Eds.), Lecture Notes in Computer Science: Vol. 10259. *Artificial Intelligence in Medicine. AIME 2017* (pp. 267–271). Springer. doi:10.1007/978-3-319-59758-4_30

Okoye, K., Islam, S., & Naeem, U. & Sharif, S. (2020). Semantic-based Process Mining Technique for Annotation and Modelling of Domain Processes. *International Journal of Innovative Computing, Information, & Control.*

Okoye, K., Islam, S., Naeem, U., Sharif, M. S., Azam, M. A., & Karami, A. (2019). The Application of a Semantic-Based Process Mining Framework on a Learning Process Domain. In K. Arai, S. Kapoor, & R. Bhatia (Eds.), *Intelligent Systems and Applications. Advances in Intelligent Systems and Computing* (Vol. 868, pp. 1381–1403). Springer Cham. doi:10.1007/978-3-030-01054-6_96

Polyvyanyy, A., Ouyang, C., Barros, A., & van der Aalst, W. M. P. (2017). Process querying: Enabling business intelligence through query-based process analytics. *Decision Support Systems*, *100*, 41–56. doi:10.1016/j.dss.2017.04.011

Van der Aalst, W. M. P. (2004). Business Process Management Demystified: A Tutorial on Models, Systems and Standards for workflow Management. Lectures on Concurrency and Petri Nets, 3098, 1-65.

Van der Aalst, W. M. P. (2016). *Process Mining: Data Science in Action* (2nd ed.). Berlin: Springer-Verlag. doi:10.1007/978-3-662-49851-4

Chapter 1
Preliminaries

ABSTRACT

This chapter looks at the relevant tools and technologies that are related/applicable to the process mining and semantic modelling techniques. Theoretically, the chapter describes some of the interrelated tools and area of topics covered by this book. In other words, the chapter introduces the background information that is essential for understanding the context and proposed method of this book. It starts by looking at the process mining term and the different types of its application when applied to solve real-time problems. Consequently, the chapter discusses the wider scope of the different semantic-aware methods that trails to provide valuable information or insights that can be utilized to support the real-time processing or decision-making purposes.

INTRODUCTION

Contextually, the chapter is structured as follows: Firstly, the idea of embracing the process mining technique and applying its methods for the purpose of this book is discussed. We start by looking at the process mining term and the different types of its application when solving real-time process-related problems. Accordingly, the chapter continues by describing the different components and practice that supports the real-time application of the process mining. We also make use of the example of the educational process mining (EPM) domain to illustrate how this is done. To this effect, this chapter describes the EPM and the other associated modelling approaches e.g.

DOI: 10.4018/978-1-7998-2668-2.ch001

educational data mining (EDM) devoted to improving process analysis by acquiring and representing non-trivial knowledge about the actual processes in reality. Essentially, the review is done in order to highlight the main benefits of using the process mining techniques to analyse data extracted from any given process domain (e.g. case study of the educational domain or learning process described in this book). Consequently, the chapter looks at the wider scope of the several semantic-aware methods that trails to provide valuable information or insights which can be used to support the real-time processing or decision-making. Therefore, the chapter discusses the broader term of Business Intelligence (BI) and other overlapping terms, such as the Business Process Management (BPM), Business Activity Monitoring (BAM), Process-Aware Information Systems (PAIS) etc. that combines tools or methodologies that are aimed at offering useful information and insights that can be utilized to support the process mining technique. Consequently, the chapter discusses the Semantic Web Search technologies, and the various associated methods or mechanisms such as the Data integration and linking, Semantic annotation and data labelling, and Ontology-based Information Extraction (OBIE) systems which are all seen as very useful methods used to support the extraction, mining and analysis of processes by influencing the level of real world (semantic) knowledge that can be derived from the readily available datasets and input models. Finally, the chapter also takes into account the Process Querying (PQ) method that is concerned with automatic management of repositories of models (of observed or unseen processes) with the goal of transforming the process-related information into decision-making capabilities. To end the chapter, the book provides a comprehensive review of the relevant works that have been conducted in context of this book – particularly focusing on the areas which covers the process discovery and pattern mining, to information retrieval and extraction, semantic-based process modelling and ontologies, and the interrelated data mining techniques such as the classifications method and the fuzzy logic. Conclusively, the work provides a systematic representation and summary of the existing methods in terms of the design approach/tools used in conducting the different studies, their findings and relevance to this book. To this effect, this chapter provides a thematic table outlining the main relevant work in this area of topic or scientific research, and are grouped in terms of their various application domains which are most closely related to the process mining and semantic modelling techniques described in this book.

PROCESS MINING (PM)

One of the many areas in which the big data research (otherwise referred to as the search for insightful and valuable analysis of captured datasets) have been applied is within the field of Process Mining (PM). Process mining has proved itself to be the missing link between model-based process analysis and data-oriented analysis techniques. One of the most influential and the best known BPM researchers, (Van der Aalst, 2016), in one of his works, referred to process mining as "data science in action". Interestingly, the author notes that data science has emerged as a new discipline in recent years which consists of methods that focus on "data extraction, data preparation, data exploration, data transformation, storage and retrieval, computing infrastructures, various types of mining and learning, presentation of explanations and predictions, and the exploitation of results taking into account ethical, social, legal, and business aspects" (Van der Aalst, 2016). Therefore, since the process mining allows for extraction of non-trivial information from captured datasets (referred to as event logs), the technique could also be seen as one of the main mechanisms of "data science". Even more, Van der Aalst (2016) opines that process mining has the capacity to provide means towards bridging the gap between *data science* and *process science*. Apparently, *Process science* has emerged due to the process-perspective that is missing in most *big data* initiative and/or the curricula of *data science*. Besides, the works in (Van der Aalst, 2011; Van der Aalst, 2016, Montani et al, 2017, Okoye et al, 2019; Lautenbacher et al, 2009; Calvanese et al, 2017) shows that the data logs extracted and stored in many organizations information system must be utilized to enhance the end to end process in reality by focusing on analysing the unseen behaviours based on the information that are present in the logs, thus, the essence of *process mining*.

Process mining research started at the Eindhoven University of Technology (TU/e) in 1999 and was first put forward by Wil van der Aalst (Van der Aalst, et al., 2003; Van der Aalst, et al., 2004). According to the forefather of process mining (Van der Aalst, 2016), as of then, there was limited availability of event logs, and the early methods used to perform process mining tasks at that time were exceptionally ineffective and naive. Remarkably, for the past few decades, the process mining methods and/or approaches has undisputedly matured (Maita, et al., 2017) because events data logs have become ever more available (Van der Aalst et al, 2019). Moreover, progress has been spectacular in the field of process mining and the technique is currently being supported by different tools and algorithms such as the method introduced in this book. Yet again, the work of Maita et al (2017) thinks that process mining research and the associated challenges, such as balancing between robustness, simplicity, accuracy, and generalization would benefit from a larger use of the technique. Even so, a number of researches and organizations are primarily working conscientiously in support of the real-time application and promotion of the process mining field (Van der Aalst et al, 2019) such as the IEEE CIS Task Force on Process Mining (IEEE, 2016; Van der Aalst et al, 2012). The IEEE Task Force on Process Mining was established in 2009 in the context of the Data Mining Technical Committee (DMTC) of the Computational Intelligence Society (CIS) of the Institute of Electrical and Electronic Engineers, Inc. (IEEE). According to Van der Aalst et al (2019), over 70 organizations are supporting the IEEE Task Force on Process Mining. As one of its many activities and principal guidelines for performing process mining tasks, the IEEE Standards Association in 2016 officially published the IEEE Standard for Extensible Event Stream (XES) (Veerbek et al, 2011) which serves as the generally accepted file format by the process mining community. The XES standard is specially proposed for achieving interoperability in event logs and/or event streams. According to the report or description in Van der Aalst et al (2019), the IEEE Task Force on Process Mining has been driving the standardization process for over six years, because the standard allows the exchange of event data between different process mining tools.

What's more? Over the past decades - whilst the initial attention of the process mining (PM) community was primarily on the *process discovery* method, the PM Field has significantly broadened to include conformance checking, operational support, model enhancement, and multi-perspective process mining. These many aspects of the process mining and more have grown into fundamental part of the several tools which supports the process of performing the different mining tasks - particularly ProM (Verbeek, et al., 2011) one of the leading process mining tool. In fact, process mining encompasses the stated methods and approaches to support the extraction and interpretation of processes in reality. Accordingly, the work in this book expands on the main three types of process mining (process discovery, conformance check, and model enhancement) which are mostly encountered or applied for any given process mining task.

Nowadays, many organizations have focused on applying the PM technique to different aspects of their business processes. Certainly, the application of the process mining techniques are not only limited to the business processes, but also provides new means to discover, monitor, and enhance any given process domain. (De Leoni & Van der Aalst, 2013; Van der Aalst, et al., 2012). According to Van der Aalst (2011), there are two main drivers for the growing interest in process mining. First, data about many organizations business processes are captured and stored at an unprecedented rate. Secondly, there is more than ever increasingly need to improve and support business processes in competitive and rapidly changing environments.

Eventually, process mining has proved its relevance and application in some important field areas and case studies. To mention but a few includes: Health care (Rojas, et al., 2016), Government sectors (Van der Aalst, 2016), Banking and Financial industries (Jans, 2011; Van der Aalst, et al., 2010), Educational organizations and settings (Cairns, et al., 2014; Okoye, et al., 2016), Airlines and Transportation industry (Van der Aalst, 2016), ICT and Cloud Computing (Chesani, et al., 2016) etc. Indeed, process mining techniques make use of the recorded events data from any of these process domain to discover useful process models, perform conformance checking of the discovered models, analyse deviations, and even more, extend and predict future outcomes or further developments.

Actually, many explanations of the process mining notion have been proposed in the literature (Van der Aalst, 2011; Cairns, et al., 2015; Ingvaldsen, 2011; Van der Aalst, 2016). To note, the founding father of the process mining (PM) (Van der Aalst, 2011) refers to the term - as a young research field that makes use of the data mining (DM) technique to find out patterns or models from event logs, and predict outcomes through further analysis of the discovered models. According to the author (Van der Aalst, 2011; Van der Aalst, 2016) PM means extracting valuable, process-related information from event logs about any domain process.

The authors in Cairns et al (2015) notes that the process mining term is concerned with the analysis of the captured datasets (i.e. events log) from a *process-perspective*. More so, Ingvaldsen (2011) notice that as soon as a particular process (e.g. business process) is being supported by some form of IT system, its operational transactions or activities executions can then be observed or recorded in the form of event logs. Likewise, the works in (Greco, et al., 2006; Van der Aalst, 2011) mentions that the process mining notion is an attempt towards extraction of meaningful and non-trivial information from the recorded event logs.

Without a doubt, references (Adriansyah, et al., 2011; Ingvaldsen, et al., 2005; Ingvaldsen, 2011; Van der Aalst, et al., 2012) are even more specific about the focus of process mining towards an explicit extraction, validation, and extension of process models, and as such, groups the process mining

5

into the following three types of process mining as discussed in details in the following section. Thus, for the aforesaid reasons and explanations, *events log* could be utilized to perform the following process mining techniques (Van der Aalst, 2016):

(i)   Process Discovery
(ii) Conformance Checking, and
(iii) Model Enhancement

DIFFERENT TYPES OF PROCESS MINING

Process Discovery

According to Van der Aalst (2016), the lion's share of attention in process mining has been devoted to the *process discovery,* i.e., extracting process models, mainly business process models from an event log (Carmona, et al., 2016). Process discovery has been lately seen as the main significant and furthermost challenge logically allied to the process mining term (Carmona, et al., 2016; Van der Aalst, 2011). In theory, the process discovery algorithms/ techniques aim to automatically construct process models, e.g., BPMN, Petri-nets, Fuzzy models etc. (Van der Aalst, 2016) from events log about any given process and describes causal dependencies between the individual activities as performed.

Practically, a typical *process discovery* method takes (as input) recorded event logs, and then produce (as output) a model without any prior information on how the activities has been earlier or formerly performed. Besides, in settings where the data sets (i.e. event logs) includes further information about the resource (e.g. roles, originators etc.), it is also possible to discover resource-related models. For instance, a shared network or server representing how teams work collectively or collaborate within a certain organization.

In a brief definition, one can make use of the process discovery methods/ algorithms to obtain models that describe reality. Various algorithms have been developed in current literature with the capability of performing process discovery tasks, namely: the α-algorithm, Fuzzy miner, Heuristic miner, Genetic miner, Inductive miner (Van der Aalst, 2016) etc. Actually, the aforementioned algorithms have also been made available in existing process mining tools such as the ProM (Verbeek, et al., 2011) and Disco (Rozinat &

Gunther, 2012) etc. Moreover, some of the main application benefits, impact, and limitations of the process discovery algorithms are discussed in details in chapter 2 of this book.

Conformance Checking

The *conformance checking* is the second type of process mining technique. The method focuses on determining (assessing) how well (fitting) the discovered process models describes the actual observation in the event logs (Ingvaldsen, 2011). In other words, the method is used to check how much the data or information in the events log matches the presented behaviour in the deployed model. Therefore, a conformance check and analysis technique references a-priori (i.e existing) process model and compares it with the events log of the specific (i.e. the same) process. Moreover, such analysis is performed in order to check if in reality, the recorded events data logs conforms to the deployed models (Munoz-Gama & Carmona, 2011; Adriansyah, et al., 2011; Rozinat & Van der Aalst, 2008; Weerdt, et al., 2011; Fahland & van der Aalst, 2012).

For instance, the outcome a conformance checking technique may imply that the discovered process model perhaps do not describe the executed process as supposed in reality, or is being executed in a different order (Fahland & van der Aalst, 2012; Van der Aalst, 2011). The results could also mean that some of the process instance (i.e. individual activities) as observed within the discovered model are skipped in the events log, or maybe the logs consist of actions (i.e. activities) that are not necessarily defined by the process model (Fahland & van der Aalst, 2012).

Therefore, a well-executed conformance check is relevant and significant especially from a business objective-alignment or auditing perspective. For example, it could be possible that the recorded logs are reiterated (i.e model replay) against the derived models in order to discover unexpected deviation or bottlenecks that may impact the business process in general. Moreover, the conformance checking could be utilized to measure the fitness of the models discovered by the PM tools, and could also be used to perform the repairing of the process models in reality. For example, one of the main standpoints of this book is related to the conformance check methodology. The book focuses on establishing to what extent can references to the semantic information and effective raising of process models from the syntactic to conceptual level enable real-time analysis or insights about the process domains in question.

Many existing PM algorithms capable of performing the conformance check has been proposed in the current literature and has been applied also in different business process settings (Adriansyah, et al., 2011; Van der Aalst, 2011). Some example of the most used algorithms includes the Inductive Visual Miner (Leemans, et al., 2014) and LTL checker (de Beer, 2005) etc. The stated algorithms can also be found in some of the existing process mining tools mainly ProM (Verbeek, et al., 2011).

Generally, in most settings the conformance checking algorithms targets to achieve the following functions as noted in the work of Van der Aalst (2016):

- Business Alignment and Auditing
- Token Replay
- Comparing Traces or Footprints
- Model Repair
- Assessing Process Mining Algorithms, and
- Connecting Event Logs and Process Models

Quite often conformance check is performed to show the replaying semantics (e.g. token replay) for models with regards to the following four quality criteria's - *Fitness, Generalisation, Precision,* and *Simplicity* (Van der Aalst, 2011). Likewise, the work describes and show the need for those four quality criteria in chapter 7 of this book. Particularly, the work indicates how the fitness of the available events data logs are being measured in a qualitative and quantitative manner, respectively. For instance, the method is used to determine the level (extent) of behaviours within the event logs which happen to be actually possible according to the discovered process models. To this effect, the conformance checking technique is applied to balance between *traces* (i.e. observed behaviours or patterns) that are *overfitting* or *underfitting* the actual model or process executions as performed in reality (Carmona, et al., 2016; Fahland & van der Aalst, 2012).

Model Enhancement

As an extension or a way to resolve the limitations with the process mining technique (especially given the drawbacks and challenges identified with the earlier types of PM techniques) the last type of process mining - *model enhancement* comes into play. The *model enhancement* aims at *augmenting* the process models with additional information extracted from the original events log. In other words, the model enhancement means extending/improving the resultant models by referencing the underlying/actual behaviours of the learned processes as represented in the original source data (Ingvaldsen, 2011).

Therefore, whilst the *conformance checking* techniques measure the fitness of the models e.g. alignment between the process models and reality, the *model enhancement* trails to extend or completely change the original (a-priori) model. Hence, the method is used to manipulate/maintain compliance about the process models learned from the event logs, or to quantify deviations by making use of the information that have been discovered (e.g. through the process discovery) and aligned (conformance checking) about the real-time process in execution.

Consequently, in terms of the process mining and analysis - the model enhancement comes in to play from two perspectives (Van der Aalst, 2016; Van der Aalst, 2011):

1) Model Repair, and
2) Model Extension

Logically, if we want to describe how the different types of process mining fit and rely on each other from a business process management or data analytics perspective: we could say that the *process discovery* and *conformance checking* approaches do not only limit their application to control-flows (or workflow management) but also allows for additional perspectives to be added to the methods by extending the discovered process models, thus, the *model enhancement*.

In addition to the different types of process mining, various other perspectives may also be considered orthogonal to the three main types of PM techniques (i.e. process discovery, conformance check, and model enhancement) namely: *Control-flow perspective*, *Case perspective*, *Organizational perspective*, *Time perspective*, *Operational support* etc. (Van der Aalst, 2011). Perhaps, owing to the fact that the *process mining* plays an important role in many organizations data analysis or process modelling procedures. The PM method spans its technical application from the fields of *data science* and *business process management* (BPM), and as such, we assume that to perform any process mining task that there has to be some kind of recorded data from an actual/real-life process.

Using one of the case study examples of this book (see: Chapter 6), the work shows in the following figure (Figure 1) that the first step (i.e. starting point) for any given *process mining* project is to capture the *event data* logs about the process (e.g. the learning process), and then produce a *process model* to show in details how the different activities that make up the process has been performed, and to reveal interesting connections between the different process elements (process instances). In consequence, the resultant process map/visualizations allow for further *analysis* and/or *extension* (enhancement) of the discovered models. Indeed, the stipulated types and application of the PM technique (as described in Figure 1) is what this work adopts to support the integration and implementation of the proposed semantic-based process mining and analysis (SPMaAF) framework in this book.

Figure 1. The different Types and Application of Process Mining techniques

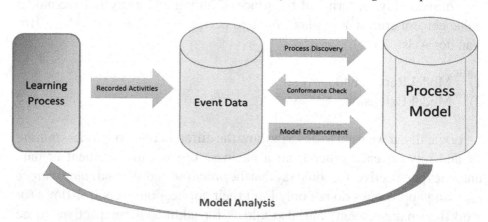

APPLICATION OF PROCESS MINING TO SOLVE REAL-TIME PROBLEMS: CASE STUDY

The need for relatable *automation and management of processes* in real-time or real-world scenarios has led to increasing demand for methods and tools that supports the accumulative large volumes of data that are extracted from the various data-sources, stored in different forms, as well as in diverse granular levels in various organizations (Bogarín, et al., 2014; Trčka, et al., 2010). Indeed, those captured datasets can be exploited by the process analyst and the business owners to understand the behaviours or patterns of the intended users, including their level of performance and/or achieved goals. Henceforth, such search for "exploration and analysis, by automatic or semi-automatic means of managing the large quantities of datasets in order to discover meaningful patterns or rules" (Ingvaldsen, 2011) motivates the increasingly research interest and real-time application of the process mining techniques in different settings (Cairns, et al., 2014).

To illustrate the influence or impact of the process mining technique in the current literature, the work chooses the Educational Process Mining (EPM) paradigm to explain the method. The educational process mining is a new domain area within the wider context of business process management that aims to apply the *process mining* techniques to find out user patterns or models from the captured sets of educational data and then trails to predict outcomes through further analysis of the discovered models. Thus, EPM refers to the application of process mining techniques within the education domain (Trčka, et al., 2010; Cairns, et al., 2014; Bogarín, et al., 2018). Bogarín et al (2018) are even more specific about the application areas of the EPM in real-time settings or processing. According to Bogarín et al (2018) one of such areas that the process mining technique is currently being applied and is gaining attention in recent years is the EPM. The authors notes that EPM means the application of process mining to raw educational data by taking into account the end to end processes rather than local patterns, as opposed to the Educational Data Mining (EDM) (Baker & Yacef, 2009; Dou, et al., 2015) which tends not to be process-centric and do not focus on event data (Van der Aalst, 2016) e.g. the rows (instances) and columns (variables) of a typical data file which does not have any meaning.

Interestingly, a number of researchers have directed their work towards the use and application of this newly advanced aspect of process mining and its application within the educational settings (Bogarín, et al., 2014; Cairns, et al., 2014; Trcka & Pechenizkiy, 2009; Trčka, et al., 2010; Okoye, et al., 2017 & 2018). Moreover, according to Cairns et al (2014), EPM emerges from the Educational Data Mining (EDM) discipline, and the drive for its incentive is primarily to discover, analyse and improve the educational processes based on the hidden information within the databases (data sources) or events log recorded by the existing systems. For example, the different sets of data could come from the Schools, Colleges, Universities, or the Professional Training Institutions information or IT systems.

EDM vs EPM

The difference between Data Mining (DM) and Process Mining (PM), is that whilst DM aims to mine and analyse event logs at *data-levels*, PM targets to mine and analyse event logs at *process-levels* (Holzhüter, et al., 2013). Likewise, those level of analysis applies to the context of the Educational Data Mining (EDM) and Educational Process Mining (EPM). Thus, whilst EDM aims to mine and analyse educational data at *data-levels*, EPM pursues to mine and analyse educational data at *process-levels*. Although, Bogarín et al (2018) notes that both the EDM and EPM apply specific algorithms to data in order to discover hidden patterns or relationships that describe the data. In fact, whichever tool one chooses to adopt, the key focus should be on achieving the purpose of adopting either of the techniques. For example, one may pursue and focus on developing process analysis methods that reproduce or mimics the individual learner activities in order to help improve the learning efficiency and/or provide useful knowledge about how the individual process elements interact with each other within the learning knowledge base. A typical example of how the learning process modelling and analysis is performed is provided in chapters 5 and 6 of this book. Besides, the effective enhancement of the learning process and its evaluated performance (see: chapter 8) is capable of providing sound arguments or point of analysis to help perceive and/or identify the benefits for different learning scenarios.

Equally, the work of Cairns et al (2015) studies the potential benefit of the process mining techniques within the educational domain by proposing a two-step clustering approach to extract the best training paths depending on an employability indicator. According to Cairns et al (2015), the embracing of abstract filtering or clustering technique could assist in reducing complexities within the learned models to improve the real-time application of the process discovery and analysis techniques in an educational setting. Although, Cairns et al (2014) observe that existing methods for extracting models within the educational processes are limited to some extent because the approaches depend on the classical process mining techniques that are purely syntactic in nature (i.e. based on the labels in event logs) to discover the process models. In so doing, the developed systems do not technically gain from the real-world knowledge that describes the processes as performed in reality, and as consequence, the actual *semantics* behind the recorded educational events log remains missing and sprouts the need for who have to interpret them. Therefore, in practice, the real-time application of the *process mining* tools or methods (e.g. within the EPM domain) poses some certain issue of *semantics* that limits its efficiency when handling the large volume of events log gathered from the complex educational systems as well as their analysis at conceptual levels (de Medeiros & Van der Aalst, 2009; Cairns, et al., 2014). However, Cairns, et al (2014) thinks that the *semantic process mining* method appears to be a promising area that can be explored in order to resolve those issues of *understanding* the different learning patterns or trace heterogeneity, and as such, to extract streamlined models that fits or represents the actual processes as performed in reality. At the same time, the authors (Cairns, et al., 2014) believes that *semantic annotation* of the captured datasets can also be utilized to address the problem or challenges of interpreting the processes in question. Henceforth, to benefit from the actual semantics behind those event tags or labels, the *semantic process mining* (de Medeiros & Van der Aalst, 2009; deMedeiros, et al., 2008) which enforces the process mining and analysis of processes at a more conceptual level has to be employed.

For this purposes, the work in this book target to provide a semantic process mining approach that is directed towards the discovery of useful models from any given process domain data, and then carries out the enhancement of the discovered process models through the conceptualization method. For instance, the work shows using data about a learning process - how event data from various process domains (e.g. the educational process) can be extracted, semantically prepared, and transformed into mining executable formats to support the discovery, monitoring and enhancement of real-time processes through further semantic analysis of the discovered models. Perhaps, the aim is not only to extract the streams of event logs from the learning execution environment but to help define formats that allow for mining and improved analysis of the captured datasets. For example, by semantically annotating the process elements with concepts they represent in real time and then linking them to an ontology built for representing the learning processes. Truly, the method proves to allow for analysis of the extracted event logs based on concepts rather than the event tags of the process. Moreover, the semantic-based analysis allows the meaning of the learning objects and the resultant models to be enhanced through the use of property characteristics and classification of the discoverable entities. This is done in order to generate inference knowledge which is then used to determine useful patterns and improve analysis of the discovered models to a more conceptual level as opposed to the syntactic nature of analysis displayed by the traditional PM techniques. To this end, the work looks at some of the different application tools or features that underlie the application of process mining for real-time processing using the case study example of the educational domain.

Learning Process Automation

The work of Holzhüter et al (2013) notes that *process mining* is the discipline capable of offering useful tools and/or sets of concept to carry out the optimization/adaptation of learning processes in real-time. In fact, the automation of the learning process means supplying simulations, contents and interactive maps in a unified and well-structured manner, moreover, this is where the process modelling, when integrated with the PM techniques, is capable of providing a useful method for analysis and better identification or interpretation of the learning problems. Thus, the main reason why the proposed method of this book is grounded on the process mining and semantic process modelling techniques.

Learning Process Management vs
Business Intelligence (BI)

Theoretically, the process mining belong to the collections of tool within the business intelligence (BI) as well as the many other overlapping terms such as business activity monitoring (BAM), business process management (BPM), process-aware information systems (PAIS) etc. (Van der Aalst, 2011; Van der Aalst, 2016) that uses, if not all, the data mining (DM) techniques described in the following Figure 2 to find out patterns or models from event logs (e.g. the learning process), and predict outcomes through further analysis of the discovered models.

For example, the authors in (Cesarini, et al., 2004; Perez-Rodriguez, et al., 2008) introduces various approaches for learning pattern control through a workflow management system (WFM) (Van der Aalst et al, 2004) but does not relate a devoted strategy for the process analysis such as the process mining technique. On the other hand, Nguyen & Phung (2008) sparks the potential benefits of enhancing learning process models particularly by studying its application within the context of Adaptive Educational Hypermedia Systems (AEHS). The authors apply the method by constructing a framework for exploiting learner models which combine the process mining techniques with the concepts of learning patterns.

Figure 2. Application of Data Mining in e-learning settings (Dżega & Pietruszkiewicz, 2013)

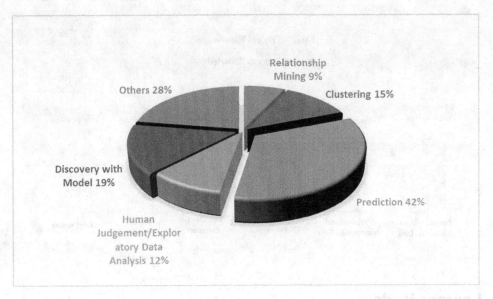

Learning Patterns Discovery

In the same way, the authors in (Trčka, et al., 2010; Pechenizkiy, et al., 2009) have worked on methods that applies the process mining technique in context of the e-learning process. The works analyses and points out tools that are currently being used to perform process mining tasks which qualifies better in support of e-learning processes. Whereas, the work in Holzhüter et al (2013) upholds that a way of supporting learners within an e-learning setting is to adopt the combined approach of using the process mining techniques with concepts of the discovered learning patterns. Generally, the learning patterns discovery describes how leaners sees, interacts or responds to a learning process, and therefore in turn measures the differences between the individual properties, or better still, help provide useful information on how to recommend (user recommendation system) certain paths or behaviours for new learners that may have or share the same properties.

Figure 3. Classical Process Mining and Analysis Framework (Holzhüter, et al., 2013)

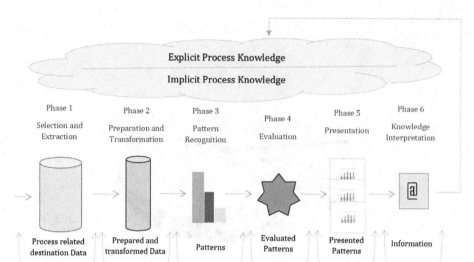

Learner Models

Typically, a learner model records the learners behaviours, and as such represents and interprets to a certain extent the characteristics (attributes) of the learners within the learning knowledge base (e.g. user ID's, task preferences, roles, abilities, categories, date and timestamps etc). These representative properties of the learners are significant and could be related to some kind of particular user-groups (e.g. through the classification method) within the learning knowledge base. In other words, the procedure/method classifies the learners as belonging to a specific or a different group, as well as integrates their usual properties within the domain models.

Learning Process Analysis and Classifications

According to the work of Holzhüter et al (2013), to perform the classification or assumptions of individual learners pattern, datasets need to be collected (extracted) from a learning system (i.e the data sources). Moreover, in view of carrying out the process analysis - the extracted datasets need to be prepared and transformed into minable formats that allow for the pattern recognition to follow. Consequently, prior to performing any other further analysis or use of the discovered information, an evaluation of the resulting learning patterns or system is carried out, and then the results are presented and interpreted as shown in Figure 3.

As gathered in Figure 3- such type of analysis often allied to the *process mining* techniques improves the process knowledge-bases in an explicit manner, Moreover, the learning processes are necessarily complemented by some implicit knowledge which may also be discovered inadvertently (Grob, et al., 2008). In other words, process mining could be applied to analyse and improve learning processes/models, or even more, used to recommend future learning patterns or behaviours.

In summary, the method and framework described in Holzhüter et al (2013) introduce the notion of process mining technique in e-learning settings to highlight the need of the approach in offering process analysts the capability of improving information values of those systems. Apparently, the authors (Holzhüter, et al., 2013) opines that process mining in combination with learning concepts could be a promising tool for learning process automation and modelling. Their arguments are concerned with how learning processes can be improved through the use of process modelling languages and rule-based controls, as well as how the process models can be generated in details taking into account the concept of learning styles or patterns. Interestingly, the outcome of their research (Holzhüter, et al., 2013) reveals that the implementation of rule-based controlled methods (e.g. workflows) into systems that support the learning process and its management still rests an important field of further investigation.

To this end, and with the intent to address such gap in literature - this book introduces the SPMaAF framework (see: chapter 3) and its main application for real-time processing which is perceived as a semantic-based PM approach (i.e extended or semantically enriched version of Figure 3) that is directed towards the discovery and enhancement of the derived process models. The work has used different case studies (see: Chapters 6 and 7) which include the learning process domain in order to show the influence and usefulness of the semantic-based approach for managing the business processes and analysis.

BUSINESS INTELLIGENCE (BI)

Business Intelligence (BI) is a broad term used to refer to methods which combine different procedures or tools by aiming at providing actionable information that can be used to support the decision-making process (Van der Aalst, 2011). Most of the time, BI is used in place of the other overlapping terms, namely - Business Process Intelligence (BPI) (Ingvaldsen, et al., 2005; van Dongen, et al., 2016). Even though, many other terms has also been used under the umbrella of BI such as the Business Process Management (BPM) (Santoro, et al., 2016), Business Activity Monitoring (BAM) (Van der Aalst, 2016), Corporate Performance Management (CPM) (Van der Aalst, 2016) etc. According to Van der Aalst (2016) the aforementioned terms have emerged as a result of the many vendors who offer BI software solutions (merchandises) and their attempts to verbally distinguish themselves from the other competitors, as well as, to show additional functionalities their product may be capable of offering.

In most cases, the usual functionalities offered by the BI products include but are not limited to the following five purposes as observed in (Van der Aalst, 2011; Van der Aalst, 2016):

- *Extract, Transform and Load* (ETL) the datasets from the different sources
- *Ad-hoc Querying* of the data and/or derived models
- *Reporting* of the newly discovered information
- *Interactive Dashboards* to help support the reporting of data and information visualization.
- *Alert Generation* useful to support the business process in general e.g. the decision-making process, user recommendation system etc.

Accordingly, some example of the state of the art BI systems (de Leoni, et al., 2012; Gatner, 2010; Van der Aalst, 2011) to mention but a few are as follows: IBM Cognos Analytics, Oracle Business Intelligence, SAP Business Intelligence, WebFOCUS, SQL Server BI, MicroStrategy, Necto Panorama Software, Qlik, SAS BI & Analytics, TIBCO Spotfire, TIBCO Jaspersoft, Pentaho Business analytics, Tableau and Alteryx[1] the recently trend in business data modelling and visualization etc.

Indeed, the process mining (Van der Aalst, 2011) field has been professed and proves to be a new collection of the BI techniques, and have closely ranked as a model-based analytic and powerful technique within the wider context of the BPM, and the industrial concepts of BAM.

Business Activity Monitoring (BAM)

BAM refers to the real-time monitoring of business processes (Van der Aalst, 2011). Apparently, the method allows and supports many organizations in extracting business performance metrics and relating those measures to the existing business operations. BAM tools as observed in (Van der Aalst, 2016; Ingvaldsen, 2011) are different from the process mining term because they assume a pre-defined or causal business process models – which means that every now and then, the resulting process models are out-dated and/or unfitting. Besides, the BAM tools aim to accomplish the business communication problems rather than the entire details or aspects of a real-life/actual business process (Adriansyah, et al., 2011).

Business Process Intelligence (BPI)

BPI is another term that is used to refer to the BI. According to the objectives and focus of one of the main discussions in BPI technologies and its applications in real-life (van Dongen, et al., 2016); BPI is an area that spans different aspects of process mining; from process discovery to conformance checking, model enhancement to predictive analytics and many other techniques which are nowadays being investigated, and altogether, are gaining attention within the research industry. In other words, the BPI notion refers to the application of the pool of different measures and analysis methods within the area of BPM (Santoro, et al., 2016). Moreover, the BPI is characterized by a common goal in relation to the process mining field. This relatedness is defined by the fact that most of the algorithms or tools that support the BPI also operates on event logs (i.e captured datasets). In turn, the algorithms are used to analyse to the different sets of activities or individual traces that can be found or as performed within the so-called processes (e.g. business process). In practice, BPI embodies the methods used for handling process executions and values by purporting several features such as process optimization, monitoring and control, to prediction and analysis etc.

On the other hand, the works in (Ingvaldsen, 2011; Erdmann, et al., 2000; Van der Aalst, 2016) observes that considering the analytical capabilities of the current systems that support BPI in practice, they are not always very intelligent and suffers from some kind of functionality limitations. Thus far, those restrictions (limitations) can be viewed from different perspectives as noted in Ingvaldsen (2011) as follows:

- **Performance Perspectives:** Where logs are not structured enough for data analysis. Process logs are designed to ease and not delay the job of the data or information processing engines.
- **Data Quality Perspectives**: Which includes noise, inconsistencies or missing data, and special codes that are not intuitive and easy to solve.
- **Semantics Perspectives**: Many times, even though the datasets are being extracted and modelled with acceptable performance to accurately reflect the execution of the processes as performed in reality, they may still be unusable for many process analysis purpose, because they lack the abstraction level required from a real-world perspective.

Actually, researchers, software vendors, and the many large scale organizations have been pursuing industriously over the years towards the development of methodologies/tools which targets at overcoming such limitations with the BPI. A typical example is the annual BPI workshop (van Dongen, et al., 2016) which predominantly strives to achieve but are not limited to the following goals: Process discovery, Intelligent Process analysis, Prediction, Handling Decisions and Exceptions, Optimization of Static processes, Optimization of Dynamic processes etc.

Business Process Management (BPM)

Another significant aspect of the process mining field is that it complements existing approaches to BPM, otherwise referred to process of continuous process improvement. Remarkably, one of the best known BPM researcher (Van der Aalst, 2016; Van der Aalst, 2011) refers to the term (BPM) as the "discipline that combines knowledge from information technology and knowledge from management sciences, and applies this to operational business process" (Van der Aalst, 2004; Weske, 2007). Moreover, BPM heavily relies on the concept of process modelling methods and has been perceived as an extension of workflow management systems (WFM) (Van der Aalst, 2011; Van der Aalst, et al., 2004). In any case, both the BPM and the traditional WFM systems (Van der Aalst, 2011) provides facts or key information on how activities are being performed within a process, and as such, are derived from the captured datasets often referred to as *event logs* (Gunther, et al., 2008; Van der Aalst, 2011). Technically, the methods or tools which are used to support the BPM approaches are mainly grounded on five important cycles as shown in the following chart (Figure 4)

Figure 4. Business Process Management (BPM) Life-cycle

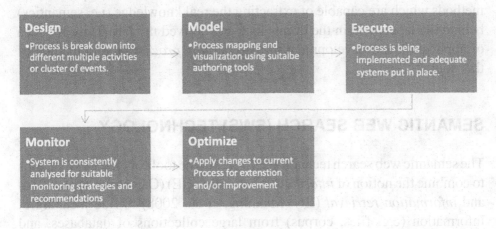

Other Terms

Also related to BI are other management tools and techniques which includes: Six Sigma (mainly used for improving operational performance), Total Quality Management (TQM) and Continuous Process Improvement (CPI) (Van der Aalst, 2011). These tools commonly have the characteristics that a process is put under scrutiny in order to check if further enhancements can be done or inadvertently possible (Van der Aalst, 2016). Interestingly, Van der Aalst (2011) notes that the BI systems and the many overlapping terms that are used to refer to the notion are not actually *intelligent* as they appear to be, and tends not to entirely encompass all the capabilities of the process mining techniques. According to Van der Aalst (2011), there is a problem with existing BI tools because they focus more on fancy looking dashboards or reports rather than carrying out an in-depth analysis of the captured datasets. To this end, the author (Van der Aalst, 2016; Van der Aalst, 2011) states that all of such BI systems are too *data centric* and are solely not aware of the processes the captured datasets are being used in. Although, the work (Van der Aalst, 2011) notes that a typical BI system provides data mining capabilities, such as Clustering, Regression, Classification, Association Rule Learning etc. Perhaps, such capabilities are not all, but one part of the techniques used for process mining to perform its tasks (e.g. the process mapping tasks, individual trace classifications etc).

In fact, nowadays the process *aware* and truly *intelligent* BI systems are potentially credible thanks to the advances within the *process mining* field (deMedeiros, et al., 2008; Van der Aalst, 2011; Okoye, et al., 2017; de Medeiros

& Van der Aalst, 2009; Okoye et al, 2019 & 2020) that aims to provide the methods which are capable of extracting the real knowledge (i.e. semantics) behind the labels within the events logs and derived models. Thus, the idea of application and development of the *semantic process mining* method of this book.

SEMANTIC WEB SEARCH (SWS) TECHNOLOGY

The semantic web search technologies refers to the tools or methods that aims to combine the notion of *information extraction* (IE) (Calvanese, et al., 2016) and *information retrieval* (IR) (Manning, et al., 2008) to find meaningful information (e.g. files, corpus) from large collections of databases, and then present the output/results to users (search initiator) based on some pre-specified information need. Basically, whilst the IR systems focuses on finding useful materials (e.g. documents) from the large collection of unstructured datasets or sources (e.g. the internet), the IE pursues to present the specified information in form or state in which the users are interested in, e.g., by providing the output in a structured format. Ultimately, the idea of combining the beneficial features of the information retrieval (IR) and extraction (IE) is the mechanism upon which the semantic technologies such as the proposed method (SPMaAF) method of this book are built. Moreover, the SWS is said to take into account the users' intent and users' data. In theory, *semantic web search* simply means finding a set of text or information that are relevant to the users' query (Ingvaldsen, 2011). Moreover, just as expressed in the name of the technology, we note that the term (semantic web search) is used to refer to the technologies that tends to integrate the two families of "semantic web" and "semantic search". Perhaps, in short definition, we define the *semantic web* technologies as methods or tools that are suitable for querying and/or retrieving information across several related information platforms, whereas, semantic search refers to the tools that proves useful for searching of information about a specific type of data in a single (domain) platform.

Interestingly, and in context of this book – the work of Cunningham (2005) notes that SWS technologies targets to add machine tractable and/or repurposable layer of annotations that are relative to *ontologies*. Even so, the method is used to match or complement the overwhelming (omnipresence) web of natural language hypertext (Fensel, et al., 2002; Bechhofer, et al., 2004) by creating semantically annotated terms, and then linking the resulting pages to ontologies. Consequently, the process turns out to be automatic or semi-automatic in nature due to the formal design, development, and inter-relation of the ontologies. According to Cunningham (2005) a typical example of such tools that support the semantic-based web search is the Knowledge and Information Management system (KIM) (Popov, et al., 2004) which offers IE-based facilities for metadata creation, storage, and semantically enriched web browsing or search. Equally, many other tools exist in literature e.g. SemTag system (Dill, et al., 2003) and Magpie (Domingue, et al., 2004) an add-on for the browser which relies on the fact that it makes use of ontologies to provide precise or tailored perspectives of the web pages which the user might be interested in (or wishes to browse) etc. Truly, all of the stated tools have one thing in common – being that the methods apply a form of metadata creation or data labelling to support the integration and/or linking of the datasets/models as described in the method of this paper (see: Chapter 3). Moreover, amongst the different characteristics that makes up the SWS technologies includes as follows (de Keyser, 2012):

- Capability to handle morphological variations regardless of the syntax
- Ability to handle synonyms
- Generalization, e.g., of object properties and restrictions.
- Concept matching
- Knowledge embedding and discovery
- Supports natural language processing (NLP) e.g. through logical queries and questions.
- Fuzziness or selection of the most relevant keywords or concepts.
- Logical queries which can be entered in a natural way and does not need to use boolean operators.
- Does not only build on some specific instances or components e.g. user behaviour, statistics, linking etc.
- Represented as process-aware information systems that can analyse its own performance (machine-understandable systems).

Interoperability for Semantic Web Search

In computing, interoperability is used to refer to methods or systems that are capable of accessing, exchanging and/or co-operatively use data in a synchronized way (HIMSS, 2020). A lot of the time, the said synchronization or exchange of data are carried out within and across different organizations and platforms to provide a unified, timely and optimized transferability of information within a given contextual domain. According to Goble et al

(2013), an understanding of how those available datasets can be compared and combined has shown to be a complex (interoperability) task that requires an ample knowledge of both the structures and content of the data collected from the different data sources. Perhaps, this also includes an understanding of how those sources could be made to work together coherently (Goble et al, 2013). Interestingly, García-Castro & Gómez-Pérez (2010) notes that attaining interoperability especially for semantic web search may not be a straightforward process because of the high heterogeneity of the semantic web technologies. Moreover, whilst the number of tools/methods which support the technology (SWS) grows, affordable mechanisms for evaluating their interoperability are needed to comprehend both the current and future capabilities of the semantic web technologies. Although, the work (García-Castro & Gómez-Pérez, 2010) argues that application of the SWS technologies within the complex scenes or platforms requires that the resultant methods correctly interoperate by interchanging, for instance, ontologies using the RDFs and OWL languages etc. To this effect, the authors (García-Castro & Gómez-Pérez, 2010) introduces an OWL interoperability method for benchmarking activities that involves evaluation of the interoperability of different SWS technologies using OWL as the interchange language.

Likewise, the work done in this book uses the OWL schema as core enabling tool for construction of the semantic-based approach as described in detail in Chapters 3 and 4. Pauwels et al (2018) also provides a brief overview of the current state of the art as it concerns interoperability for semantic web search in terms of standardization and community efforts in general. The work (Pauwels et al, 2018) notes that maintaining data consistency throughout the whole lifecycle of any given real-time process, especially during the design and construction phases, is a fundamental challenge to the different organizations. To this end, the authors (Pauwels et al, 2018) states that to address the aforementioned challenges, flexible mechanisms are required to facilitate data exchange between the different entities (process instances) that are involved at the different phases of the process, and in turn, help to provide the required interoperability between the different process elements or components (e.g. data, tools, devices and systems).

To summarize interoperability in relation to SWS, HIMSS (2020) highlights four levels of interoperability especially as it concerns its adoption and implementation in any given process and/or context as illustrated in the following Figure 5.

Figure 5. Four main levels of adoption and implementation of Interoperability for business process management (HIMSS, 2020)

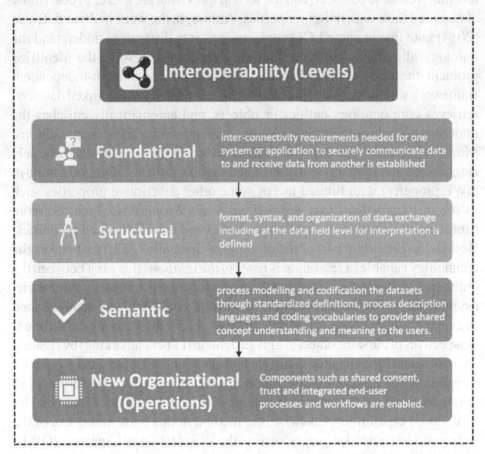

As gathered in the figure (Figure 5) the fundamental aim and outcome of interoperability for any given process must be focused on achieving seamless and timely communication and use of data both within and between the stakeholders e.g. organizations, entities and individuals (which includes governance, policy, social, legal and organizational considerations) to facilitate a secure business process management and operations in general (HIMSS, 2020).

Data Integration and Linking

One of the many areas in which the semantic technologies have experienced exponential growth over the past few decades is the Linked Open Data (LOD) cloud (Poggi et al, 2008; Zhao & Ichise, 2014). LOD consists of a number of machine-readable datasets (e.g. the RDF triples) that are useful in describing classes and their underlying properties. Although, the work in Zhao & Ichise (2014) note that in some LOD applications - it is difficult to understand the ontology alignments between multiple datasets. To resolve the identified problem, the authors (Zhao & Ichise, 2014) introduce a domain-independent framework which decreases the ontology heterogeneity in the linked datasets, retrieves core ontology entities or objects, and automatically enriches the underlying ontology by adding the domain, range, and properties annotations. Moreover, another problem with the LOD cloud is that the datasets are largely categorized into domains and interlinked mainly with *owl:sameAs* (a built-in OWL property) with limited use of some other descriptive properties such as the *owl:equivalentClass* and *owl:equivalentProperty* - which are more useful method for linking equivalent classes and their associated properties. Besides, an important part of the ontologies (specially OWL) that makes the technology capable of reasoning is *types of the relations* that exist between the ontological concepts (e.g. functional, inverse functional, transitive, symmetric, asymmetric, reflexive and irreflexive) (Motik et al, 2012) as demonstrated in chapter 5 of this book. Similarly, Pfaff et al (2018) measures the different perspectives of the same object in a given domain (IT benchmarking) by creating an ontological formalization of all relevant elements, attributes, and properties integration using the expressive functionalities of the OWL (Bechhofer et al, 2004) with logical reasoning (Horrocks et al, 2004) and querying (Baader et al, 2003) capabilities. Likewise, the method of this book makes use of the property description languages such as the Web Ontology Language (OWL) (Bechhofer et al, 2004), Semantic Web Rule Language (SWRL) (Horrocks et al, 2004), and Description Logic (DL) queries (Baader et al, 2003) to provide a semantic-based process mining method that supports real-time description of the process elements or labels. This is done by allowing the meaning of the process elements to be enhanced through the metadata creation or data labelling. Thus, semantical annotations by using the formal and expressive properties of the semantic schema/vocabularies.

Semantic Annotation and Data Labelling

One of the biggest challenge when performing process mining task is to discover the correct (right) information and to understand what they mean (Rozinat, 2016; Carmona et al, 2016; Rozinat, 2010). The works in (Lautenbacher et al,

2009; Born et al, 2007; Lautenbacher et al, 2008; Okoye et al, 2019, Okoye et al, 2020) shows that the semantically annotated logs or models are necessary for the conceptual analysis, and consequently, the model enhancement to follow. Specifically, the work in (Okoye et al, 2019; Okoye et al 2020) notes that the semantic annotation (data labelling) is an essential component in realizing such tools that support the semantic process mining. This is done by automatically conveying the formal structures (meaning) of the derived models or extracted logs. Theoretically, the semantic annotation is defined formally as a function that returns a set of concepts from the ontology for each node or edge in the resultant graph or models (Lautenbacher et al, 2009; Lautenbacher et al, 2008). Equally, Born et al (2007) note that the semantic annotation process could be carried out either manually, or automatically computed bearing in mind the similarity of words to generalize the individual entities or properties within the domain processes in view. Recently, Jonquet et al (2018) studied ontology metadata practices by analysing metadata annotations of different ontologies and reviewing the most standard and relevant vocabularies. The work (Jonquet et al, 2018) systematically compared different metadata implementation in various ontology repositories (reference libraries) in order to build a new metadata model that can be used to describe ontologies.

In the same manner, the work in this book introduces a technique for annotating unlabelled activity sequences using the semantic schema/vocabularies (see chapter 5). The book demonstrates the method using a series of case study experimentation such the learning process domain (see: chapter 6) and data about the business process (Carmona et al, 2016) (see: chapter 7). Fundamentally, the method is used to transform the extracted datasets and models into minable executable formats (e.g. through the use of property description languages) to support the discovery and improved process models. In other words, the method for semantically annotating the unlabelled activity sequences or workflows makes use of the ontological schema (e.g. OWL, SWRL, DL queries, restriction properties) to provide metadata or object-property assertions that allow for the discovering of useful information and/or relevant rule expressions within the existing knowledge-base.

Interestingly, we note that OWL (Bechhofer et al, 2004; W3C, 2004) has emerged as the standard format for defining the semantic web ontologies, and has since in recent years, widely been accepted and used towards advanced structuring of information and knowledge engineering. The OWL is specially built for the purpose of depiction of inference rules and modelling of the different associations they hold between the entities that can be found within the available datasets or input models. For example, as utilized in chapter 5 and

6 of this book to support the process descriptions (assertions) and reasoning of the derived process models at a more conceptual level. Moreover, as a set(s) of annotated terms and relations, the resulting ontologies or semantic model supports information extraction particularly compared to the *Ontology-based Information Extraction* (OBIE) systems (Wimalasuriya & Dou, 2010).

Over the next sections of this chapter, the work subsequently looks at the Ontology-Based Information Extraction systems (OBIE) and how they can be applied to support meaningful information extractions and management of processes in different contexts or settings, especially within the process mining field.

ONTOLOGY-BASED INFORMATION EXTRACTION (OBIE) SYSTEMS

Ontology-Based Information Extraction systems (OBIE) refer to tools or methods that aim to identify and extract information in form of texts (concepts) and describes the relations (properties) which are relatedly expressed in an ontology for any given process domain (Yankova, et al., 2008). The OBIE notion spans and is inspired by the *Information Extraction* (IE) terminology. According to the observation in Cunningham (2005) typical IE systems take as input - texts and even at times speech, to produce fixed format explicit data as outputs. Obviously, such method of information extraction means that IE systems only presents relevant (specific) information or knowledge in a form in which the users are interested in. Actually, this feature is where OBIE systems draw its incentive due to the fact that *ontology* is one of such tools that have the capacity of providing information in a structured format. For example, the automatic population of ontologies in OBIE applications means that the resulting systems are capable of identifying instances within a text document or process models that belong to a particular class, and trails to add those learned instances within their correctly inferred locations. Moreover, the work of Yankova et al (2008) observes that such method for information aggregation has proved to be advantageous by increasing the confidence of the extracted information, as well as, formal storage of the updated information within the process knowledge bases. For instance, if an employee's new role is added to his/her description in an OBIE system, it is expected that the role restriction will be added to a new identity criterion, and not necessarily changing the entire function or a-priori details in the system.

On the other hand, Yankova et al (2008) reveal that one fundamental problem to be addressed when providing a structure for distribution of conceptual knowledge such as the OBIE system is the question of *identification* and *integration* of the entities (instances) which are extracted from different data sources. Perhaps, the process should aim at identifying newly extracted facts (e.g. from texts, models, web pages) and linking them to their previously mentioned references. To this end, example work in this area of research (Cunningham, 2005) notes that OBIE poses two main challenges especially as it concerns the development of the methods which are mainly directed towards:

(i)   identification of concepts from the ontologies, and
(ii)   automatic population of ontologies with instances in the texts or databases.

Moreover, if the ontology in question is already populated with instances, the task of an OBIE system may perhaps be simply to identify and integrate those instances from the ontology in the text or data sources (Cunningham, 2005). According to Cunningham (2005), with such methodology, it appears to be more useful as opposed to the traditional IE systems because they make use of an ontology rather than a flat gazetteer. Practically, the work (Cunningham, 2005) notes that for such systems which are *rule-based*, the procedures or method used to integrate the instances in the ontologies are pretty direct (straightforward). But for the systems which are *learning-based*, it appears to be somewhat challenging because a *training dataset* is most often required. In turn, the method for collection of the training datasets is likely to be a constraint or bottleneck. Perhaps, to address such problems; new training datasets have to be manually or semi-automatically created, which appears to be time-consuming and are sometimes a burdensome task. Although, new methods and systems are currently being developed with the intent to help support such metadata creation (Jonquet et al, 2018; Lautenbacher et al, 2009; Zhao & Ichise, 2014; Pfaff et al, 2018). Besides, a number of OBIE supported systems have also been proposed and used in different settings in current literature(De Giacomo, et al., 2018; d'Amato, et al., 2008; deMedeiros, et al., 2008; Okoye, et al., 2016; Yankova, et al., 2008, Okoye et al, 2019).

In summary, it is important to note that one common feature of the methods described in those works (De Giacomo, et al., 2018; d'Amato, et al., 2008; deMedeiros, et al., 2008; Okoye, et al., 2016; Yankova, et al., 2008, Okoye et al, 2019 & 2020) is that unlike the traditional IE systems (where the extracted information are only classified as appropriate for pre-defined data types) the methods seek to discover data structures that aim at generating reference links between the objects (process instances) inherent in the knowledge-bases as well as their mentions within the contextual domain of interest (Cunningham, 2005). In other words, the ontology-based systems do not only contain representations of the specified domains, but they also provide information about the identity of the process instances (entities) as well as their mention within the knowledge-base (e.g. through the object/datatype properties). Thus, a suitable OBIE system must contain a set of well-defined concepts (classes, object properties, and individual assertions) with their full semantic descriptions.

OBIE in Context of Process Mining

In relation to the work done in this book and application of the OBIE systems in practice, the work in Calvanese et al (2016) looks at the OBIE in context of the process mining by highlighting the extreme challenges encountered when extracting the different events data logs or models. The work reveals the necessity for appropriate methods that are deemed beneficial towards extracting events log from the relational databases. According to the authors (Calvanese, et al., 2016), the *information extraction* processes or methods spans across several levels of abstractions; ranging from the high-level (i.e. the domain-independent notions which are characterized at the conceptual level by the so-called domain ontology), to coming down to the concrete level at which sets of data are effectively stored.

Even though, a number of process mining tools such as the XESame (Verbeek, et al., 2011), ProMimport (Verbeek, 2014; Gu¨nther & Van der Aalst, 2006), and ProM (Verbeek, et al., 2011) that all support events log extraction, and the commercial tools (such as Disco Rozinat & Gunther, 2012) and many other overlapping tools - MinIt, Celonis, MyInveno etc.) that makes it easier to transform excel or CSV files into an eXtensible Event Streams (XES) (IEEE 1849-2016, 2016; Verbeek, et al., 2011) or Mining eXtensible Markup Language (MXML) (deMedeiros, et al., 2008) log format has already been developed. On the one hand, Calvanese et al (2016) observe that none of those tools or process mining platforms, in reality, considers the domain-specific information in the loop. In consequence, the process of extracting valuable information or populating the ontologies are a lot of the time ad-hoc because in such settings, the data might be duplicated for dissimilar interpretations, and the semantics of the available datasets perhaps cannot be traced back in most cases. On the other hand, the authors (Calvanese, et al., 2016) notes that some works have similarly been done on semantically annotated events log (deMedeiros, et al., 2008; Allahyari, et al., 2014; Erdmann, et al., 2000; Calvanese, et al., 2017; Ingvaldsen, 2011) which focus on exploiting such ontological information during the data analysis process, but yet, do not put profusely in consideration the process of extracting the events log. However, to overcome such challenges, the work (Calvanese, et al., 2016) argues that the data analytics methods, or yet still, the process mining could be theoretically applied only if realistic datasets (i.e. event logs) that follows the accepted standards (e.g. XES) (Verbeek, et al., 2011) are available, and in view of that, proposes a novel framework that supports domain experts in the extraction of XES events log information from legacy relational databases (Calvanese, et al., 2016).

Practically, in order to demonstrate the capability of the ontology-based framework in context of the process mining, the work in Calvanese et al (2016) resort to a well-established Ontology-Based Data Access (OBDA) model which allows one (e.g. the said process analysts) to link the raw data to the underlying domain ontologies (i.e. hierarchical datasets or taxonomy), and in so doing, overcome the impedance mismatch. Having constructed the taxonomical framework or the domain information structure, the process analysts can focus more on the ontological levels only, whilst the associations within the underlying knowledge-base/datasets are managed automatically by the OBDA system (De Giacomo, et al., 2018; Poggi, et al., 2008). In other words, the ontology-based approaches such as the OBIE can provide basis for the development of process mining tools and algorithms that are capable of extracting conceptual information - either by explicitly materializing it or by retrieving the information on demand.

Likewise, the work in this book is grounded on the process mining and semantic (i.e ontological) modelling techniques. Consequently, the book introduces an ontology-based system that is able to perform information retrieval and/or query answering in a more abstract way compared to other standard logical procedures used for information management and data analysis (semantic data engineering).

OBIE in Context of Knowledge Extraction for BI

Business Intelligence (BI) are information gateways or systems which assist business analysts with the tasks of discovering, gathering, aggregating, and analysing of information. For instance, a simple BI task could mean a search for documents within a colossal amount of data or electronic note. Quite often, it is up to the user of such system to dig into the large amounts of the readily available data to find relevant facts that supports the so-called businesses or the decision making processes e.g. credit ratings, measuring probability of the business success, discovering appropriate business partners, or getting up-to-date facts about companies, places, people etc (Yankova, et al., 2008).

The work of Yankova et al (2008) explains the application of OBIE systems within the Business Intelligence (BI) context through their project named MUSING project (Yankova, et al., 2008). The method focuses on integrating human language applications with semantic technologies in order to address the problem of identifying and integration of the different process elements which can be found within the various datasets - which are every now and again extracted from the different data sources. Theoretically, the works in (Yankova, et al., 2008; Calvanese, et al., 2017; De Giacomo, et al., 2018) shows that the answer to such problem relies on applying process modelling and natural language processing (NLP) (Maynard, et al., 2007) approaches to complement the supposed *unstructured-data sources*. Actually, such integrating of the human language applications with the semantic technologies is related to the OBIE supported systems. Perhaps, the planned methods for knowledge extraction should aim at allowing the transformation of the different data extracts into a well-structured representation that fits the said higher level (conceptual) of analysis. For example, the MUSING project (Yankova, et al., 2008) has been developed with a key focus on identifying newly extracted business facts, e.g. from text or models, and aims to link them to their prior references through formal structures (e.g. population of ontologies). The authors (Yankova, et al., 2008) has developed the project using the general architecture text engineering (GATE) platform (Cunningham, et al., 1995). Moreover, the GATE system is a text (engineering) developer tool that offers a wide range of applications that have proved useful towards the development of OBIE systems, especially with regards to its ability to support ontology-based projects. The main component and lesson learned here (i.e. the key element of the system) is the *annotations* that are created by using the method. Thus, the annotation of the different texts (corpus or datasets) is done through encoding of an ontological information system (*mention* annotations) that makes references to targeted ontologies, as well as, the concepts referenced by the strings of texts or labels. Equally, the method of this book introduces a technique for semantic annotation of the process models by making use of the ontological schema/vocabularies, thus, allows the meaning of the process elements to be enhanced through the metadata creation or encoding of the ontological information.

MEASURING PERFORMANCE AND FLEXIBILITY IN OBIE SYSTEMS

To run through the importance of the OBIE systems and its application to solve real-time problems, for instance, by weighing the impact of the classification tasks or method, and the influence of the underlying logic – the work in Maynard et al (2008) discusses the different ways and/or means for measuring the performance of OBIE systems. The work (Maynard, et al., 2008) looks at why the traditional *precision* and *recall* evaluation metrics usually applied for systematic information extraction methods are somewhat insufficient when ontologies are involved. In turn, the authors propose the Balanced Distance Metric (BDM) (Maynard, et al., 2006) which measures the flexibility of the ontology-based systems, as well as, takes into account the similarities between the different (ontology-based) systems. Specifically, the experimentations in Maynard et al (2008) based their arguments on the reason why the traditionally discovered entities (classes) does not incorporate one another? Whereas with ontology-based settings, there exists *subClasses* or *superClass* types to reason or integrate. Hence, discrepancies amongst what is thought as correct or incorrect (i.e. true or false) classes are not clear. Interestingly, the authors (Maynard, et al., 2008) observes that with traditional or standard IE systems, a process instance (entity) that is recognized as a *person* may either be true or false when measured using *precision* method. However, when measured by *recall*, the instances which should have been recognized as a *person* are either identified or not at all. Moreover, the dissimilarities are fuzzier (Günther & Van der Aalst, 2007; Zadeh, 1971; Rozinat, 2010), especially when making ontological classifications after all. Nonetheless, Maynard et al (2008) argue that such method of evaluation of the models or systems can at times be conventionally realized by assigning a half-weight to *things* (e.g. entities) considered to be partially correct, yet, are still not enough to provide a proper (balanced) differentiation between the levels of accuracy or precision. Even though, credit should be given for partial correctness.

Surely, the balanced distance metric (BDM) (Maynard, et al., 2008) follows some of the guidelines proposed by (King, 2003). Henceforth, an effective ontology-based application and performance metrics should:

- reach its highest value for perfect quality
- reach its lowest value for worst possible quality
- be monotonic
- be clear and intuitive
- correlate well with human judgment
- be reliable and exhibit as little variance as possible
- be cheap to set up and apply
- be automatic

Without a doubt, the preliminary observations in the work (Maynard, et al., 2008) shows that two-fold (binary) decisions are not appropriate for evaluation of ontology-based systems, especially in settings where the objects or class hierarchies (taxonomy) are being considered. As gathered in the observations (Maynard, et al., 2008), both the Balanced Distance Metrics (BDM) and Learning Accuracy (LA) metrics are more useful when compared to the distance-based or flat metric. In other words, the Balanced Distance Metrics (BDM) or Learning Accuracy (LA) metrics are more resourceful when evaluating information or extraction of concepts based on hierarchical rather than a flat structure (Maynard, et al., 2008).

Interestingly, the most notable and applicable outcome of the evaluation in the work (Maynard, et al., 2008) with regards to the context of this book - is the usefulness of the performance measures (metrics) in *population of ontologies*. In practice, the evaluation metrics were specifically centered on structures of an ontology to analyse similarities between the concepts defined within the ontologies as utilized in the method of this book. Moreover, since based on the *description logic* (Baader et al, 2003) - the ontologies are not only able to allow for semantic interpretations, but can also measure the concepts similarities by making use of the underlying descriptions/assertions. Overall, Maynard et al (2008) note that such kind of semantic similarity would make more sense than the structure-based measures especially for complex systems or ontologies that contain different types of relations. Besides, the method could be applied to help provide more flexibility and support for task-specific processes and systems which are believed to be *aware* of the processes they trail to support as discussed in the next section.

PROCESS-AWARE INFORMATION SYSTEMS (PAIS)

Process-Aware Information Systems (PAIS) comprises of the methods that aim to provide more flexibility and support for task-specific processes (Dumas, et al., 2005; de Leoni, et al., 2008). Perhaps, a typical example of PAIS is the traditional workflow management systems (WFM) (Van der Aalst et al, 2004). Moreover, many other process control and management systems which overlaps or could be classed under the umbrella of PAIS exists – which includes but to name a few: SAP (Oracle), Enterprise Resource Planning (ERP), Customer Relationship Management (CRM), WebSphere (High-end middleware), Rule-based systems, Call Centre software etc.

Even though PAIS tends not to necessarily control the process via some generic work-flow engine, they share a common attribute which is that the information systems are entirely aware of each and every process they trail to support, and also, for the fact that there exists an explicit process view or interpretation (Van der Aalst, 2011). According to Van der Aalst (2011) many database systems or programs may well be utilized for executing/mapping of the activities sequence (i.e. steps) within a given process (e.g. business process). However, those systems are most often not aware of the methods or processes they are being used to support. For that reason, the systems or programs appear not to be dynamically involved in the transposition or management of the processes they are involved in. Therefore, the more flexibility (generalization) a PAIS allows for, the greater the diversity of behaviours that can be derived from the supported processes. Moreover, only in situations where the process in question shows a great level of flexibility, would the resultant models offer the best values when compared to other methods that could be used to perform the task-specific processing such as the business activity monitoring (BAM), or better still, the business process management (BPM) systems (Van der Aalst, 2016).

Totally, the process mining technique embodies PAIS, because process mining aims to mine and analyse event logs at *process-level*, and at the same time, are entirely aware of the *facts* or details (to a greater extent) of how the various activities have been performed. Indeed, such a method/means of data analysis which also is related to the proposed SPMaAF framework described in this book (see: chapter 3) - makes use of semantic annotations to add meanings to the discovered models, and in consequence, enables an automatic inference (e.g. process querying – see the conclusion) of new and abstract knowledge from the underlying knowledge-bases. This is done with the goal of bringing the process-related information to a more conceptual level of human (real-world) understanding. Thus, the method of this paper is exclusively considered to support *machine-understandable* system rather than just *machine-readable* system.

Process Querying

Process querying is an emerging method for automated management of real-world or envisioned processes, models, repositories, and knowledge within the field of business process management or organizational data analysis (Polyvyanyy et al., 2017; Polyvyanyy et al, 2016). According to Polyvyanyy et al (2017) the process querying technique concerns automatic methods for handling (e.g. through filtering or manipulating) repositories of models of observed and unseen processes as well as their associated relationships. This is done with the intention of transforming the process-related information into decision-making capabilities. In theory, the work in Polyvyanyy et al (2016) notes that the process querying research spans a range of topics from theoretical studies of algorithms and the limits of computability of process querying techniques to practical issues of implementing the querying capabilities in software products. Besides, the work in Polyvyanyy et al (2017) observes that such methods which aim to combine the process models and ontologies (particularly ontologies for process management) are increasingly gaining attention in recent years. According to Polyvyanyy et al (2016), one reason for the growing interest is that ontologies permit the adding of semantics to the discovered or pre-existing models by enabling an automated discovery (inference) of knowledge from the domain processes in question. Consequently, the derived knowledge (semantic information) could then be used to manage any given process (e.g. business process) both at the design or execution time etc. To this end, the work carried out in Polyvyanyy et al (2017) proposes a process querying framework used for enabling business intelligence (BI) through query-based process analytics. The framework structures the state of the art components built on generic functions that can be configured to create a range of querying techniques, and also points to gaps in existing research and use cases within the BPM and BI fields. According to the observations in Polyvyanyy et al (2017), process querying methods need to address those gaps. For instance, organizations often fail to convert the high volume of data recorded in their various information system into strategic and tactical intelligence. This is owing to the lack of dedicated technologies that could be designed to effectively manage the informations that are encoded within the said business models or data records. Perhaps, an effective application of the ontology-based framework is useful to better support the process querying or strategic decision-making and to provide the next generation of business intelligence (Polyvyanyy et al., 2017). Interestingly, the proposed framework in Polyvyanyy et al (2017) is an abstract system in which components can be selectively replaced to result in a new process querying method.

For the purpose of the work done in this book, we focus particularly on the *Process Querying with Rich Annotations* (Polyvyanyy & et al, 2016) which studies the use of rich ontological annotations of process models for the purpose of process querying. Thus, the proposed method combines the derived process models with ontologies. Moreover, Montani et al (2017) notes that a trace abstraction technique (e.g. the Process Querying) for any semantic-based analysis such as the process mining method of this book should present the methods/frameworks which are able to convert traces found within the discovered models into higher level concepts based on the domain knowledge, thus, the term *conceptualization* method. Clearly, the proposed SPMaAF framework (see: chapter 3) sits as the central footing for the associated process querying method described in this book. Besides, the SPMaAF takes into account the different stages of the process mining and analysis - which includes the initial phase of collecting and transformation of the readily available events data logs, to discovering of useful (insightful) process models, and then, expounds the result of the standard process mining technique to semantical preparation of the extracted models for further analysis and querying at a more abstraction level.

RELATED WORKS AND SYSTEMATIC REVIEW

Most of the existing tools and methods for analysing large growing knowledge bases (such as the big data or process analysis) focus on creating techniques or approaches to help the said knowledge-bases automatically or semi-automatically extend. Miani & Hruschka (2015) observes that a vast number of such systems which constructs or supports the large knowledge-bases continuously grow, and most often, they do not contain all of the facts for each process instance or elements. As a consequence, the resultant process models may tend to be vague or missing value datasets. Henceforth, well-designed information retrieval or mining system should present the results or the discovered models in a formal and structured format qua being interpreted as domain knowledge, as well as, supports the further enhancement of the existing knowledge-base (Dou, et al., 2015).

Information Retrieval and Extraction

One of the main challenges with the process discovery (e.g. the information retrieval and extraction) techniques when applied to any given process domain - is that they rely exclusively on the syntax of labels in the datasets, and are very sensitive to data heterogeneity, label name variation and frequent changes (Cairns, et al., 2014). As a result, a majority of the process models are discovered without some kind of hierarchy or structuring. Although to address the said challenges, the work of Cairns et al (2014) shows how by linking labels in the events log to the underlying concepts (semantics) that describes the discovered models, one can bring process discovery (mining) to the conceptual level. This can be done in order to provide a more accurate mining and compact analysis of the processes at different levels of abstraction. Moreover, Cairns et al (2014) proposes a semi-automatic procedure used to associate semantics to training labels through the method for extraction of process models which are annotated with semantic information (metadata). The authors (Cairns, et al., 2014) used the Ontology Abstract Filter plug-in in ProM (Verbeek, et al., 2011) as input to a semantically annotated log to produce as output events log where the names of tasks, i.e. training labels, are replaced by the names of a set of chosen concepts. The resulting or produced log is then exported as Semantically Annotated Mining eXtensible Markup Language (SA-MXML) (deMedeiros, et al., 2008) file format, and subsequently perform a control-flow mining by using the Heuristic Miner algorithm (Weijters & Ribeiro, 2010; Weijters, et al., 2006) to extract the process models based on the concepts that has been derived.

Semantic-Based Process Analysis Through Conceptualization Method

Indeed, the methods for semantic-based process mining and analysis focuses on information about resources hidden within a process knowledge-base, and how they are related (deMedeiros, et al., 2008; de Medeiros & Van der Aalst, 2009; Okoye, et al., 2016; Okoye, et al., 2017; Jareevongpiboon & Janecek, 2013). The semantic-based process analysis allows the meaning of the process domain entities and object properties to be enhanced through the use of property characteristics and classification of discoverable entities. The objects/data properties and the classification aptitude (e.g. by making use of the reasoner) is used to support/permit for analysis of the extracted event logs based on concepts rather than the event tags or labels about the process. Currently, there are not too many algorithms that support such kind of semantic-based (conceptual) analysis and there are few existing applications that demonstrate the capabilities of the semantic-based approach (deMedeiros, et al., 2008; de Medeiros & Van der Aalst, 2009; Okoye, et al., 2017; Jareevongpiboon & Janecek, 2013, Okoye et al, 2019 & 2020). Remarkably, the works in (Okoye, et al., 2016; Okoye, et al., 2017; Okoye et al, 2019; Okoye et al, 2020) shows how the semantic annotations and reasoning method can be used to provide a more improved analysis (i.e enhancements) to the process models or input data logs through concept matching (i.e. ontology classifications). Specifically, the works in (Okoye, et al., 2016 & 2020) performs the semantic modelling and integration of the resulting process mappings with annotated terms, and then present the domain-specific information for the activity workflows and concepts defined in an ontology - by using process description languages such as the Web Ontology Language (OWL) (Horrocks, et al., 2007; W3C, 2012) and Semantic Web Rule Language (SWRL) (Horrocks, et al., 2004). Indeed, reasoning on the ontological knowledge plays an important role in the semantic representation of the supposed processes in view (Calvanese, et al., 2017). Besides, semantic reasoning allows for the extraction and conversion of the explicit information that underlies the process model into some implicit information. For example, the intersection or union of classes, description of relationships and concepts, or the different role assertions.

Process Modelling and Pattern Discovery

Elhebir & Abraham (2015) notes that the pattern discovery algorithms make use of the statistical and machine-learning techniques to build models that are capable of predicting the behaviour of the captured datasets. The authors concede that one of the most pattern discovery techniques used to extract knowledge from pre-processed data is Classification. Moreover, the work (Elhebir & Abraham, 2015) observe that most of the existing classification algorithms or methods attains good performance for specific problems but are not robust enough for all kinds of process discovery (mining) problems. To this effect, the authors (Elhebir & Abraham, 2015) propose that a combination of multiple classifiers (e.g. hybrid algorithms) could perhaps be considered as a general solution for pattern discovery because they obtain better results compared to a single classifier as long as the components are independent or have diverse outputs.

Classification and Reasoning

According to the works of (Han & Kamber, 2004; Han, et al., 2011) *classification* is one of the most common data mining (DM) technique that aims at finding models or functions that describes/distinguishes data classes (or concepts). Clearly, one of the many benefits of applying such DM technique in the method of this book is to help annotate and explain the classification labels (concepts) in line with the set of relations (assertions) defined in an ontology. The method is particularly useful for semantic enhancement of the input datasets and the discovered models. Perhaps, the semantic information encoded and/or discovered as a result of the classification tasks has the potential not only to influence the real-world understanding of the labelled data (i.e annotated logs or models) but also to handle the large number of unlabelled data (i.e the input or original data) (Allahyari, et al., 2014; Balcan, et al., 2013). For instance, Balcan et al (2013) incorporated ontology as consistency constraints into multiple related classification tasks by classifying multiple categories of unlabelled data in parallel to determine labels that violate the ontology. Although, d'Amato et al (2008) argue that classification is a fundamental task for a lot of intelligent systems and that classifying through logical reasoning may be both too demanding and frail because of inherent incompleteness and complexity in the knowledge bases. On the one hand, the work (d'Amato, et al., 2008) observes that the methods adopt the availability of an initial drawing of ontology that can be automatically enhanced by adding or refining concepts, and have been shown to effectively resolve process modelling problems (Okoye et al, 2016 & 2020) by using process description languages such as the (OWL and SWRL) (Bechhofer et al, 2004, Horrocks et al, 2004) and logic queries (Baader et al, 2003) particularly those based on classification, clustering and ranking of individuals. On the other hand, the works in (d'Amato, et al., 2008; Okoye, et al., 2016; Okoye et al, 2020) explicitly shows that the problem of modelling domain processes can be solved by transforming the ontology population problem to a classification task (reasoning method): where for each entity within the ontology, the concepts (classes) to which the entities belong to have to be determined, hence, *classified*.

Fuzzy Logic vs Fusion Theory

The works in (Baati, et al., 2016; Baati, et al., 2017) defines the Possibility theory, introduced by Zadeh (1965) and further developed by Dubois et al (1988) as a fusion theory based on the concept of fuzzy sets and are devoted to represent and combine imperfect information in a qualitative and yet quantitative manner. The authors (Baati et al., 2016) proposes two kinds of possibilistic classifiers which they applied on numerical data namely - (i) one that extends the classical and flexible Bayesian classifiers by applying a probability-possibility transformation to Gaussian distributions, and (ii) the second, that directly express or manipulates data in possibilistic formats using the idea of proximity between data values. Perhaps, one could say that information imperfections treated by possibility theory may be used to represent the uncertainty due to the variability of observations, uncertainty due to poor information, the information ambiguity, or the information imprecision etc (Khaleghi, et al., 2013). On the one hand, Baati et al (2017) notes that in many cases, the minimum-based possibilistic combination is likely to lead to a final decision that may have very close possibility estimate to other alternatives, and in such situations, the quality of decision may be seriously altered since the final classification tasks are likely to be inaccurate. On the other hand, to resolve such problem, the authors (Baati, et al., 2017) states that the Generalized Minimum-based (G-Min) algorithm (Baati, et al., 2016) can be applied to avoid the ambiguity between the final decision and the rest of the existing classes. Thus, to find a decision with a possibility estimate that is deemed to be widely away from other alternatives. According to the work (Baati, et al., 2017), the G-Min algorithm requires the matrix Π of possibilistic estimates. Moreover, the method is based on two main steps or analysis: (i) the first method which aims to build a set of possible decisions, and (ii) the second which aims to filter those set in order to find a final class with a high score of reliability (Baati, et al., 2016). Consequently, at the semantic level, the basic function in possibility theory could be defined as a possibility distribution (denoted as π) which assigns to each possible class c_j from C a value in either 1 (i.e true) or 0 (i.e false). The possibility value assigned to a class c_j stands for plausibility i.e. the belief degree that this class is the right one. By convention, $\pi(c_j) = 1$ means that c_j is totally possible and if, $\pi(c_j) = 0$, c_j is considered as impossible.

Likewise, the work in this book introduces a semantic-fuzzy mining approach that applies the *conceptualization method* (abstraction analysis) to turn the fuzzy models into a classification task or semantic-based reasoning system, for instance, using the case study of the business process with a training set and a test set (Carmona, et al., 2016; Van der Aalst, 2016) where the discovered models needs to decide whether traces found as a result of applying a *classifier* over the models are fitting (true) or not (false). Technically, the proposed method focuses on making use of semantic annotations to link the different process elements in the events log and models with concepts they represent in an ontology. Moreover, the purpose of the semantic annotation is to seek the equivalence between the *concepts of the fuzzy models* derived by applying the fuzzy miner algorithm on the datasets and the *concepts of the well-defined ontologies* or process domain.

Thematic Table/Representation of Related Literature

To summarize the related works, the method proposed in this book as opposed to the other benchmark techniques/algorithms within the field of process mining - makes use of the semantics of the sets of activities within the domain process and models to generate rules and events relating to the task. This is done in order to allow for automatic discovery and ascertaining of the various process instances that can be found within the models as well as the relationships they share amongst themselves within the knowledge-base. Clearly, the methodology of this book is put forward in an attempt to address the identified challenges with process mining techniques. Interestingly, the contributions and knowledge of this book can be used by the process owners in understanding their everyday processes, and more importantly, grasp information on how to improve on them by performing a real-time application of the method. Another benefit provided by the proposed method of this book is the ability to describe the semantics behind the labels in the represented models and events log which are considered useful for discovery of new knowledge about the domain processes in question. The main opportunity here is that the process knowledge-base is enhanced as a result of its analysis being based on concepts rather than event tags or labels. After all, when those real conceptual knowledge are inferred, and the semantic rules are executed, the knowledge base is updated with the newly discovered knowledge. Thus, providing the users (e.g. process owners or analysts) with new ways of extracting and analysing the input data logs. In general, the ample application of ontologies for any process mining or management system should focus on generating new or improve on the existing methods for the process analysis.

Therefore, as collated in this chapter, the work methodically presents in the table (Table 1) a systematic review of the related works considered appropriate to the method and proposals of this book. The review is carried out by critiquing and analysing the applicable studies that covers either of the process mining techniques or the semantic technologies. In other words, the analysis in Table 1 is a thematic look at the different methods, tools, case studies and its main application domains, as well as, the findings that are closely related to the semantic-based process mining and analysis method proposed in this book.

CONCLUSOIN

The work collates and analysed in this chapter - the main technologies and motives that have led to the emergence and use of the process mining technique, its trailed theories, and influence within the wider scientific community. Perhaps, this is owing to the fact that the process mining techniques builds on computational intelligence and the data mining techniques, which has led to its significant influence on how the process owners/analysts perceive and analyse the readily available large volumes of data captured from the various IT systems. For this purpose, the book deemed it necessary to look at the main tools and the other overlapping terms within the process mining field that are pertinent for the proposed approach in this book. In consequence, the chapter investigates the practical use of the process mining and the semantic modelling techniques in the current literature. For instance, the book reviews some of the approaches that are entirely aware of the several processes which they trail to support and are used to extract meaningful patterns from the event logs captured about those processes. This is done as a way of transforming and analysing the input datasets and models in order to provide real knowledge (semantics) and understanding of the processes in reality. Moreover, the chapter looks at the promising and applicable mechanisms (technique) towards the semantical improvement of the information values of the readily available events logs and models.

Table 1. Systematic Review of the related works in terms of the Scope of the study, Design methods used, and Finding relevant to the process mining and Semantic modelling techniques

Works/Papers	Field relevant to this work	Scope	Are findings relevant to proposals and method of the paper?	If yes, then what Design Method/Approach was used?	Main Tools
Bogarín et al (2018)	Yes	Educational process mining (EPM), Intentional mining, Sequential pattern mining, and Graph mining	Yes, the authors observe that the application of process mining to raw educational data takes into account the end to end processes rather than local patterns, as opposed to the Educational Data Mining. They suggest that Semantic concepts can be layered on top of existing learner information assets to provide a more conceptual analysis of the processes in reality	The paper reviews existing techniques used for EPM and elaborates on some of the potentials of those technologies. It reviews some of the relevant, related areas and highlights the components of the EPM framework. It also describes the tools, data sources, techniques and models used in EPM	Process Discovery and Conformance Checking Techniques, Dotted Chart and Social Network Analysis, Massive Open Online Courses (MOOCs), Learning Management System (LMS), Hypermedia LE's, Curriculum Mining, Computer-Supported Collaborative Learning, Software Repositories etc.
Cairns et al (2014)	Yes	EPM, Process discovery and Information Retrieval (IR), Semantics particularly ontologies, Learning Process Automation	Yes, the authors observe that one of the problems with existing process mining techniques is that they rely exclusively on the syntax of the labels in the databases or events log, and are very sensitive to data heterogeneity, label name variation, and frequent changes. As a result, a majority of the process models are discovered without some kind of hierarchy or structuring.	The work proposes a semi-automatic procedure used to associate semantics to training labels by extracting process models annotated with semantic information in order to provide a more accurate mining and compact analysis of the said processes at different levels of abstraction.	Ontology Abstract Filter plug-in in ProM, Semantically Annotated Mining eXtensible Markup Language (SA-MXML), Heuristic Miner algorithm
deMedeiros et al (2008)	Yes	Semantic Process Mining (SPM), Events Logs Annotation, Ontologies	Yes, the authors opine that the three core building blocks i.e Annotation of events logs, Ontologies, and Semantic reasoning; if adequately utilized, could cater for a much more robust and accurate process mining and analysis technique as opposed to the traditional means of process mining.	The paper proposes the Semantic LTL Checker Algorithm by extending the existing LTL Checker (conformance and analysis) plug-in in ProM. Their approach applies concepts in an *ontology* as input to parameters of a Linear Temporal Logic (LTL) formulae used to answer questions about the process elements through the WSML2Reasoner.	Conformance analysis plug-in in *LTL Checker* in ProM, Semantic Annotation, Semantic Reasoning, and LTL formulas and Template.
Han et al (2011) d'Amato et al (2008) Elhebir & Abraham (2015)	Yes	Classification, Clustering techniques, Data mining (DM), Ontology, Classes, and Concepts.	Yes, the works observe that Classification is one of the most common DM technique that aims at finding models or functions that describes concepts. The works show that the problems of modelling domain processes can be resolved by transforming ontology population problem to a *classification* one; where for each entity within the ontologies, the concepts (classes) to which the entities belong to have to be determined, thus, classified.	Combination of multiple classifiers (hybrid algorithm) and Ontologies which are incorporated as consistency constraints to multiple related classification tasks, clustering, and ranking of individuals. In addition, pattern discovery algorithms that use statistical and machine-learning techniques to build models that predict the behaviour of captured datasets, or input data models.	Data Mining (DM) techniques, Semantic labelling, Process Description logics, and multiple Classifiers.

continued on following page

44

Table 1. Continued

Works/Papers	Field relevant to this work	Scope	Are findings relevant to proposals and method of the paper?	If yes, then what Design Method/Approach was used?	Main Tools
Baati, et al (2016, 2017) Zadeh (1999) Peña-Ayala & Sossa (2013)	Yes	Fuzzy Logic, Fuzzy Sets, Fusion Theory, Fuzzy Mining and Reasoning, Standard percent of Classification.	Yes, the works observes that information imperfections treated as possibility theory may represent information or data uncertainty due to variability of observations, the uncertainty due to poor information, ambiguity, or information imprecision etc., which in turn, could affect or seriously alter the quality of the decision-making since the final classification tasks is likely to be inaccurate.	The works make use of the Fusion theory (i.e. a combination of two or more algorithms, classifiers etc.) based on fuzzy sets theory that is devoted to represent and combine imperfect information in a qualitative or yet quantitative manner. A number of the approach organizes *ontologies* which are used to define the meanings of concepts, casual relations, fuzzy rules bases etc.	Extended Bayesian classifiers, Generalized Minimum-based (G-Min) algorithm, OWL Schema and declaration sentences such as Classes, Datatype Properties, Functional Properties, and Individuals or process instances etc.
Peña-Ayala (2013)	Yes	Intelligent and adaptive educational learning systems (IAELS), AI's, User Modelling, Content Representation, and Case studies Application	Yes, the author looks at the collection of methods and parameters that could be raised or paramount to the idea of using the process mining in the combination of semantic modelling techniques to manage perspectives of the different process domains (e.g. educational learning systems)	The book introduces various approaches for user attribute which are semantically described in form of concepts (e.g within ontologies) by enabling classification of identified users (e.g leaners) based on qualitative observation of the ascertained properties. In other words, Concepts and Entities Relationship Prediction, user modelling methods etc	Computer-based and Business Intelligence (BI) tools, Workflow management system (WFM), Learner Models, OWL, and the property descriptions.
Van der Aalst (2016) de Leoni et al (2012) de Leoni et al (2016) Van Dongen et al (2016) Ingvaldsen (2011)	Yes	Process Mining, BPI, BI, BPM, BAM, Corporate Performance Management (CPM), Process-Aware Information Systems (PAIS) etc.	Yes, the works look at ways towards effective Extraction, Transformation, and interpretation of events logs about any given process domain. Although, the works observe that all of such BI systems are too data centric and are solely not aware of the process the captured datasets are being used in or to support.	The works include various approaches and methods that combines tools and methodologies which aims at providing actionable information that can be used to support decision making particularly in terms of process mining, even the latter, semantic process mining.	Process Mining tools e.g. PROM, Disco etc. Data mining techniques e.g. Clustering, Regression, Classification, Association Rule Learning, Predictive Analytics, and WFM systems, BI tools e.g. SAP, WebFOCUS, SQL Server, TIBCO, Pentaho, Tableau etc.
Calvanese et al (2016) Yankova et al (2008) Cunningham (2005) Calvanese et al (2017) Maynard et al (2008) Maynard et al (2016)	Yes,	Semantic Web Search Technologies, OBIE, Information Extraction (IE), Information Retrieval (IR), Process Mining, and Database Management.	Yes, the works seek ways to structure information or knowledge engineering for the purpose of enriching the input datasets and depiction of inference rules. Predominantly, in terms of identification of concepts from the ontologies, and automatic population of ontologies with instances within the knowledge-bases.	The works developed tools and methods that support semantic-based process analysis by offering either OBIE, IR or IE based facilities for metadata creation, storage, and semantically enriched queries or search methods.	XESame, ProMimport, eXtensible Event Streams (XES), Ontology-Based Data Access (OBDA) model, OWL, Balanced Distance Metric (BDM), Learning Accuracy (LA) Knowledge and Information Management system (KIM), SemTag system, Magpie etc.

continued on following page

Table 1. Continued

Works/Papers	Field relevant to this work	Scope	Are findings relevant to proposals and method of the paper?	If yes, then what Design Method/Approach was used?	Main Tools
Polyvyanyy et al (2017) **Polyvyanyy et al (2016)** **Montani, et al (2017)**	Yes	Process Querying, Trace Abstraction and Classifications, Ontologies for process management, BPM, BI, Semantic Modelling and Annotations.	Yes, the papers study techniques which concern automatic methods for handling (e.g. filtering or manipulating) repositories of models of observed and unseen processes as well as their relationships, with the intention of transforming process-related information into decision-making capabilities.	The work proposes a process querying framework used for enabling BI's through query-based process analytics. The framework structures state of the art components built on generic functions that can be configured to create a range of querying techniques, and also points to gaps in existing research and use cases within the BPM and BI fields.	Ontology, semantic annotations, Process Models, process querying tools, reasoners etc.
Okoye, et al (2016, 2017, 2018, 2019, 2020)	Yes	Process Mining, Semantic Modelling, Process Models and Events Log Annotation, Ontologies, Semantic Reasoning, Fuzzy Mining, BPMN notation, semantic process mining etc.	Yes, the authors observes that most of the existing process mining techniques appears to be vague or limited when confronted with unstructured data because they depend on the tags or labels (rather than concepts) within the events logs to analyse the input data and models, and therefore, seeks ways on how best to use the semantic-based approaches to manage the perspectives of process mining.	The work introduces a framework (SPMaAF) and sets of semantically motivated algorithms for the construction of semantic-based process mining technique that exhibits a high level of intelligence and conceptual reasoning capabilities using a combination of the semantic labelling (annotation), representation (ontology) and reasoning (reasoner) method	Process Mining tools such as Disco and PROM, Process Modelling tools such Bizagi Modeler, Fuzzy and BPMN Models, Ontologies and Process description Languages such as OWL, Semantic Web Rule Language (SWRL), Description Logics (DL), Reasoners e.g. Pellet, OWL API etc.

Indeed, most organizations/business processes are complex, because the amount of data available today has outgrown both the human expectations and processing capabilities of the various IT systems. Yet, the opportunities, methods, and good news from the available literature in diaspora remains that there are solutions. Many researchers are working unwaveringly to meet these expectations. Certainly, if the process owners, process analysts, software vendors, IT experts etc. (whose tasks are to provide the methods and tools to manage such increasingly huge amounts of data) can understand the data with an *advanced level of intelligence*, then they can start to realize the power of *semantic process mining* and its technologies. Without a doubt, the process mining methods could be employed for diagnostic purposes (e.g. detection of bottlenecks, process deviations, and semantic gap), and subsequently utilized to improve those complex processes (e.g. model enhancement, semantic-based model analysis) in reality. Even though, that is only if the process analysts should take the additional step of providing the real knowledge (*semantics*) that describes the said processes.

"Process Mining" *represents* "Data Science in Action"
"Data Science" *represents* "Augmented Intelligence" (AI)
"AI" *represents* "Computing + Human Input"

"Human Input" *represent* "the Process Analyst, Software vendors & IT experts" Agreeing to (Van der Aalst, 2016) "Start Today"

REFERENCES

W3C. (2004). *OWL Web Ontology Language*. Available at: http://www.w3.org/TR/owl-ref/

W3C, S. W. (2012). *Web Ontology Language (OWL)*. Oxford, UK: OWL Working Group.

Adriansyah, A., Van Dongen, B., & Van der Aalst, W. M. P. (2011). Conformance Checking using Cost-Based Fitness Analysis. *IEEE International Enterprise Computing Conference (EDOC 2011)*. IEEE Computer Society. 10.1109/EDOC.2011.12

Adriansyah, A., Van Dongen, B., & Van der Aalst, W. M. P. (2011). Towards Robust Conformance Checking. *Proceedings of the 6th Workshop on Business Process Intelligence (BPI2010)*, 122-133. 10.1007/978-3-642-20511-8_11

Allahyari, M., Kochut, K. J., & Janik, M. (2014). Ontology-based text classification into dynamically defined topics. *IEEE International Conference on Semantic Computing (ICSC) 2014*, 273-278. 10.1109/ICSC.2014.51

Baader, F. (2003). *Description Logic Handbook: theory, implementation, and applications* (1st ed.). New York, NY: Cambridge University Press.

Baati, K., Hamdani, T. M., Alimi, A. M., & Abraham, A. (2016). A New Possibilistic Classifier for Heart Disease Detection From Heterogeneous Medical Data. *International Journal of Computer Science and Information Security*, *14*(7), 443–450.

Baati, K., Hamdani, T. M., Alimi, A. M., & Abraham, A. 2017. Decision quality enhancement in minimum-based possibilistic classification for numerical data. *Proceedings of the 8th International Conference on Soft Computing and Pattern Recognition (SoCPaR 2016)*.

Baker, R., & Yacef, K. (2009). The state of educational data mining in 2009: A review and future visions. *Journal of Educational Data Mining*, *1*(1), 3–17.

Balcan, N., Blum, A., & Mansour, Y. (2013). Exploiting ontology structures and unlabeled data for learning. *Proceedings of the 30th Int. Conference on Machine Learning 2013*, 1112-1120.

Bechhofer, S. (2004). *OWL Web Ontology Language Reference*. Manchester, UK: Technical report W3C Proposed Recommendation.

Bechhofer, S. (2004). *OWL Web Ontology Language Reference*. Manchester, UK: Technical report W3C Proposed Recommendation.

Bogarín, A., Cerezo, R. & Romero, C. (2018). A Survey on Educational Process Mining. *Wiley Interdisciplinary Reviews: Data Mining and Knowledge Discovery (WIRES), 8*(1).

Bogarín, A., Romero, C., Cerezo, R., & Sánchez-Santillán, M. (2014). *Clustering for improving educational process mining*. New York, NY: ACM.

Born, M., Dörr, F., & Weber, I. (2007). User-Friendly Semantic Annotation in Business Process Modeling. In M. Weske, M. Hacid, & C. Godart (Eds.), Lecture Notes in Computer Science: Vol. 4832. *Web Information Systems Engineering – WISE 2007 Workshops. WISE 2007* (pp. 260–271). Berlin: Springer. doi:10.1007/978-3-540-77010-7_25

Cairns, A. H. (2014). Towards Custom-Designed Professional Training Contents and Curriculums through Educational Process Mining. *IMMM 2014: The Fourth International Conference on Advances in Information Mining and Management*, 53-58.

Cairns, A. H. (2014). Using Semantic Lifting for Improving Educational Process Models Discovery and Analysis. *CEUR Workshop Proceedings*, 150-161.

Cairns, A. H. (2015). Process Mining in the Education Domain. *International Journal on Advances in Intelligent Systems, 8*(1-2).

Calvanese, D., Kalayci, T. E., Montali, M., & Tinella, S. (2017). Ontology-based Data Access for Extracting Event Logs from Legacy Data: The onprom Tool and Methodology. *Proceedings of 20th International Conference on Business Information Systems 2017*, 220-236. 10.1007/978-3-319-59336-4_16

Calvanese, D., Montali, M., Syamsiyah, A., & van der Aalst, W. M. P. (2016). Ontology-Driven Extraction of Event Logs from Relational Databases. Lecture Notes in Business Information Processing, 140-153. doi:10.1007/978-3-319-42887-1_12

Carmona, J., de Leoni, M., Depair, B., & Jouck, T. (2016). *Process Discovery Contest @ BPM 2016*. Rio de Janeiro: IEEE CIS Task Force on Process Mining.

Cesarini, M., Monga, M., & Tedesco, R. (2004). Carrying on the e-learning process with a workflow management engine. *Proceedings of ACM Symposium on Applied Computing*, 940-945. 10.1145/967900.968091

Chesani, F., Ciampolini, A., Loreti, D., & Mello, P. (2016). Process Mining Monitoring for Map Reduce Applications in the Cloud. *ACM Digital Library - Proceedings of the 6th International Conference on Cloud Computing and Services Science, 2*(1), 95-105.

Cunningham, H. (1995). *GATE: General Architecture for Text Engineering*. Available at: https://gate.ac.uk/

Cunningham, H. (2005). *Information Extraction, Automatic*. Sheffield, UK: University of Sheffield.

d'Amato, C., Fanizzi, N., & Esposito, F. (2008). Query answering and ontology population: An inductive approach. In *Proceedings of the 5th Euro. Semantic Web Conference, ESWC2008*. Springer. 10.1007/978-3-540-68234-9_23

de Beer, H. T. (2005). *The LTL Checker Plugins: a (reference) manual*. Eindhoven, The Netherlands: processmining.org.

De Giacomo, G. (2018). Using Ontologies for Semantic Data Integration. In S. Flesca, S. Greco, E. Masciari, & D. Saccà (Eds.), *A Comprehensive Guide Through the Italian Database Research Over the Last 25 Years. Studies in Big Data* (pp. 187–202). Cham: Springer. doi:10.1007/978-3-319-61893-7_11

de Keyser, P. (2012). *The Semantic Web*. Available at: https://www.sciencedirect.com/topics/computer-science/semantic-search

de Leoni, M., Van der Aalst, W., & ter Hofstede, A. (2008). Visual Support for Work Assignment in Process-Aware Information Systems. In M. Dumas, M. Reichert, & M. Shan (Eds.), Lecture Notes in Computer Science: Vol. 5240. *Business Process Management. BPM 2008* (pp. 67–83). Berlin: Springer. doi:10.1007/978-3-540-85758-7_8

De Leoni, M., & Van der Aalst, W. M. P. (2013). Data-Aware Process Mining: Discovering Decisions in Processes Using Alignments. *ACM Symposium on Applied Computing (SAC 2013)*, 1454-1461. 10.1145/2480362.2480633 de Leoni, M., Van der Aalst, W. M. P., & Dees, M. (2016). A General Process Mining Framework for Correlating, Predicting and Clustering Dynamic Behaviour Based on Event Logs. *Information Systems, 56*(1), 235–257. doi:10.1016/j.is.2015.07.003

de Leoni, M., Van der Aalst, W. M. P., & ter Hofstede, A. H. M. (2012). Visual Support for Work Assignment in Process-Aware information Systems: Framework Formalisation and Implementation. *Decision Support Systems, 54*(1), 345–361. doi:10.1016/j.dss.2012.05.042

de Medeiros, A. K. A., & Van der Aalst, W. M. P. (2009). Process Mining towards Semantics. In T. Dillon, E. Chang, R. Meersman, & K. Sycara (Eds.), Lecture Notes in Computer Science: Vol. 4891. *Advances in Web Semantics I* (pp. 35–80). Berlin: Springer. doi:10.1007/978-3-540-89784-2_3

deMedeiros, A., van der Aalst, W. M. P. & Pedrinaci, C. (2008). *Semantic Process Mining Tools: Core Building Blocks.* ECIS.

Dill, S. (2003). SemTag and Seeker: Bootstrapping the semantic web via automated semantic annotation. *Proceedings of WWW'03.* 10.1145/775152.775178

Domingue, J., Dzbor, M., & Motta, E. (2004). Magpie: Supporting Browsing and Navigation on the Semantic Web. *Proceedings ACM Conference on Intelligent User Interfaces (IUI).* 10.1145/964442.964479

Dou, D., Wang, H., & Liu, H. (2015). Semantic Data Mining: A Survey of Ontology-based Approaches. *9th IEEE Int. Conference on Semantic Computing,* 244 – 251. 10.1109/ICOSC.2015.7050814

Dubois, D. (1988). *Possibility theory: an approach to computerized processing of uncertainty 2* (2nd ed.). New York: Plenum Press. doi:10.1007/978-1-4684-5287-7

Dumas, M., van der Aalst, W. M. P., & ter Hofstede, A. H. M. (2005). *Process-Aware Information Systems: Bridging People and Software through Process Technology* (1st ed.). New York, NY: Wiley. doi:10.1002/0471741442

Dżega, D., & Pietruszkiewicz, W. (2013). Intelligent Decision-Making Support within the E-Learning Process. In A. Peña-Ayala (Ed.), *Intelligent and Adaptive Educational-Learning Systems: Achievements and Trends* (pp. 497–521). Springer. doi:10.1007/978-3-642-30171-1_20

Elhebir, M. H. A., & Abraham, A. (2015). A Novel Ensemble Approach to Enhance the Performance of Web Server Logs Classification. *International Journal of Computer Information Systems and Industrial Management Applications*, 7, 189–195.

Erdmann, M., Maedche, A., Schnurr, H. p., & Staab, S. (2000). From manual to semi-automatic semantic annotation: about ontology-based text annotation tools. *Proceedings of the COLING-2000 Workshop on Semantic Annotation and Intelligent Content*, 79-85.

Fahland, D., & van der Aalst, W. M. P. (2012). Repairing Process Models to Reflect Reality. Lecture Notes in Computer Science, 7481, 229-245. doi:10.1007/978-3-642-32885-5_19

Fensel, D., Hendler, J., Wahlster, W., & Lieberman, H. (2002). *Spinning the Semantic Web: Bringing the World Wide Web to Its Full Potential* (1st ed.). Cambridge: MIT Press.

García-Castro, R., & Gómez-Pérez, A. (2010). Interoperability results for Semantic Web technologies using OWL as the interchange language. *Journal of Web Semantics*, 8(4), 278–291. doi:10.1016/j.websem.2010.08.008

Gatner. (2010). *Magic Quadrant for Business Intelligence Platforms.* Available at: www.gartner.com

Goble, C., Bechhofer, S., & Wolstencroft, K. (2013). Semantic Web, Interoperability. In W. Dubitzky, O. Wolkenhauer, K. H. Cho, & H. Yokota (Eds.), *Encyclopedia of Systems Biology*. New York, NY: Springer. doi:10.1007/978-1-4419-9863-7_1111

Greco, G., Guzzo, A., Pontieri, L., & Sacca, D. (2006). Discovering Expressive Process Models by ClusteringLog Traces. *IEEE Transactions on Knowledge and Data Engineering*, 18(8), 1010–1027. doi:10.1109/TKDE.2006.123

Grob, H. L., Bensberg, F., & Coners, A. (2008). Regelbasierte steuerung von geschaftsprozessen-konzeption eines ansatzes auf basis des process mining. Die Wirtschaftsinformatik.

Gunther, C., Ma, S. R., Reichert, M., Aalst, W. M. P. V. D., & Recker, J. (2008). Using process mining to learn from process changes in evolutionary systems. *International Journal of Business Process Integration and Management*, 3(1), 61–78. doi:10.1504/IJBPIM.2008.019348

Gu¨nther, C. W., & Van der Aalst, W. M. P. (2006). A generic import framework for process event logs. In J. Eder & S. Dustdar (Eds.), *Business Process Management Workshops* (pp. 81–92). Berlin: Springer. doi:10.1007/11837862_10

Han, J., & Kamber, M. (2004). *Data Mining: Concepts and Techniques* (1st ed.). San Francisco, CA: Morgan Kaufmann Publishers Inc.

Han, J., Kamber, M., & Pei, J. (2011). *Data Mining: Concepts and Techniques* (3rd ed.). Burlington, MA: The Morgan Kaufmann Series in Data Management Systems, Morgan Kaufmann Publishers.

HIMSS. (2020). What is Interoperability? *Healthcare Information and Management Systems Society Library*. Available at: https://www.himss.org/library/interoperability-standards/what-is-interoperability

Holzhüter, M., Frosch-Wilke, D., & Klein, U. (2013). Exploiting Learner Models Using Data Mining for E-Learning: A Rule Based Approach. In A. Peña-Ayala (Ed.), *Intelligent and Adaptive Educational-Learning Systems: Achievements and Trends* (pp. 77–105). Berlin: Springer Berlin Heidelberg. doi:10.1007/978-3-642-30171-1_4

Horrocks, I. (2004). *SWRL: A Semantic Web Rule Language Combining OWL and RuleML*. Network Inference, Canada and Stanford University: W3C Member Submission - 2004 National Research Council of Canada, Network Inference, and Stanford University.

Horrocks, I., Patel-Schneider, P. F., McGuinness, D. L., & Welty, C. A. (2007). Owl: a description logic based ontology language for the semantic web. In *The Description Logic Handbook: Theory, Implementation, and Applications* (2nd ed., pp. 458–486). New York, NY: Cambridge University Press. doi:10.1017/CBO9780511711787.016

IEEE 1849-2016, X., 2016. (n.d.). *OpenXES - reference implementation of the First XES standard*. Available at: http://www.xes-standard.org/openxes/start

IEEE CIS Task Force on Process Mining. (2016). *1849-2016 - IEEE Standard for eXtensible Event Stream definition*. Available at: http://www.xes-standard.org/

Ingvaldsen, J. E. (2011). *Semantic process mining of enterprise transaction data* (PhD Thesis). Norwegian University of Science and Technology.

Ingvaldsen, J. E., Gulla, J. A., Hegle, O. A., & Prange, A. (2005). Revealing the real business flows from enterprise systems transactions. *7th International Conference on Enterprise Information Systems*.

Jans, M. J. (2011). Process Mining in Auditing: From Current Limitations to Future Challenges. *International Conference on Business Process Management Workshops. BPM 2011*, 394-397.

Jareevongpiboon, W., & Janecek, P. (2013). Ontological approach to enhance results of business process mining and analysis. *Journal of Business Process Management, 19*(3), 459–476. doi:10.1108/14637151311319905

Jonquet, C., Toulet, A., Dutta, B., & Emonet, V. (2018, August). Harnessing the Power of Unified Metadata in an Ontology Repository: The Case of AgroPortal. *Journal on Data Semantics, 7*(4), 1–31. doi:10.100713740-018-0091-5

Khaleghi, B., Khamis, A., Karray, F. O., & Razavi, S. N. (2013). Multisensor data fusion: A review of the state-of-the-art. *Information Fusion, 14*(1), 8–44. doi:10.1016/j.inffus.2011.08.001

King, M. (2003). Living up to standards. *Proceedings of the EACL 2003 Workshop on Evaluation Initiatives in Natural Language Processing*.

Lautenbacher, F., Bauer, B., & Forg, S. (2009). Process Mining for Semantic Business Process Modeling. *13th Enterprise Distributed Object Computing Conference Workshops*, 45-53. 10.1109/EDOCW.2009.5332017

Lautenbacher, F., Bauer, B., & Seitz, C. (2008). *Semantic Business Process Modeling - Benefits and Capability*. California, USA, AAAI Spring Symposium: AI Meets Business Rules and Process Management, Stanford University.

Leemans, S. J. J., Fahland, D., & van der Aalst, W. M. P. (2014). Process and Deviation Exploration with Inductive visual Miner. *Proceedings of the BPM Demo Sessions 2014*.

Maita, A. (2017). A systematic mapping study of process mining. *Enterprise Information Systems, 0*(0), 1–45.

Manning, C. D., Raghavan, P., & Schütze, H. (2008). *Introduction to Information Retrieval*. Cambridge: Cambridge University Press. doi:10.1017/CBO9780511809071

Maynard, D. (2007). Natural Language Technology for Information Integration in Business Intelligence. In W. Abramowicz (Ed.), Lecture Notes in Computer Science: Vol. 4439. *Business Information Systems. BIS 2007* (pp. 366–380). Berlin: Springer. doi:10.1007/978-3-540-72035-5_28

Maynard, D., Peters, W., & Li, Y. (2008). Evaluating Evaluation Metrics for Ontology-Based Applications: Infinite Reflection. *Proceedings of the International Conference on Language Resources and Evaluation.*

Miani, R. G. L., & Hruschka, E. R. Jr. (2015). Exploring Association Rules in a Large Growing Knowledge Base. *International Journal of Computer Information System and Industrial Management, 7*, 106–114.

Montani, S. (2017). Knowledge-Based Trace Abstraction for Semantic Process Mining. In A. ten Teije, C. Popow, J. Holmes, & L. Sacchi (Eds.), Lecture Notes in Computer Science: Vol. 10259. *Artificial Intelligence in Medicine. AIME 2017* (pp. 267–271). Springer. doi:10.1007/978-3-319-59758-4_30

Motik, B., Patel-Schneider, P. F., Parsia, B., Bock, C., Fokoue, A., Haase, P., . . . Smith, M. (2012). *OWL 2 Web Ontology Language Structural Specification and Functional-Style Syntax* (2nd ed.). W3C Recommendation 11. Available at: https://www.w3.org/TR/owl2-syntax/

Munoz-Gama, J., & Carmona, J. (2011). Enhancing Precision in Process Conformance: Stability, Confidence and Severity. *Proceedings of CIDM 2011.* 10.1109/CIDM.2011.5949451

Nguyen, L., & Phung, D. (2008). Learner model in adaptive learning. *World Academy of Science, Engineering and Technology, 45,* 395–400.

Okoye, K. (2016). Using semantic-based approach to manage perspectives of process mining: Application on improving learning process domain data. *Proceedings of 2016 IEEE International Conference on Big Data (Big Data),* 3529-3538.

Okoye, K. (2018). Semantic-based Model Analysis towards Enhancing Information Values of Process Mining: Case Study of Learning Process Domain. *Proceedings of SoCPaR 2016 Conference,* 622-633. 10.1007/978-3-319-60618-7_61

Okoye, K., Islam, S., & Naeem, U. (2020). Semantic-based Process Mining Technique for Annotation and Modelling of Domain Processes. *International Journal of Innovative Computing, Information and Control.*

Okoye, K., Islam, S., Naeem, U., Sharif, M. S., Azam, M. A., & Karami, A. (2019). The Application of a Semantic-Based Process Mining Framework on a Learning Process Domain. In K. Arai, S. Kapoor, & R. Bhatia (Eds.), *Intelligent Systems and Applications. Advances in Intelligent Systems and Computing* (Vol. 868, pp. 1381–1403). Springer Cham. doi:10.1007/978-3-030-01054-6_96

Okoye, K., Naeem, U., & Islam, S. (2017). Semantic Fuzzy Mining: Enhancement of process models and event logs analysis from Syntactic to Conceptual Level. *International Journal of Hybrid Intelligent Systems*, *14*(1-2), 67–98. doi:10.3233/HIS-170243

Pauwels, P., Poveda-Villalón, M., Sicilia, Á., & Euzenat, J. (2018). Semantic technologies and interoperability in the built environment. *Semantic Web*, *9*(6), 731–734. doi:10.3233/SW-180321

Pechenizkiy, M. (2009). Process Mining Online Assessment Data. *Proceedings of EDM*, 279-288.

Peña-Ayala, A. (2013). *Intelligent and Adaptive Educational-Learning Systems: Achievements and Trends* (1st ed.). Springer-Verlag Berlin. doi:10.1007/978-3-642-30171-1

Peña-Ayala, A., & Sossa, H. (2013). Proactive Sequencing Based on a Causal and Fuzzy Student Model. In A. Peña-Ayala (Ed.), *Intelligent and Adaptive Educational-Learning Systems: Achievements and Trends* (pp. 49–76). Berlin: Springer Berlin Heidelberg. doi:10.1007/978-3-642-30171-1_3

Perez-Rodriguez, R., Caeiro-Rodriguez, M., & Anido-Rifon, L. (2008). Supporting PoEML educational processes in Moodle: A middleware approach. *Proceedings of SPDECER*.

Pfaff, M., Neubig, S., & Krcmar, H. (2018). Ontology for Semantic Data Integration in the Domain of IT Benchmarking. *Journal on Data Semantics*, *7*(1), 29–46. doi:10.100713740-017-0084-9 PMID:29497460

Poggi, A. (2008). Linking Data to Ontologies. Journal on Data Semantics, 4900(1), 133-173. doi:10.1007/978-3-540-77688-8_5

Polyvyanyy A. (2016). *Process Querying*. Available at: http://processquerying.com/

Polyvyanyy, A., Ouyang, C., Barros, A., & van der Aalst, W. M. P. (2017). Process querying: Enabling business intelligence through query-based process analytics. *Decision Support Systems*, *100*, 41–56. doi:10.1016/j. dss.2017.04.011

Popov, B. (2004). KIM – Semantic Annotation Platform. *Journal of Natural Language Engineering*, *10*(3-4), 375–392. doi:10.1017/S135132490400347X

Rojas, E., Munoz-Gama, J., Sepúlveda, M., & Capurro, D. (2016). Process mining in healthcare: A literature review. *Journal of Biomedical Informatics*, *61*(1), 224–236. doi:10.1016/j.jbi.2016.04.007 PMID:27109932

Rozinat, A. (2010). *Process Mining: Conformance and Extension* (PhD thesis). Eindhoven, The Netherlands: Technische Universiteit Eindhoven.

Rozinat, A. (2016). *Data Quality Problems for Process Mining*. Eindhoven, The Netherlands: Fluxicon.

Rozinat, A., & Gunther, C. (2012). Disco User Guide - Process Mining for Professionals. Eindhoven, The Netherlands: Fluxicon.com.

Rozinat, A., & Van der Aalst, W. M. P. (2008). Conformance Checking of Processes based on Monitoring Real Behaviour. *Journal of Information Systems*, *33*(1), 64–95.

Santoro, F. M., Rosa, M. L., Loos, P., & Pastor, O. (2016). *14th International Conference on Business Process Management*. Available at: http://bpm2016. uniriotec.br/

Trcka, N., & Pechenizkiy, M. (2009). From Local Patterns to Global Models: Towards Domain Driven Educational Process Mining. IEEE Computer Society.

Trčka, N., Pechenizkiy, M., & van der Aalst, W. M. P. (2010). Process Mining from Educational Data. In C. Romero, S. Ventura, M. Pechenizkiy, & R. S. J. D. Baker (Eds.), *Handbook of Educational Data Mining* (pp. 123–142). Boca Raton, FL: Chapman & Hall/CRC Data Mining and Knowledge Discovery Series, CRC Press. doi:10.1201/b10274-11

Van der Aalst, W. M. P. (2004). Business Process Management Demystified: A Tutorial on Models, Systems and Standards for workflow Management. Lectures on Concurrency and Petri Nets, 3098, 1-65.

Van der Aalst, W. M. P. (2011). *Process Mining: Discovery, Conformance and Enhancement of Business Processes* (1st ed.). Berlin: Springer. doi:10.1007/978-3-642-19345-3

Van der Aalst, W. M. P. (2016). *Process Mining: Data Science in Action* (2nd ed.). Berlin: Springer-Verlag Berlin Heildelberg. doi:10.1007/978-3-662-49851-4

Van der Aalst, W. M. P. (2019). *Process Mining Conference Series: IEEE Task Force on Process Mining*. Available at: https://icpmconference.org/2019/general-information/ieee-task-force/

Van der Aalst, W. M. P., Adriansyah, A., & de Medeiros, A. K. A. (2012). Process Mining Manifesto. *Lecture Notes in Business Information Processing*, *99*, 169-194.

Van der Aalst, W. M. P., van Hee, K., van Werf, J. M., & Verdonk, M. (2010). Auditing 2.0: Using Process Mining to Support Tomorrow's Auditor. *IEEE Computer*, *43*(3), 90–93. doi:10.1109/MC.2010.61

Van der Aalst, W. M. P., Weijters, A. J. M. M. & Maruster, L. (2004). Workflow Mining: Discovering Process Models from Event Logs. *International Journal of IEEE transactions on Knowledge and Data Engineering, 16*(9), 1128-1142.

Van Dongen, B., Claes, J., Burattin, A., & De Weerdt, J. (2016). *12th International Workshop on Business Process Intelligence 2016.* Available at: http://www.win.tue.nl/bpi/doku.php?id=2016:start#organizers

Verbeek, H. (2014). *Process Mining research tools and application.* Available at: http://www.processmining.org/promimport/start

Verbeek, H., Buijs, J., van Dongen, B., & van der Aalst, W. M. P. (2011). XES, XESame, and ProM 6. In *Information Systems Evolution.* Springer.

Weerdt, J. D., Backer, M. D., & Vanthienen, J. (2011). A Robust F-measure for Evaluating Discovered Process Models. *Proceedings of CIDM*, 148–155.

Weijters, A. J. M. M., & Ribeiro, J. T. S. (2010). *Flexible Heuristics Miner (FHM).* Eindhoven, The Netherlands: BETA Working Paper Series, WP 334, Eindhoven University of Technology.

Weijters, A. J. M. M., Van der Aalst, W. M. P. & de Medeiros, A. K. A. (2006). *Process Mining with the Heuristics Miner-algorithm*. Eindhoven, The Netherlands: Technical report, EUT, Eindhoven, BETA Working Paper Series, WP 166.

Weske, M. (2007). *Business Process Management: Concepts, Languages, Architectures* (1st ed.). Berlin: Springer Berlin.

Wimalasuriya, D. C., & Dou, D. (2010). Ontology-based information extraction: An introduction and a survey of current approaches. *Journal of Information Science, 36*(3), 306–323. doi:10.1177/0165551509360123

Yankova, M., Saggion, H., & Cunningham, H. (2008). *Semantic-based Identity Resolution and Merging for Business Intelligence*. Sheffield: University of Sheffield, UK.

Zadeh, L. (1965). Fuzzy sets., Information Science. *Information and Control, 8*(3), 338–353. doi:10.1016/S0019-9958(65)90241-X

Zadeh, L. A. (1971). Similarity relations and fuzzy orderings. *Information Sciences, 3*(2), 177–200. doi:10.1016/S0020-0255(71)80005-1

Zadeh, L. A. (1999). Fuzzy sets as a basis for a theory of possibility. *Fuzzy Sets and Systems, 100*(1), 9–34. doi:10.1016/S0165-0114(99)80004-9

Zhao, L., & Ichise, R. (2014). Ontology Integration for Linked Data. *Journal on Data Semantics, 3*(4), 237–254. doi:10.100713740-014-0041-9

Chapter 2
State-of-the-Art Components, Tools, and Methods for Process Mining and Semantic Modelling

ABSTRACT

This chapter describes the state-of-the-art technologies, tools, and methods that are closely connected to the work done in this book. The chapter describes in detail the key components of the process mining and semantic modelling methods and the different technologies that enable the practical application of the techniques. In essence, the chapter explains the main tools and mechanisms that are applied in this book, ranging from the events log to the different tools that are applied for process mining, and the existing algorithms used to discover the process models and to support the interpretations and/or further analysis of the models at semantic levels.

INTRODUCTION

The chapter describes in details the key components of the process mining and semantic modelling methods, and the different technologies that enable the practical application of the techniques. In essence, the chapter explains the main tools and mechanisms that are applied in this book; ranging from the events log to the different tools that are applied for process mining, and

DOI: 10.4018/978-1-7998-2668-2.ch002

the existing algorithms used to discover the process models and to support the interpretations and/or further analysis of the models at semantic levels.

- the need for events data from the different information systems or databases for process mining.
- the different information which are expected to be existing in the events data logs for process mining and further steps of semantic-based process mining.
- the data quality challenges that may be encountered in reality when performing the process mining tasks, as well as
- how the identified challenges with process mining can be addressed.

Consequently, the chapter looks at current tools and methods which support the semantic-based process mining approaches – ranging from the annotation of events log, to the ontological representation of the resulting models and the semantic reasoning aptitudes. This is then followed by an illustration of how the different tools/components are integrated and can be applied to carry out the analysis of the event logs and derived process models at a more abstraction level. Finally, the chapter summarizes the presented state of the art components or approaches, and then subsequently propose a semantic-based process mining framework (in chapter 3) that integrates the different tools/components towards the application and development of the semantic process mining approach.

EVENT LOGS

Process mining algorithms use the event logs to learn and reason about processes by coupling in a technical manner: *event history data* and *process models* (Van der Aalst, 2011). Indeed, data logged in IT systems can be utilized (analysed) towards the provision of a better understanding or insights about the real-time processes. This is done in order to improve the quality of the discovered models, support an abstract analysis of the individual process elements, or help to detect deviations. In fact, the process mining combines techniques from the data mining to process modelling and analysis, as well as several other disciplines, otherwise referred to as "computational intelligence" tools to analyze the captured datasets. Perhaps, many approaches which incorporate such use of data mining techniques to interpret datasets have been proposed in the existing literature. On the one hand, the works in

(Dou, et al., 2015; De Leoni & Van der Aalst, 2013; Han, et al., 2011) refers to data mining as the techniques that are used to analyse recorded datasets in order to find unpredicted relations, and then trails to process or interpret the data in a more novel way that are both meaningful, understandable, as well as beneficial to the data owners.

Likewise, process mining allows for the same practice or theory as the data mining methods but on the contrary aims to analyse the recorded event data at *process-levels* (Van der Aalst, 2016). In consequence, the advanced analysis of the captured data at the "process-levels" helps to address the problem of determining unwavering connections amidst the low-level elements that can be found within the events log about the processes in question. Perhaps, such kind of analysis is performed especially in alignment with the discovered process models in order to reflect reality (i.e how the different activities that make up the process have been performed in the real-world settings or environment). Apparently, this is where the process mining techniques can be of paramount, because many of the existing data mining methods appear to be overly data-centered in providing an inclusive or full understanding of the end to end processes during the execution time (e.g. from a business process or operational perspective). Certainly, this means that the process mining techniques are not limited to automatic discovery or interpretation of patterns within any given process, but are also built on or integrates the *data mining* and *process modelling* techniques.

In essence, process mining assume that a typical dataset (i.e. the event logs) consist of at least information about a *single process* and every event within the (data) logs has to refer to a single process *trace*, by specifying the process as group of *activities* such that the *life-cycle* (e.g. sequence of activities) of a single process trace is established. Therefore, we can safely argue that the *events log* serves as the first step (i.e starting point) for any given process mining task. By definition, the event logs are a multiset of *traces* where each trace describes the life-cycle of a particular case (*sequence of activities*) in terms of how they have been executed or performed within the said process in view. Thus:

- The *"Case ID"* and *"Activity"* labels represent the bare minimum to perform a process mining task (Van der Aalst, 2016).

Other additional information may be required for ample implementation of the process mining technique, depending on the level or type of analysis that is needed:

- **Event ID**: For the ordering of information to discover casual dependencies in process models.
- **Timestamp**: Useful when analysing performance-related properties (for instance, the waiting time between two activities).
- **Resources**: The persons executing the activities
- **Other Attributes**: e.g. Cost, Roles, Abilities, Preferences, Place etc.

In simple term, the *event logs* describe executed operations for a given process, and classically contains *timestamps* as to the periods during which the operations were performed including the *names* and *identifiers* of the activities that were performed. There could also exist references to the sets of the *resource(s)* that was involved during the execution of the mentioned process. Moreover, the resources could be the different departments that are involved in the process, the users (originators) that carried out the operations, or the documents and products listing etc.

DATA SOURCES

One of the most essential and integral phase in carrying out any process mining task is the *data extraction* process. According to Van der Aalst (2016) societies, people and organizations are *Always On,* i.e., data are collected *about anything*, *at any time*, and *at any place*. Therefore, the idea of performing process mining is to analyse those captured datasets from a process-oriented perspective aimed at answering some of the business questions and to provide insights or actionable procedures about the operational processes in view. Typically, many organizations have IT systems with more or less event logs which are stored as audit trails, history or transaction logs etc. (Goedertier, et al., 2009). However, most of those systems tend to store the captured informations or data in an unstructured format. For instance, event logs that are distributed or spread across different tables or are needed to be extracted from another IT system.

Interestingly, Van der Aalst (2016) notes that the process of extracting the datasets have to be inspired as a result of business-minded questions that needed to be answered or resolved, rather than, the presence of a large amount of event data logs. In so doing, the process analysts are able to answer and provide solutions to a wide range of *"data-to-process"* driven questions to help in support or improvement of the business processes in reality. For instance, the following questions could be established (Van der Aalst, 2016):

- What really happened in the past? (reporting)
- Why did it happen? (diagnosis)
- What is likely to happen in the future? (prediction)
- When and why do organizations and people deviate? (alignment)
- How to control the process better? (recommendation)
- How to redesign a process to improve its performance? (extension)

Moreover, it is also important to note that the said datasets may come in form of simple flat file e.g. Excel or CVS spreadsheets, Tables within databases, Transactional logs, web pages, e-mails, Documents in form of text or pdf etc., and quite often, the datasets are sometimes not well-structured. Even now and then, the event logs may also be distributed across the various data platforms (sources) due to technical and/or organizational reasons, and a lot of the time, additional effort is being required in order to collect the relevant data.

Therefore, it is indispensable and fundamental that the design of the process mining techniques should relate to the events (elements) within the captured data often referred to as *trace* (i.e *sequence of related events*). Moreover, the measurement or dimension of what makes the events to be associated (i.e relates) relies entirely on the nature of the prospective process mining task, especially when considered in terms of the trailed domain processes in view or of interest. For example, in more or less situations, events about similar items/product may well describe or determine the resulting traces or sequence of related events. Besides, traces are found and are always present in any process mining task particularly when the process analyst is focused on determining how the events or operations are executed to reach some common business goal or decision.

Nonetheless, irrespective of the process-related questions or viewpoint chosen by the process analysts and/or the concerned organizations, there may also be the need for data cleaning otherwise referred to as *filtering* (i.e. removing events of a particular type). Practically, filtering is an iterative process that corresponds to drilling down (fine-grained scoping) of the available event logs based on an initial effort or analysis of the extraction process. For instance, the process analyst could choose to pay more attention to the activities that are performed most frequently in order to keep the model simple at the modelling stage. Perhaps, this form of process modelling and analysis method could be said to be in line with the Occam's razor principle (Thorburn, 1918; Hiroshi, 1997). The Occam's razor principle follows the natural rule that process analyst must aim for the "simplest models" which are capable of explaining the behaviours or what is observed within the datasets. In essence, in a format that takes its own advice "keep things simple".

STANDARD FORMAT FOR STORING EVENT LOGS

A number of events log format has been made available for the purpose of standardizing the data input formats for process mining. In practice, the standard format for storing the events log is by using XML-based formats (Van der Aalst, 2016). The XML-based formats are standard event logs layouts used by many process mining algorithms: whereby the process and activity names are normally assumed to be unique by assigning a *case identifier* and/ or using both *start* and *end* times to obtain activity durations respectively. Over the next sub-sections, the work looks at some of the relevant events log file formats currently used to perform process mining tasks as well as their individual attributes, benefits, and limitations.

Mining eXtensible Markup Language (MXML)

MXML is one of such XML-based file format used for event log representation/ storage (deMedeiros, et al., 2008). The MXML format first emerged in 2003 and ever since then have been adopted by a number of process mining tools such as ProM (Verbeek et al, 2011). In contrast to the other file formats, the most important part (or unit) of an MXML log file is the *Workflowlog* (Van der Aalst & Van Hee, 2004). The workflowlog assemblies some group of process elements (i.e entities) as well as contains a well-ordered list of *AuditTrailEntry* events - where every single event is expected to have a name, thus the term *WorkflowModelElement*.

More so, another compulsory attribute present in the MXML file layout is the *EventType* which identifies the lifecycle transition of the elements in the logs (e.g. states if an event denotes a task that is in its start state, or complete state etc.). Other optional attributes that are present in MXML files are the event *Timestamps* (i.e. the precise dates and time the events occurred), and *Originator* (the name of the resources that initiated the events) etc. On the one hand, the ad-hoc extensions of the MXML format such as the Semantic Annotated Mining eXtensible Markup Language (SA-MXML) (de Medeiros & Van der Aalst, 2009) unveils the fixed format limitation of the files. Whereas, on the other hand, the shortcomings has spanned the emergence and advancement of the eXtensible Event Stream (XES) file format as discussed in the following subsection.

eXtensible Event Stream (XES)

XES is the successor of MXML file format (Van der Aalst, 2011). XES has been proven in the current literature, as well as, in the industrial application settings to be a reliable and trustworthy XML-based format used for process mining. This is because the XES file appears to be less restrictive and truly extendible (Verbeek, et al., 2011; IEEE CIS Task Force on Process Mining, 2016). The standard (XES) first emerged in 2010, and in the meantime has been accepted by the process mining community (IEEE CIS Task Force on Process Mining, 2016, Van der Aalst et al, 2019) as the standard format for process mining. This is so since the standard can simply define the attributes which could explicitly be identified practically in any settings as well as enables the capability of interchanging events data logs across different application platforms or the PM tools. Currently, the XES standard format is being used and supported by a lot of process mining tool including ProM (Verbeek, et al., 2011; Verbeek, 2014), Disco (Rozinat & Gunther, 2012), XE-Same (Verbeek, et al., 2011) and OpenXES (IEEE 1849-2016, 2016), and the many other commercial tools that supports the process mining framework such as: Celonis, MinIt, ProcessGold, My-Invenio, Worksoft, QPR ProcessAnalyzer etc.

Furthermore, the report by the IEEE CIS Task Force on Process Mining (2016) sets the following objectives as guiding principles in the design of the XES standard format (or layout) as follows: *Simplicity - Flexibility - Extensibility –* and *Expressivity.* Interestingly, Rozinat (2016) notes that one of the most frequently encountered issues with the use of XES or any of the other data file formats for process mining - remains with *semantics*. For instance, in settings where there exist no devoted distinctive *activity name* field (or variables) within a dataset; how do the process analysts attach meaning (semantics) to the available data? or in other words, know what the exact attributes mean in reality?

Nonetheless, the introduction of XES has made available to the process mining community the concept or idea of file *extension* primarily for the purpose of the semantic issues. According to the works in (Van der Aalst, 2011; Rozinat, 2016) XES *extension* defines a number of *standardized attributes* for each and every *level* in the events log hierarchy (e.g. log, trace, attributes) together with their *type* (e.g. String, Boolean, Char etc) as well as their specific attribute *keys*. In fact, currently there are five standard extensions or properties which are integrated in the XES format as shown in the following Figure 1. Moreover, those extension are defined in terms of the;

(i)   *Concept*
(ii) *Life-Cycle,*
(iii) *Organizational*
(iv) *Time,* and
(v)   *Semantics* (IEEE Standards, 2016).

Figure 1. Standard format (properties) of the XES file format

```
<global scope="event">
    <string key="concept:name" value="name"/>
    <string key="lifecycle:transition" value="transition"/>
    <string key="org:resource" value="resource"/>
    <date key="time:timestamp" value="2015-04-05T14:30:13.876+01:00"/>
    <string key="Activity_Name" value="string"/>
    <string key="Event_Type" value="string"/>
    <string key="Performer" value="string"/>
    <string key="Role" value="string"/>
</global>
<classifier name="Activity" keys="Activity_Name"/>
<classifier name="Resource" keys="Performer"/>
<string key="lifecycle:model" value="standard"/>
<string key="creator" value="Fluxicon Disco"/>
<string key="library" value="Fluxicon Octane"/>
<trace>
    <string key="concept:name" value="L08"/>
    <string key="creator" value="Fluxicon Disco"/>
    <event>
        <string key="concept:name" value="Define Research Topic"/>
        <string key="lifecycle:transition" value="start"/>
        <string key="org:resource" value="John"/>
        <date key="time:timestamp" value="2014-05-24T12:45:00.000+01:00"/>
        <string key="Activity_Name" value="Define Research Topic"/>
        <string key="Event_Type" value="Completed"/>
        <string key="Performer" value="John"/>
        <string key="Role" value="Research Student"/>
    </event>
```

For example, as gathered in the figure (Figure 1) the *Concept* extension may describe a *Case* or *Activity* attributes of types; *case_id* and *activity_name* respectively. Equally, such file extension matches the $\#case\_id(e)$ and

$#activity\_name(e)$ attribute as utilized in this book to carry out the classification of the individual traces that can be found in the provided events log in chapter 7. Practically, the work uses the *classifier* to define the *identity* of the events in the logs by simply defining the sets of data attributes by their *attribute keys*. Whereby, two events are considered to be similar, if they have the same values for each of the attributes.

In fact, one of the usefulness of XES format is that it does not only provide semantics for commonly used attributes, but also supports the *semantic extensions* which are capable of making use of the underlying information about the event logs to create new knowledge, or even more, utilized to enhance existing ones (Van der Aalst, 2011). Besides, the works in (Van der Aalst, 2016; Verbeek, et al., 2011; IEEE CIS Task Force on Process Mining, 2016) opines that if a log can actually describe a specific process in terms of their various domains, then the Application developers or analysts can also easily define their own domain-specific extensions. Interestingly, the works (Van der Aalst, 2016; Verbeek, et al., 2011; IEEE CIS Task Force on Process Mining, 2016) notes that, indeed, additional attributes that are not defined by any extension are always allowed. Henceforth, the one reason why the pursuits and streams in XES extensions have also inspired the advent of the latter - XESEXT (Gunther, 2009) as discussed in the next subsection.

eXtensible Event Stream Extension (XESEXT)

XESEXT (Gunther, 2009) has been developed as an extension to the XES file format. Typically, the XESEXT can have essential child element tags which include - *log, trace, event,* and *meta*. Truly, the XESEXT function serves as an enfolding container for the attributes tags definition: where the attributes that are defined in the tags are applicable to their conforming entities (i.e process elements) in line with the structure of the XES core standards. In other words, whilst the XES core standard do not necessarily have a generic understandable purpose (i.e. does not have semantics and is mainly focused on describing the general structures of the event data logs), the actual information that are enclosed within the logs are stored in the attributes. Therefore, to define the semantic information for any events log - the XES core standard makes use of the extension interface to perform such functions, whereas XESEXT permits the definition of an explicit extension to the XES standards. Perhaps, this type of function results in a fixed set(s) of attribute for any structural levels especially with the XES core standard (Gunther, 2009).

Semantic Annotated Mining eXtensible Markup Language (SA-MXML)

The SA-MXML format (deMedeiros, et al., 2008; de Medeiros & Van der Aalst, 2009) is a semantically annotated version of the MXML file standard that incorporates an additional attribute called the *modelReference* for all elements in the log except for *AuditTrailEntry* and *Timestamp*. The SA-MXML standard format is inspired by the limitations with the MXML file extension. Basically, the extension incorporates *reference* between elements in the events log and concepts in an ontology - which is a great way to define or compliment the way we look at processes. In practice, this is utilized by associating meaning to the tags or labels within the datasets (i.e. event logs). In other words, the *modelReference* attribute points and links between the various elements or instances in the log, and a list of concepts in the ontologies in order to provide a standard structuring particularly useful for implementing the semantic-based process mining approaches as shown in Figure 2. Moreover, the SA-MXML format is supported by tools such as ProM 5.2 (Verbeek, 2014) and ProMImport (Gu¨nther & Van der Aalst, 2006) open source frameworks for process mining.

Figure 2. Fragment of the SA-MXML file format

```
<ProcessInstance id="L08" description=""  modelReference="file:/C:/Users/KINGSLEY/Desktop/Process%20mining%20files/ProcessInstanceOntology.
wsml#ProcessInstance " >
    <AuditTrailEntry>
        <Data>
            <Attribute name="Role"  modelReference="file:/C:/Users/KINGSLEY/Desktop/Process%20mining%20files/DataFieldOntology.wsml#Role " >Research
            Student</Attribute>
            <Attribute name="Event Type"  modelReference="file:/C:/Users/KINGSLEY/Desktop/Process%20mining%20files/DataFieldOntology.wsml#EventType " >
            Completed</Attribute>
        </Data>
        <WorkflowModelElement modelReference="file:/C:/Users/KINGSLEY/Desktop/Process%20mining%20files/TaskOntology.wsml#DefineResearchTopic " >Define
        Research Topic</WorkflowModelElement>
        <EventType modelReference="file:/C:/Users/KINGSLEY/Desktop/Process%20mining%20files/EVO.wsml#Start " >start</EventType>
        <Timestamp>2014-05-24T12:45:00.000+01:00</Timestamp>
        <Originator modelReference="file:/C:/Users/KINGSLEY/Desktop/Process%20mining%20files/OriginatorOntology.wsml#John " >John</Originator>
    </AuditTrailEntry>
```

PROBLEMS WITH DATA QUALITY FOR PROCESS MINING

Having looked at the different types of file formats used to carry out the process mining task. The work discusses in this section some of the problems that may be encountered especially with regards to the data quality for process mining. Indeed, the quality of data is imperative to any data processing or analysis procedures such as the Process Mining. According to Rozinat (2016) the co-founder of fluxicon.com and Disco process mining tool (Rozinat & Gunther, 2012) in one of her article published in the Flux capacitor blog (Rozinat, 2016) - the outcomes of process mining algorithms in relation to quality of the recorded data can be likened to the longstanding computing phrase "Garbage in, Garbage out". In view of that, we can argue that it is important that the event logs which serves as *input* to the different process mining tools/techniques are relatively of high quality in order to ensure the quality of the *outputs*. Moreover, Rozinat (2016) opines that for an effective analysis of data or process mining tasks that the quality of the underlying data is important, or else, the process analysts may run the risk of drawing the wrong conclusions. Even so, the work in Rozinat (2016) notes that "the value of data is reflected in the value of decisions made" a quote written by Mark Norton in his comment on a blog post about the monetary value of data by Forrester Analyst - Rob Karel (Karel, 2011) who states that:

"...If you don't have the data, decisions can't be made (by definition), and if decisions can't be made, the organization cannot create value. So there is also an 'opportunity cost' associated with non-existent or bad data..." Mark Norton wrote in (Karel, 2011)

To this end, for example, and as a solution to resolving some of the data quality problems, namely; Incorrect logging, Insufficient logging, Semantics, Correlation, and Timing - the work in this book shows in chapter 8 that to measure the quality of process mining algorithms/techniques, it is essential that one must first focus on the accuracy of the classification results (i.e. the outcomes of the classifier over the given data sets) rather than just focusing on the seen (observed) instances. In turn, having the outcome of the classifier over the given datasets, the analyst finds it effective to further predict good classification for unseen (unobserved) instances within the available datasets. Basically, in Chapter 8 the work has used the test event logs in (Carmona, et al., 2016) with a complete total of 200 traces to evaluate the accuracy, error-free rate, recall and precision of the proposed classification method of this book by making use of the standard Percent of Correct Classification (PCC) (Baati, et al., 2017) to assess the performance of the classifiers.

Therefore, in the following sub-sections, this book looks at the predominant problems with the quality of data for process mining in more details. Essentially, the work looks at some of the issues in relation to data quality that the process analyst may come across during any process mining or analysis task, and consequently expound on how those data quality problems can be resolved.

Incorrect Logging

Noise is used in process mining field to refer to exceptional behaviours that are classed as not being present in the actual log (Van der Aalst, 2016). In the same way, if a specific process mining tool has the capability to abstract low frequently behaviours by displaying only the most frequent (main) process flows, then it could be referred to have the capacity to deal with noise. Even though, in most cases, the process mining algorithms finds it difficult to differentiate between incorrect loggings from the said frequent events. Therefore, *incorrect logging* could be referred to mean that the *recorded data is wrong* (Rozinat, 2016). Besides, the problem noted here is that the available datasets tends not to mirror the underlying certainty about the processes in question, but instead provides wrong information about the process in reality. For example, data logs from a company's supply bill invoice in a typical ERP system may be automatically scanned. However, due to mistakes during the process of scanning the document, the "invoice ID" may be misunderstood or misinterpreted as "invoice Date" and in consequence, the activities with timestamps referring to years with numbers (e.g. 2013, 2016, 2019, 2020 etc.) may appear in the logged data.

Furthermore, another typical example of incorrect logging with regards to the data quality for process mining is the inconsistencies that may appear within the logged data due to human errors or alterations. For instance, an employee in an organization could mistakenly press the *complete* button in a workflow system right at the start of a task, or another employee may press the *start* button at the end (complete) of a task. By chance, such kind of problems could only be addressed during the process analysis phases that is only if, the originators (employees) become aware of such inconsistencies. To this end, according to (Rozinat, 2016) it is imperative when carrying out a process mining task, that the process analysts and/or owners are cautious about datasets which are manually generated because they are often less reliable than datasets which are created automatically. Needly and practice-wise, the data quality should first be inspected prior to performing the process mining/analysis tasks, even if there exist no doubts about the reliability or consistency of the data. Moreover, as noted earlier in this chapter - the results of process mining algorithms in relation to the quality of the recorded data is allied to the longstanding computing phrase "Garbage in, Garbage out". Therefore, the accuracy of the classification results, i.e., the outcome of the classifier over a given dataset (see: chapter 8) could as well indicate that the input data is reliable and/or at the same time consistent.

Insufficient Logging

Modern tools/method for collection of data and management of information from the many existing IT systems are often updated and in most settings simply overwritten. In so doing, past entries or existing loggings may be lost. Moreover, in a number of cases, the databases only make available the informations about the current state of the systems which they support, but not the complete (full) history about what has occurred in the past. Characteristically, many of those systems adopts the *batch logging* method of processing - where activities may be entered all at once at the end of or in a day. In consequence, every change that might have been made intermediately (i.e. halfway) could be lost, and the recollection of when and what has happened (i.e the process history) may not be remodelled.

Therefore, whilst *incorrect logging* is about wrong data, *insufficient logging* is about missing data (Rozinat, 2016; Van der Aalst, 2011). For example, Van der Aalst (2011) notes that the minimum requirement for any process mining project must include the: *Case ID*, *ActivityName* and/or *Timestamp*s to be able to model the *history* of the events or activities as performed in reality. Whereas, Rozinat (2016) observes that most of the data mining, or yet still, online analytical processing (OLAP) systems does not need the entire history of a particular process to analyse the captured datasets. So for these reasons, data extracted from many database systems (i.e the warehouse) may not carry or include all the information (i.e. data fields or variables) that are necessary to carry out the process mining tasks.

Notably, one can argue that the quality of the outcome of any process mining task does not depend on logging too much data but relies exclusively on the minimum data requirements to carry out the process mining task. Even though, for some particular type of process mining/analysis tasks - additional data may be needed. For instance, when analysing a specific organizations business operations - a "person" and/or "department" that executed a particular set(s) of activity, as a prerequisite, needs to be present within the extracted data logs. More so, it is expected that both "start" and "end" timestamps are available within the events logs, for any process mining algorithm to be able to compute the *execution-times for activities* etc.

Semantics

Most of the time, the biggest encounters when performing a process mining task is to discover the correct information and to comprehend (i.e understand) what they mean (Rozinat, 2016; Carmona, et al., 2016; Rozinat, 2010). According to the work in Rozinat (2016), it could be anything between really easy or very complicated to figure out the semantic informations (i.e metadata and assertions) from existing logs in many organizations databases or IT systems. Moreover, quite often the outcomes of the analysis mainly depend on how distant the logs are from the actual business logic. For example, a typical scenario is a case where a specific business process operations (events logs) could be logged directly in relation to the corresponding activity names as performed, or in settings where a process analyst may perhaps require to some extent a kind of process mappings between the actual business activities and some kind of hidden action code in order to be able to analyse the process.

Although, according to the work of Rozinat (2016) and evidently from current researches in the advanced area of semantic process mining (deMedeiros, et al., 2008; de Medeiros & Van der Aalst, 2009, Okoye et al, 2019, Okoye et al, 2020) and business process intelligence (Ingvaldsen, et al., 2005; Van der Aalst, 2004; van Dongen, et al., 2016); it is best practice when carrying out the process mining tasks to work alongside process analyst who are able to mine the correct datasets (information) as well as interpret the implication of the various components that constitute the said process in question. Ultimately, in context of the process mining techniques and use/application of the different tools that supports the method, the work in Rozinat (2016) notes that it helps not to try to understand everything at once but instead to focus first on the three essential elements:

(i)   How to differentiate the process instances?
(ii)   Where to find the activity logs? and
(iii) The start and/or completion timestamps for activities?

According to the author (Rozinat, 2016) when these essential three elements have been identified and addressed, subsequently, one may further look for additional informations (i.e metadata and assertions) that might help improve the process mining outcomes and analysis - especially from a specific domain of interest or different perspectives. Accordingly, the method of this book proposes a semantic-based process mining framework and sets of semantically motivated algorithms that are directed towards the enhancement of the process mining results and analysis. Technically, the method shows that a system which is formally encoded with semantic labelling (annotation), semantic representation (ontology) and semantic reasoning (reasoner) has the capability to enhance the process mining results and analysis from the syntactic level to a much more conceptual level. In turn, the outcome is a process mining approach that is able to induce new knowledge based on previously unobserved behaviours, and a more intuitive and easy way to envisage the relationships that exist between the various process instances that can be found within the discovered models.

Correlation

Correlation is about stitching all the different elements that are contained in the events log together, and in the correct way. Without a doubt, correlation is another important task that is essential for ensuring the quality of data for process mining, since the PM techniques are technically based on the *history* of processes. Besides, the logic behind the design and implementation of the process mining algorithms is that each and every element (i.e. the process instances) in the underlying process has to or are mapped (modelled) from the available event data logs. Rozinat (2016) is even more specific about the notion of the Correlation. The work (Rozinat, 2016) notes that correlation is a very important factor when considering the quality of data for process mining, and to this end, looks at the correlation of data from the following examples:

- Nowadays, the business processes often span multiple IT systems and usually, each of the IT systems has its own local IDs. Therefore, one needs to correlate the local process IDs in order to combine log fragments from the different systems (e.g. local ID from system-1 and local ID from system-2). Perhaps, this is done, for example, as a way of getting (grasping) the full picture of the processes as performed in reality, i.e., from start to end.
- Also, even within the same systems, the correlation of the event logs may be necessary. For example, in an ERP purchase-to-pay process, the purchase orders are identified by the order IDs and later on the invoices are characterized by invoice IDs. Therefore, to get an end-to-end perspective of the said processes, the corresponding purchase order IDs and invoice IDs need to be matched.

- Moreover, from time to time, there exist some hierarchical (structured) processes which means that the activity instances need to be distinguished (e.g. through ontological modelling) in order to correlate lower-level events that belong to those (activity) sub-processes.

In general, to resolve the problem of correlation, it makes sense to start in a simple manner in order to identify the low-level information needed to interpret or demonstrate the value of the process mining task. Perhaps, such kind of analysis is often allied to the Occam's Razor Principles (Hiroshi, 1997) as noted earlier in this chapter.

Timing

Timing is another important factor that is considered for many process mining tasks. It is used especially for ordering the events found within the captured logs. Essentially, the timing permits the ordering of activities in the discovered models due to the fact that the process mining tools/algorithms calculates the history of the process elements (instances) or activities as they are sequentially performed. Thus, if the recorded timestamp(s) are incorrect or not sufficiently accurate, it may then become problematic for the process mining tool to produce the right order (i.e. sequence) of events history from the available data. For example, the work in Rozinat (2016) identifies more or less the complications that one may encounter with timing when carrying out a process mining task as follows:

- **When The Timestamp Resolution is Too Low:** for example, only the date of a performed activity (but not the time) is recorded. But even if the time is recorded, it may be necessary to record it at least with millisecond accuracy if many events follow each other in an automated system or perhaps are performed in a sequential manner.
- **Different Timestamp Granularities on Different Systems:** for example, the timestamps in one system may be rounded to minutes. Whereas, in another system (which is also executing a part of the same process) records events with 1-second resolution. As a consequence, when the captured (extracted) logs from the two different systems are put together, the order of some of the events in the log may be wrong due to the granularity difference.

- **Different Clocks on Different Systems:** for example, if multiple computers record the same type of data, then peradventure the computers may have different system clock settings. As a result, when the events logs from the different computers are merged, the time differences perhaps can create problems, since they void the correct order of events.

Eventually, in an ideal world, the timing of event logs must not be synchronized or summed up (especially if different systems are involved) but should be exact and accurate (Rozinat, 2016).

To summarize the problems with data quality for process mining in this section, it is certain that the quality of data is an indispensable problem or challenge that has to be firstly addressed even before commencing the process mining task. In fact, it is an undertaking which must not be ignored especially when the quality of the eventual analysis and/or output are of paramount. Besides, to discover proper or fitting models, one expects that the available datasets must consist of a *descriptive* example behaviour (Van der Aalst, 2011; Cairns, et al., 2015) - which implies that most often the problems encountered while using any type of process mining algorithm or carrying out the process modelling task in reality, is closely related to the available *event logs*. For all intents and purposes, it could take even more time to perform pre-processing of data than the actual time required to perform the said mining task in question. Nonetheless, it is important to note that not every dataset are incorrect and it's beneficial to start simple (Rozinat, 2016; Hiroshi, 1997).

Predominantly, the method of this book focuses primarily on the *semantics* aspect of the data quality issues to provide an easy and accurate way to effectively carry out the process mining tasks. The work lays emphasis on how to differentiate the process instances (i.e. classifications) for the purpose of achieving the overall book aim - which is to extract streams of event logs from any given process execution environment (using the series of case studies) and describe formats that allows for mining and improved model analysis of the captured datasets. To this effect, this book describes how data from various process domains are being extracted, semantically prepared, and transformed into minable executable formats to support the discovery, monitoring, and enhancement of real-time processes through further semantic analysis of the discovered models. As noted in the earlier chapters particularly in Introduction section and Chapter 1, the semantic viewpoint is captured by exploring the elements (i.e the process instances) that can be found within the event logs based on two types of probes/analysis, namely - (i) how to make use of the semantics that describes the available data? and (ii) how to mine the semantic information from the discovered models? (deMedeiros, et al., 2008).

PROCESS MINING ALGORITHMS, TOOLS AND SUPPORT

A lot of software vendors including the IT experts and developers offer intelligent tools/methods that provide support towards the implementation (carrying out) of process mining tasks or projects. Amongst the many existing tools that supports the process mining is ProM (Verbeek, et al., 2011) an open source tool that supports or integrates altogether a vast number of algorithms, methods, and aspects of process mining. Although, several other commercial tools exist which also supports the process mining application for real-time processing such as Disco by fluxicon (Rozinat & Gunther, 2012), and the other commercial vendors like Celonis15, MinIt16, ProcessGold17, MyInvenio18, Worksoft19, QPR ProcessAnalyzer20 etc.

Therefore, for the rest of this section, the work provides comprehensive insight on the strength and weaknesses of some of the different algorithms that are used to perform/guide the right use, interpretation, and extension of the process mining and the resulting process models. Essentially, the work explains the main ideas behind the development of the existing PM algorithms, their successful application towards the real-time visualization and analysis of the event logs, as well as the problems one may need to deal with when using any of those algorithms.

Alpha Algorithm (α-algorithm)

One of the very first algorithms developed for the primary purpose of process mining is the *Alpha algorithm* denoted in short form as *(α-algorithm)* (Van der Aalst, 2011). The α-algorithm was first put forward by Van der Aalst et al (2004), and ever since then many extensions of it has been proposed. Technically, a typical α-algorithm takes an event log and produces a *Petri net* (Van der Aalst, 2011) that can replay the different low-level activities that can be found within the discovered model by explaining the behaviours (i.e traces) recorded in the log. Whereas, the *Petri net* (Van der Aalst, 2016) is one of the oldest and best-investigated process modelling language that allows for concurrency which consists of *places* and *transitions* that are run by firing rules *tokens* through the *split* and *join* notations, e.g., AND, XOR, OR gateways etc. Indeed, one major function or characteristics of the Petri net models is that the discovered patterns (often referred to as footprints) are represented as Workflow nets (WF-net) (Van der Aalst & Van Hee, 2004). Interestingly, according to the work in Van der Aalst (2011), α-algorithms are able to discover a huge amount of workflow nets that are perceived to be valid.

However, there are also some limitations when using α-algorithm to carry out a process mining task. For example, there may exist several workflow nets (WF-net) that appears to have similar behaviours (i.e trace equivalent) but the models can be *structurally* different. This means that even though the discovered models are capable of representing the behaviours as observed within the event logs, the resultant Workflow nets may still be unnecessarily complex (representational bias).

Heuristic Miner (HM)

Heuristic Miner (HM) (Weijters & Ribeiro, 2010; Weijters & Van der Aalst, 2003) is one of the existing process mining algorithms that make use of representations similar to Casual nets (C-net) (Van der Aalst, 2016) to construct process models by taking into account the *event frequency*. The main idea with heuristic mining algorithms/methods remains in its ability to ignore paths which are not frequently executed within the process. Moreover, the supporting approaches (Heuristic Miner) are additionally robust than the majority of existing process mining techniques. This is due to its ability to focus on the frequent paths, and thus, overcomes the problem of representational bias provided by the C-nets and/or WF-nets. Besides, the work in Van der Aalst (2016) notes that even though in a practical sense, casual nets are more expressive and intuitive than the traditional heuristic nets, the process models discovered by using the heuristic miner still appears to be highly structured and rather sequential.

Furthermore, Buijs (2014) notes that the heuristics miner (HM) has been developed to be more resistant to exceptional behaviour than most of the other process discovery algorithms. For instance, when compared to outputs of the Petri nets, the work (Buijs, 2014) observes that the resulting process tree from the heuristic miner can correctly replay all the behaviour that can be found within the events log because there exist a lot of silent transitions that allow for different combinations of activities being executed. Perhaps, this function is as opposed to the Petri nets which could produce WF-nets that have similar behaviours (i.e trace equivalent) but the models may be structurally different.

Nonetheless, the work in Buijs (2014) notes that the results of the heuristics miner are in general relaxed sound, which for most analysis techniques is not sufficient. In other words, even though the HM is able to handle exceptional behaviours, the method results in low replay fitness scores especially in settings where the behaviours are slightly more complicated. Besides, the heuristics miner tools and the resulting applications trails to consider *precision* because the behaviour of the process models are restricted, and as such, comes at the cost of *generalization*. In consequence, the resulting process models are not easy to interpret since the different relationships between the various activities are encoded with separate transitions (Buijs, 2014).

Inductive Miner (IM)

Inductive Miner (IM) algorithm supports a wide range of *process discovery* methods. The results of the IM approaches are represented in form of *process trees*, i.e., notations used to signify *block structured models* that are seen to be sound in representation (Van der Aalst, 2016; Leemans, et al., 2015). According to the work of Van der Aalst (2016), whereas many of the other process discovery models such as the WF-nets, Petri nets, BPMN, EPCs, YAWL, UML etc. might suffer from dead-locks, live-locks, and other anomalies, the *process trees* discovered by the inductive miner are usually sound by construction. Furthermore, the work (Van der Aalst, 2016) notes that the IM frameworks are extremely extendible and also permits for a lot of variations of the elementary method. Notably, the *family of the inductive mining* techniques (Leemans, et al., 2013; Leemans, et al., 2014; Leemans, et al., 2014a; Leemans, et al., 2015) has different variations which are capable of handling behaviours that are not frequent, and also deals with large amount of models including its analysis whilst making sure the proper (correct) measures are conformed. For instance, the IM algorithms have the capability of rediscovering the original models within the actual limit. Hence, IM methods are capable of discovering a much-wider class of events or activities and can learn sound models in settings where the α-algorithm including the several other methods for process discovery fails.

Currently, many extensions and/or refinements of the IM algorithms have been developed, thanks to the basic ideas presented by the family of the inductive mining methods. Typical examples of such family of IM algorithms which are also available in ProM (Verbeek, 2014) are as follows: Inductive Miner-infrequent (IMF), Inductive Miner-incompleteness (IMC), Inductive Miner-directly-follows based (IMD), Inductive Miner-infrequent-directly-follows based (IMFD), and Inductive Miner-incompleteness-directly-follows based (IMCD) (Leemans, et al., 2013; Leemans, et al., 2014; Leemans, et al., 2014a; Leemans, et al., 2015; Van der Aalst, 2016).

Indeed, IM is currently one of the leading process discovery techniques (Van der Aalst, 2016) due to its ability to discover process models that are thought to be sound in nature. Thus:

- Flexible and Scalable
- Formal or Fitness guarantees
- Ability to convert the resulting process trees to other notations. For example BPMN models or Petri nets etc.
- Simplicity - due to its block-structure (i.e. activities are not duplicated)

Nevertheless, one of the limitations of the IM is the *fall-through* (Van der Aalst, 2016) which may create underfitting models in settings where there exist no process trees without silent and/or duplicate activities during the process of creating the observed behaviours. Moreover, the experiment carried out in Buijs (2014) indicates that the IM algorithms take a constructive approach whereby more emphasis is put on replay *fitness* than on *precision*.

Genetic Process Mining

Genetic process mining algorithms are *search methods* that mimic the process of evolution in biological systems in order to discover process models. The genetic process mining methods are used to carry out the process mappings by randomly distributing a finite number of points into the search space (de Medeiros, 2006; Van der Aalst, 2016). According to the work of Van der Aalst (2016) whilst the α-algorithm and the many other techniques (e.g. the fuzzy and heuristics miner) provides the models in a deterministic and direct way, the genetic algorithms appears not to be fixed but instead depends on unsystematic (random) approach to discover new methods for the process modelling and/or interpretation. The work (Van der Aalst, 2016) also notes that the genetic process mining steps are very general, and certain choices need to be made when actually implementing the technique. For instance, the precarious choice needed for representation of the Individuals, Initialization,

Fitness function, Selection strategy (i.e. tournament and elitism), Crossover, and Mutation etc.

Interestingly, on one hand, de Medeiros (2006) observes that even though such choices may be necessary, they are not sufficient enough since generally there may be more than one individual(s) that are capable of reproducing the behaviours within the log. However, on the whole, by method (i.e genetic process mining), there also exist the risks of discovering underfitting (*over-general*) or overfitting (*over-specific*) individual populations. Likewise, the work in Van der Aalst (2016) notes some limitations with the genetic process mining. According to the observations of the work (Van der Aalst, 2016), the realization of the main ideas beneath the genetic mechanisms (i.e. crossovers and mutations) is not as simple as they may suggest. Usually, in many settings; model repairs are often required when the crossovers and mutations are completed. Besides, the work (Van der Aalst, 2016) notes that the genetic approach appears not to be somewhat effective particularly when a large amount of models are being considered, and it could take longer computational times to derive models which have a fitness that is satisfactory. Nevertheless, to benefit from the unique characteristics of the genetic process mining approach, Turner et al (2008) outlines an incremental procedure that can be applied to achieve optimal fitness of the discovered models. This includes the initial step of performing an effective reading the events logs to ensure that the dependency relation between the different activities that make up the process are well calculated. The process is then followed by building the initial population and calculating the individual fitness. Consequently, the results (crossover and mutation) helps to create the next population vice versa (Turner et al, 2008).

On the other hand, the authors in de Medeiros et al (2007) argues that such kind of algorithms (genetic miner) which mimic the process of evolution could be potentially used to effectively mine and analyse event logs. This could be done by pursuing to make use of the *conformance checking* technique to select the representative models, which are in turn, then used to produce the next generation of process models. In other words, the genetic mining approach can be used to repair the process models to reflect reality (Fahland & van der Aalst, 2012). Although, the work in Fahland & van der Aalst (2012) notes that similarity of the repaired model to the original model (including simplicity of the repaired model in general) is harder to achieve and may require trade-offs. For example, allowing for all possible noisy behaviours with respect to other quality dimensions for comparing the process models.

In turn, the approach can result in spaghetti-like or complex models (Van der Aalst, 2016).

Nevertheless, genetic process mining approaches have some benefits when compared to the other process mining algorithms. The work in Van der Aalst (2016) observes that a combination of the heuristic miner with the genetic approaches is quite meaningful and advantageous. Accordingly, in order to demonstrate the benefit of such mixture of methods (hybrid algorithms) the work of de Medeiros (2006) observes in its experiments that a combination of the heuristics with genetic process mining algorithm is superior when compared to situations where it is used without the heuristic, or heuristics without the genetic operators. In the experimental setup, de Medeiros (2006) tested the genetic algorithm on event logs from 25 different process models assumed to be noise-free (Van der Aalst, et al., 2004). Essentially, the author (de Medeiros, 2006) set up four scenarios while running the genetic algorithm:

- *Scenario 1* - without heuristics to build the initial population and without genetic operators
- *Scenario 2* - with heuristics, but without the genetic operators
- *Scenario 3* - without heuristics, but with genetic operators
- *Scenario 4* - with heuristics and genetic operators.

Remarkably, the results of the experiment with *heuristics and genetic operators* (scenario 4) indicate that the hybrid (combined) algorithm is superior to the other scenarios. This is owing to the fact that - the *scenario 4* combines the strong ability of the heuristics to correctly capture the local causality relations, with the benefits of using the genetic operators (especially mutation) to introduce the non-local causality relations. Overall, the set up in scenario 4 (i.e. *hybrid genetic algorithm*) produces much more complete and precise models than the other approaches. Likewise, the proposed method of this book appears to represent itself as a fusion theory that semantically integrates the fuzzy models with other tools in order to enhance the informative values of such type of models. This is done by carefully integrating and tuning the semantic metrics that those models (fuzzy models) lack.

Fuzzy Miner (FM)

Fuzzy Miner (FM) algorithms are practically used to discover process models in a more or less precise way. In other words, used to visualize complex processes. The algorithm (fuzzy miner) is considered to be effective in discovering flexible and less-structured models (Rozinat, 2010; G"unther, 2009). According to the work of Rozinat (2010), the fuzzy miner algorithms are applied with the goal to show understandable models for very unstructured processes. Interestingly, Ingvaldsen (2011) mentions that the FM is one of the many existing algorithms that aim to address the problem of mining complex processes (which appears to be unstructured in nature) by utilizing a mixture of clustering and abstraction techniques. This implies that models discovered as a result of applying the fuzzy miner algorithms on the captured datasets are able to abstract from details and aggregate behaviours that are not of interest to the process analysts (i.e excludes visual noise) into cluster nodes (Rozinat, 2010). Although, by referring to the unstructured processes, we could realize that the fuzzy miner algorithms are used to produce simplified models to directly address the problems of large numbers of activities and/ or highly unstructured datasets or behaviours. However, the fuzzy models tend to lack some kind of formal description. For instance, successive pattern recognition such as the *simple choice* (OR split), *parallel choice* (AND split), or *multiple choice* (XOR split) otherwise linked to the lack of semantic representation - when compared to the class hierarchy (classifications), or better still, *taxonomies* that can be described through the semantic-based fuzzy mining approach of this book (see: Chapter 7).

Consequently, the work in Rozinat (2010) notes that the results of the fuzzy miner algorithms are *relaxed* in nature especially when compared with the semantics of the other process modelling languages/notation such as Petri nets or BPMN. The work (Rozinat, 2010) observes that if a task in a fuzzy model has multiple successor tasks, then all of those successors will be activated once the task has been executed, even though, they do not need to be executed. In so doing, there is no explicit distinction possible between the *simple choice*, *parallel choice* and *multiple choices*. Although by chance, those patterns may emerge implicitly but are not necessarily enforced by the model semantics (Rozinat, 2010).

Practically, in tools that supports the FM algorithm (e.g. ProM and Disco), users have the capacity to control the levels of detail displayed by the resulting process maps through the attributes sliders (e.g. frequent paths or performance indicators) that are used to set the threshold-values. Usually, the resulting models are not often suitable for enacting a process on a workflow system, but instead, are used to provide means to explore the complex processes in an interactive manner and/or on variable levels of abstraction.

Nonetheless, one of the main strengths of the fuzzy models is that they are conceived to be easily adaptable (i.e. extendible) (Rozinat, 2010). For example, with the fuzzy miner, the nodes and edges can be automatically removed or clustered by moving a slider along a particular connotation or correlation threshold scale. To this end, the relaxed nature (one of the main characteristics) of the fuzzy model semantics can be summarized in terms of the workflow patterns as follows (Van der Aalst, 2016):

1. **Instantiation:** The process may start at any arbitrary node in the fuzzy model, i.e., there is no exclusive starting point.
2. **Branch Semantics**: Every node in the fuzzy models has an AND split semantics, i.e., an executed node enables all successor nodes.
3. **Join Semantics**: Every node has memory-less XOR join semantics, i.e., it can be executed as soon as it has been enabled by any of its predecessor nodes, but in most cases does not *recall* how often it has been enabled.
4. **Termination:** The process terminates implicitly whenever no further nodes are executed, i.e., there is no exclusive ending point, and possibly, remaining enabled nodes are ignored.

Unfortunately, even with the relaxed execution semantics (as explained above) and the adaptive simplification mechanism exhibited by the fuzzy miner - the resulting models are mainly useful only as a descriptive method for complex and unstructured processes which eventually would produce the so-called *spaghetti* models (Van der Aalst, 2016) if they would be precisely represented (G"unther, 2009). Therefore, one can say that the fuzzy models are ambiguous and tends to lack the real descriptions (semantics) behind the event logs. Besides, the definition characteristically means that fuzzy models are only useful when the process analyst is interested in how the activities have been performed or the paths the process instances follow during the execution - but does not actually describe the semantics about relationships the process instances share within the underlying knowledge-base which shows the limitation of such hierarchical decomposition.

Yet, fuzzy mining approaches are very useful especially in settings where the analyst is interested in process discovery algorithms that are capable of producing simplified process models. Besides, the proposed method of this book reveals how the ambiguous problem of the fuzzy models and the lack of real descriptions (semantics) behind the events log or labels can be resolved by bringing the analysis of the resulting models to a more conceptual level, thus, the semantic-fuzzy mining approach. More so, because the fuzzy models are conceived to be easily adaptable (i.e. extendible) by utilizing the mixture of clustering and abstraction techniques which are similar to the classification and abstraction (conceptual) method of analysis used in this book, this work focuses on resolving the *semantics* limitations that are associated with the fuzzy algorithms by aiming to integrate semantic knowledge into the resulting fuzzy models. Technically, the work illustrates this method through the series of experimentation and the proposed semantic fuzzy miner approach. In fact, this work has shown that it is possible to improve the information values of such type of models (fuzzy models) to some greater extent by carefully integrating and tuning the semantics metrics that those models lack.

SEMANTIC PROCESS MINING AND ITS ENABLING TECHNOLOGIES

The semantic technologies and its application have of late gained a significant interest within the field of process mining (de Medeiros & Van der Aalst, 2009; De Giacomo, et al., 2018; Okoye et al, 2019; Okoye et al, 2020). Truly, the growing interest has prominently spanned the emergence and advanced notion of the *semantic process mining* which is currently being embraced and technically applied as a tool towards the extension and enhancement of event logs and process models derived by using the traditional process mining techniques.

By definition, the semantic process mining and its enabling technologies aim to utilize the semantic information (i.e. metadata) about the process instances that can be found within the event logs and/or process models to create new techniques for process mining or improve the level of analysis of the existing ones. Perhaps, this is done in order to better support humans in obtaining a much more detailed and accurate result for process mining that are closer to human understanding. Consequently, the methods means that the *semantic-based analysis* helps to present the process mining results and outcomes at a much more conceptual level that can be easily grasped by the process owners, process analysts, or IT experts etc.

In principle, the *semantic process mining* techniques takes advantage of the rich semantics (Polyvyanyy & et al, 2016; De Giacomo, et al., 2018) embedded in the event logs or models (i.e. tags or labels) about any given process, and links them to concepts in an *ontology* in order to extract useful patterns by means of *semantic reasoning*. To this effect, the three basic blocks for any given semantic process mining task can be said to include – the semantic annotated logs/model, ontologies, and semantic reasoning (de

Mederios et al, 2008; Okoye et al, 2018 & 2020). Certainly, the *semantic annotation* helps in describing the meaning behind the events log labels or attributes of the process models. Whereas, *ontologies* are used to define or provide useful information (semantics) on how the different activities that make up the process depend on each other within or during the process execution environment, and are essential for extracting models capable of creating new knowledge by supporting the making of inference through the *semantic reasoner*. Perhaps, semantic reasoning is supported due to the formal definition of the ontological concepts and expression of relationships that exist within the event logs and the derived model about the processes in view.

Essentially, the semantic-based approach has emerged due to the limitations identified with the majority of the existing process mining techniques. Most of the existing process mining techniques depend on tags or labels in event logs information to discover the process models, and perhaps, to a certain extent are limited because they do not technically gain from the real knowledge (semantics) that describe the tags or labels. Therefore, to cater for this problem, the methods which supports the semantic-based process mining approaches prompts the main benefits provided by its utilization - which is the ability to describe the semantics behind the tags or labels in any given events log or resultant process models. Moreover, the methods are considered especially useful for the discovery of new knowledge or real-world understanding about the said processes in question.

In the short term, the semantic process mining approaches are purely grounded on the three basic building blocks (deMedeiros, et al., 2008) namely:

- Annotated event logs or models
- Ontologies, and
- Semantic Reasoning (ontology reasoners)

Interestingly, the semantic process mining is a new area within the field of process mining and there are few existing approaches that demonstrate the capabilities of the technique (de Medeiros & Van der Aalst, 2009; De Giacomo, et al., 2018; Okoye et al, 2019; Invangsen, 2011, Cairns et al, 2014). For example, the work in Okoye et al (2019) introduces the semantic-based process mining and analysis framework that is directed towards the discovery and enhancement of the sets of behaviours that can be found within a process execution environment. The method (Okoye et al, 2019) which integrates the three basic building blocks (i.e annotated events logs or model, ontologies, and semantic reasoner) is developed in order to address the problem of determining the presence of different patterns or traces that can be found within any given process knowledge-base. Moreover, the study focuses on identifying meaningful information about the different process elements in the available event logs, and enriching the information values of the resulting models based on the proposed framework, semantic-based algorithms, and its main application in real-time.

Semantic LTL Checker Algorithm

The Semantic LTL Checker (deMedeiros, et al., 2008) is one, if not the only existing process mining algorithm that aims to analyse event logs based on concepts by presenting the analysis of the processes (which they are used to support) at a more abstraction level. In practice, the Semantic-LTL checker applies concepts in an *ontology* as input to parameters of a Linear Temporal Logic (LTL) formulae to formulate and answer questions about the process elements (instances) by making use of the WSML2Reasoner (Bishop, et al., 1999) to infer all the necessary associations. Initially, the authors in deMedeiros et al (2008) proposed the algorithm to help support the development of a semantic process mining tool and its application when auditing logs. The authors (deMedeiros, et al., 2008) applies the method by extending the existing LTL Checker conformance and analysis plug-in (de Beer, 2005) in ProM. Basically, the process is carried out by exploiting the semantic annotation and the creation of ontologies. Moreover, the standard LTL Checker has proved to be useful for verification of properties that are defined in terms of Linear Temporal Logic (LTL) particularly for events log auditing. Although, the standard LTL Checker plugins only work on labels or tags in the event logs. This means that setting values for the parameters in the LTL Checker interface is perceptibly based on the event logs tags (or labels) that eventually produces results which are syntactic in nature. As a result, the standard LTL Checker does not benefit from the actual semantics behind those labels; which if adequately utilized could cater for a much more robust and accurate process mining and analysis technique. For this reason, the Semantic LTL Checker algorithm is developed with the primary aim of extending the original LTL Checker through the addition of the choices (i.e. options) to provide and accept concepts as input to parameters of the Linear Temporal Logic (LTL) formulae.

In principle, the work in deMedeiros et al (2008) has modified the LTL Checker algorithm in the following ways:

- The input formats were extended to support semantic annotations, thus, paving the way for further development of semantic process mining techniques.
- The Semantic LTL checker has been integrated with the WSML2Reasoner framework (W2RF). The authors chose the WSML2Reasoner because their work is part of the SUPER European project, in which ontologies are defined in WSML format (Lausen, et al., 2005).

In theory, the Semantic LTL checker (i.e. a semantically motivated version of the conformance analysis plug-in *LTL Checker*) was developed based on the stated reasons. The algorithm (Semantic-LTL Checker) is only available in previous versions of ProM (ProM 5.2). To note, the algorithm was originally built to provide support for analysis of business processes in order to carry out semantically augmented auditing of events data logs. However, the algorithm can now be applied to analyse datasets from any given process domain of interest or context as long as the recorded data contains the bare minimum requirement to perform process mining, and are in the standard format for storing event logs for process mining and analysis.

Accordingly, in order to demonstrate how the Semantic LTL Checker structured and could be applied for the purpose of semantic process mining/analysis tasks, this work have utilized the algorithm to show the need for the three basic building blocks (i.e. *annotated event logs, ontologies,* and *a reasoner*) for any semantic-based process mining method. For example, this work utilizes the *Semantic LTL Checker* algorithm to provide an answer to a real-world learning question by pointing to concepts within the defined ontologies as shown in Figure 3.

As shown in the figure (Figure 3), the work uses the Semantic LTL Checker in ProM to carry out the annotation and construction of the ontologies from the events log about the learning process (Okoye et al, 2016) based on attributes (labels) in the logs. The following are examples of the resulting ontologies: TaskOntology, OriginatorOntology, ProcessInstanceOntology, ProcessOntology, EventOntology, SourceOntology, DataFieldOntology, WorkFlowLogOntology etc. Subsequently, based on the underlying ontologies (concepts or class taxonomies) and the use of the reasoner, the work carries out a more conceptual analysis of the events logs as illustrated in Figure 3.

Thus, by *checking* (computing) the formulae in Figure 3:

*"forall_activities_and_persons_always_event_E_implies_eventually_event_F"*Where:

Figure 3. Typical events log analysis for a Learning Process using the Semantic LTL Checker

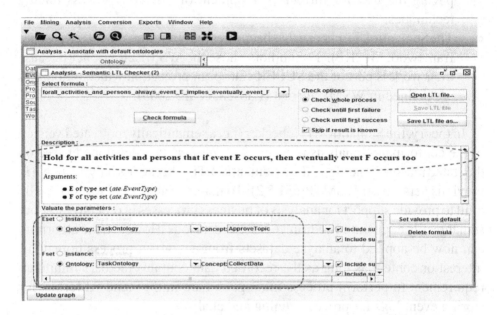

- Parameters: **E** set points to **Ontology** = TaskOntology, and **Concept** = ApproveTopic.
- Parameters: **F** set points to the **Ontology** = TaskOntology, and **Concept** = CollectData

Indeed, the result of executing the formula is an association that holds for all Activities and Persons that *IF* event **E** (ApproveTopic) occurs *THEN* eventually event **F** (CollectData) occurs too. Truly, such kind of analysis is essentially important, for instance, in measuring the progress of a learner within the learning execution environment and the purpose is not only to match the questions one would like to answer (as shown in Figure 3) but also, the ability to identify and monitor deviations/bottlenecks, distinguish and establish the attributes the process elements (instances) share within the learning knowledge-base. Moreover, such information can be of paramount and important especially when measuring the transition or progress of a learner within the learning knowledge-base. For instance, since the *ApproveTopic* is within the *Define Topic Area*, it can be logically deduced that there exists a *necessary condition* for a Learner to complete the task *ApproveTopic* before they can eventually move on to or perform the task *CollectData* etc.

Notably, the associations or references to the *concepts* within the domain ontologies reveals interesting connection or attributes between the different entities that are found in the process. Besides, the method also provides a better understanding of how the different elements within the learning process-base relate and interact with each other. Clearly, such a *conceptualization method* of analysis is based on the incentives of the semantic process mining which of certain forms the primary focus and is central to the objective of this book. Obviously, the ontological *references* or *terms* associate meanings to labels (i.e. objects/datatypes properties, individual restrictions etc.) in the event log by pointing to the defined concepts in the ontologies. Moreover, the *reasoner* supports reasoning over the ontologies in order to derive new knowledge (deMedeiros, et al., 2008; Okoye, et al., 2016; De Giacomo, et al., 2018).

For the next sections of this chapter, the work looks in details the main technologies which are used to support or enable the semantic process mining technique as proposed in this book. The section starts by looking at the ontological concepts/schema and its main functions that allow for the implementation of the semantic-based process mining and analysis framework as described in chapter 3. This is followed by a description of the importance of the semantic annotation, as well as, the logic behind using the inference capability of the reasoner to support the conceptual analysis of the derived models.

ONTOLOGIES

Ontologies, as a collection of *concepts* and *predicates*, has the ability to perform logic reasoning and consequently bridge the underlying challenges (*semantic gaps*) beneath the event logs and models discovered especially by using the conventional process mining techniques. This is done by integrating the said events log or process models with rich semantics. Technically, in order to make the *semantic knowledge* available, semantic annotations are incorporated with the process models (for instance, the semantic fuzzy models described in this book) to pre-determine the model structures (taxonomies) as well as allows for the enhancement of the informative values of the knowledge-base in general. In other words, the method/schema serves as a way of representing or bridging the distances (semantic gap) between the labels in the models and concepts within the defined ontologies.

By definition, an ontological schema aims to transform a process map into a *bipartite graph* (also referred to as *Ontograph*) to denote both the process models and its elements in a uniformed structure. So, whenever an *inference* (semantic reasoning) is made, a generalized association (classification) of the individual process elements is created, and in turn, infers the class hierarchies (taxonomies) as well as performs a consistency check for those predicates.

Remarkably, for any ontological approach, the ability to make *consistency inference* is usually represented as constraints which help to bring the analysis or information values of the model to a more conceptual level by making use of the restriction properties (e.g. the object/datatype properties, SWRL rules and assertions etc.). Moreover, the sets of constraints which are driven or supported by the underlying ontologies have the capacity to recognize inconsistent data and outputs particularly during the pre-processing stage, the different sets of algorithm execution stage, filtering or interpretation stage, as well as the results generation or outputs.

Interestingly, a number of definitions/application of the ontology term has been proposed in the literature which every now and then concerns the varied domains of interest. According to the work of Hashim (2016) the term *ontology* is borrowed from the philosophy field which is concerned with being or existence study. The author (Hashim, 2016) notes that in the context of computer and information science, ontology symbolizes as an *artifact that is designed to model any domain knowledge of interest*. Even more, Gruber (1995) refers to the ontological term as a *formal explicit specification of a conceptualization*, and till date, has been the most widely cited definition of ontology in the computer field. Apparently, the definition (Gruber, 1995) means that ontology is able to explicitly determine (i.e. specifies) the *concepts* and *relationships* that are pertinent for modelling any process domain of interest. Moreover, such kind of specification can be represented in the form of *Classes, Relations, Constraints* and *Rules* which are all aimed to provide more meanings to the use of the schema (i.e expressions or terms) when carrying out any process modelling task as described in the method of this book (see: chapter 6).

Furthermore, ontology has proved to support the following three functions, namely: *Formal - Explicitness – Conceptualisation*. Ultimately, these functions are used to provide hierarchical structures and to support the abstract representation of informations and/or knowledge. Basically, ontologies help in the description of the various concepts as well as the relations or associations that hold amongst those concepts that can be found within the process domains. Hence, the ontologies range from taxonomies, classifications, database schemas to fully axiomatized theories which state facts. Besides, ontologies are nowadays an essential tool to a lot of intelligent systems and applications which are used for information (data) analysis – ranging from the information retrieval and extraction systems, to information management and integration of hybrid intelligent systems, scientific-knowledge portals, including e-commerce and web services etc.

Indeed, ontology has been broadly used in many sub-fields of the computer science ranging from the AI or Data Science, to Deep Learning and Semantic Web search particularly in the areas which concerns information retrieval and extraction (IR) (Manning, et al., 2008), IE (Cunningham, 2005), to OBIE systems (Calvanese, et al., 2016; M'uller, et al., 2004; Hosseini, et al., 2013), database management systems (Alkharouf, et al., 2005; Calvanese, et al., 2009), information management and intelligent systems integration (Seng & Kong, 2009; De Giacomo, et al., 2018), knowledge representation (Brewster & O'Hara, 2007; Kumar, et al., 2011), and specially in context of this book, semantic-based process mining (Ingvaldsen, 2011; deMedeiros, et al., 2008; de Medeiros & Van der Aalst, 2009; Okoye, et al., 2017).

Truly, the representation of knowledge by using the ontological schema/ vocabularies helps in organizing *datasets* of complex structures, for instance, the fuzzy models (Günther & Van der Aalst, 2007). Moreover, the work in this book proves that by using the ontology as a conceptual consistency constraint, a typical fuzzy model with unlabelled data can be tuned into one (semantic model) that have the best consistency especially based on the prior knowledge or information that can be found within the model. Besides, the metadata (conceptual) descriptions means that the syntactic nature of the input datasets or models are semantically synchronized with information about the process elements which are then encoded in form of entities (concepts or classes) within the ontologies (Sheth, et al., 2002; Okoye, et al., 2016; De Giacomo, et al., 2018). As the end result, the formal representations and the resulting metadata (process description and assertions) properties allows for automatic reasoning of the whole ontology with the aim of retrieving or producing meaningful/useful knowledge which are automatically being inferred (Dolog & Nejdl, 2007). In other words, the reasoning aptitude ensures that the process specifications within the ontologies are logically interpreted in a suitable manner by allowing for the automatic reasoning or computation of explicit knowledge about the domain processes in view (Yarandi, 2013; Gruber, 1993).

Therefore, the main functional benefits of ontologies can be summarised in two forms:

(i)   encoding knowledge about specific process domains, and

(ii)   advanced analysis and reasoning of the input datasets or models at more conceptual levels.

Accordingly, it is important to note that encoding ontologies with specific process domains often requires the use of formal languages (Brewster & O'Hara, 2007; Yarandi, 2013) such as the OWL, SWRL etc. as described in this book (see: Chapter 5). In other words, the ontological languages/ vocabularies are the foundation upon which the construction of the domain (specific) knowledge-bases are built, and most of the time, the method consists of semantic rules that are applied to support the automatic reasoning and/or capabilities of the resultant systems.

In the meantime, many languages or vocabularies have been theoretically proposed over the years primarily for the purpose of constructing ontologies. For example,

- the Knowledge Interchange Format (KIF) which are based on logic expressions (Obitko, 2007)
- LOOM8 which are based on description logics (DL) (Baader et al, 2003).
- FLogic (Kifer, et al., 1995)
- CycL (Witbrock et al, 2004)

And also, many other advanced languages or formats which are particularly based on the XML syntax, namely:

- Resource Description Framework (RDF) Schema (Horrocks, et al., 2003; W3C, 2004)
- Ontology Exchange Language (XOL) (Karp, et al., 1999),
- SHOE (Heflin & Hendler, 2000) etc.

Interestingly, over the past few decades, three additional languages have been developed on top of the families of the RDFs with the main intention of improving the RDFs features and to overcome its weaknesses. These includes:

(i)   Ontology Inference Layer (OIL) (Fensel, et al., 2000)
(ii) DAML+OIL (Horrocks, 2002), and
(iii) OWL (Patel-Schneider, et al., 2004; Horrocks, et al., 2007)

For example, one of the limitations with the RDFs which the aforementioned three additional languages trails to overcome is - the lack of proper explicit specification of resource in the ontologies, property descriptions limits, and the domain ranges.

Currently, there exist different kinds of ontology editors which eventually makes use of the different schema or vocabularies to describe and represent the knowledge. Some examples of the commonly used ontology editors include - Protégé, NeOn Toolkit, SWOOP, Neologism, TopBraid Composer, Vitro, Knoodl, Anzo for Excel, OWLGrEd, Fluent Editor, Semantic Turkey, VocBench etc.

Moreover, software developers or editors can create their own ontology, if they cannot find a relevant vocabulary that suits their kind of work. For example, if the existing languages are not good enough, or not suitable for the use case scenarios or domains of interest. To throw more light on the functionalities of the ontologies, the work specifically looks at (see the following subsection OWL Ontologies and Schema) the OWL ontology schema and the main different types used by the many existing ontology-based approaches for formal structuring of the processes. Besides, the method of this book also makes use of the OWL schema for the development and implementation of the proposed semantic-based process mining and analysis technique.

OWL Ontologies and Schema

For all intents and purposes, the work in this book focuses primarily on the Web Ontology Language (OWL) (W3C, 2012; Obitko, 2007; Horrocks, et al., 2007). The work has chosen the language over the other existing methods because it is the current state of the art *logical layer* upon which the semantic architectures or tools are currently built in the literature (Lisi, 2008; Lisi & Esposito, 2007). In spite of the different facilities being offered by the various existing ontology languages, the OWL (started by the World Wide Web Consortium – W3C) (W3C, 2012) has proved itself to be the most recent and widely accepted standard for ontology tools, design and development. According to Lisi & Esposito (2007) whilst debate around a unified language for web rules e.g. the Semantic Web Rule Language (SWRL) (Horrocks, et al., 2004) is still ongoing, the OWL Mark-up language is already undertaking its standardization process at the World Wide Web consortium (W3C).

To note, one of the main benefits of the OWL is that the resultant ontologies are capable of declaring the different classes and object/datatype properties in any given process domain. In turn, the OWL schema classifies those classes and properties in a taxonomy (i.e *superClass* → *subclass* and/or *subProperty* hierarchy) by assigning the *domains* and *ranges* in the same way as the RDF schema (W3C, 2004; Yarandi, 2013).

Certainly, the OWL has a better-off set(s) of operators than many of the other type of ontologies. For example, the *union, intersection,* and *inverse* properties of the OWL which makes it possible for *concepts* to be logically *defined* for any named process. Moreover, the resulting models allows for the use of a *reasoner* to check (compute) if or not all of the definitions or expressions defined in the ontologies are equally consistent and/or recognizes which concepts fit under which class. For instance, the ability to recognize what the meaning of the individual specific properties are (Kumar, et al., 2011). More so, it is important to note that the OWL is based on *Description Logic* (DL) (Baader, et al., 2003) which makes it possible for a complete realization of the meanings of the propositions or schema. Apparently, this is owing to the fact that building ontologies which are perceived to be fitting (especially for performing semantic-based process analysis and/or deploying the methods in an application) requires perhaps a system with high level of *semantic reasoning* capability. Moreover, the main application of the OWL based on the DL (Baader, et al., 2003) allows for use of some of the existing reasoners that supports DL queries or classification method. A typical example is the Pellet reasoner (Sirin & Parsia, 2004) as used in this book which undoubtedly has proven to be very effective in its ability to reason particularly at a more abstraction level. In principle, state of the art tools used for constructing ontologies (e.g., Protégé, SWOOP, and TopBraid Composer) makes use of those reasoners to make available the inference knowledge (i.e. the underlying inferred classes) to the developers or users predominantly in understanding the logically impacts (implication) of their developed ontologies and designs (Horrocks, 2008; De Giacomo, et al., 2018).

Different Types of OWL Ontologies

The OWL ontologies support three main expressive sublanguages, namely: (i) OWL Lite (ii) OWL DL, and (iii) OWL Full (Obitko, 2007). Predominantly, these sublanguages are specifically designed by either a particular community of software developers or the end-users for specific use in the development of their various ontology projects. In turn, each of them (OWL sublanguages) has its own different computational *complexities* and *expressiveness* (Horrocks, et al., 2007) as described in details in Table 1.

Table 1. Computational Complexities and Expressive functionalities and limitations of the different types of OWL ontologies

	OWL Lite	OWL DL	OWL Full
User Support	Supports those users primarily needing a classification hierarchy and simple constraint features.	Supports those users who want the maximum expressiveness without losing computational completeness and decidability of reasoning by the systems.	Meant for users who want maximum expressiveness and the syntactic freedom of RDF with no computational guarantees.
Property Restrictions	whilst OWL Lite supports cardinality constraints, it only permits cardinality values of 0 or 1	OWL DL includes all OWL language constructs with restrictions such as type separation, thus, a class cannot be an individual or also a property, or a property cannot be an individual or also a class. OWL DL is so named due to its correspondence with Description Logics (i.e. first order logic).	In OWL Full, a class can be treated simultaneously as a collection of individuals, and as an individual in its own right. Thus, it differs from the OWL DL in the sense that an owl:DatatypeProperty can be marked as an owl:InverseFunctionalProperty. Moreover, OWL Full allows an ontology to augment the meaning of the pre-defined (RDF or OWL) vocabulary.
Functionality (Expressiveness & Decidability)	It should be simpler to provide tool support for OWL Lite than its more expressive relatives (i.e. the OWL DL and OWL Full), and provide a quick migration path for vocabularies and other taxonomies.	OWL DL was designed to support existing DL reasoning. It has decidable inference, which means, that the formal reasoning facilitates the use of deduction to infer new knowledge from the information explicitly available in an ontology due to its ability to automatically compute classification hierarchies as well as perform inconsistency checks.	OWL-full uses all OWL language primitives. Besides, it is syntactically and semantically an extension of RDF and RDFS. With such feature, the expressivity of OWL-full is more than the other two sub-languages which leads to it being undecidable. It is unlikely that any reasoning software will be able to support every feature of OWL Full.

As gathered in the table (Table 1), each of the OWL sublanguage types is characteristically an extension of its simpler predecessor - both in what can be legally expressed and in what can be validly concluded. Perhaps, it is imperative for the developers or users (e.g the OWL ontology with Description Logics as used in the method of this book) to put into consideration what type of the OWL sub-language(s) best suits their requirements. For example, the OWL DL proves to provide the users with a more expressive restriction construct than the OWL Lite. Moreover, the optimal choice between the OWL Lite and OWL DL relies exclusively on the level of the requirement by the users in terms of expressiveness.

Furthermore, as shown in the table (Table 1), the choice between OWL DL and OWL Full depends mainly on the level of the requirement by the users in terms of meta-modeling functionalities of the RDF Schema. In essence, OWL DL is not fully compatible with the RDFs as opposed to the OWL Full. This means that not all RDF text is necessarily a legal OWL DL document, whereas on the contrary, every OWL DL document is in-fact an RDF text.

Moreover, *reasoning* support appears to be less likely when using OWL Full as opposed to the OWL DL. For example, when defining superClasses in ontologies as expanded in details of this book. Therefore, the OWL DL ontologies have lesser expressiveness influence (i.e. a reduced amount of computing complexities) than the OWL full. On the other hand, reasoners used by the OWL DL e.g. the Pellet (Sirin & Parsia, 2004) and FaCT++ reasoner (Tsarkov & Horrocks, 2006), when dealing with a decidable sublanguage appears to be subject to more worst-case complexities than reasoners for OWL Lite that frequently have a desirable computational property. Even though, the Pellet reasoner has been proven to be very effective in reasoning particularly at a more conceptual level.

Likewise, as described in this book (see: Chapter 5 and 7) - the work makes use of the OWL as it concerns protégé (Musen, et al., 2015) to provide additional new functions that allows for formal descriptions and structuring of the concepts (e.g. object property assertions) for any given process domain of interest. This is shown through the series of use case studies in this book (see: Chapter 6). Indeed, the method especially as defined later in this chapter, involves the use of the main functions/component of the OWL schema, i.e, Classes, Restriction Properties, Instances (individuals), and Reasoning capabilities (such as the Pellet) to support the semantic modelling of the various elements (entities) that makes up the processes in question or in view. Consequently, the semantic-based approach allows for the automatic classification and/or inference of the different concepts as defined within the resultant model or knowledge-bases.

SEMANTIC ANNOTATION

Clearly, the first step towards achieving the semantic-based process mining and analysis tasks as described in this book - is aimed at making use of process description languages/assertions to link elements in the logs and models with concepts that they represent in an ontology. Thus, the idea of *semantic annotation* of the input datasets. Essentially, the purpose of the semantic annotation technique is to seek the equivalence between the concepts of the models derived by applying the process mining algorithms on the readily available events log and the concepts of the defined ontologies. In essence, as discussed earlier and subsequently applied in chapters 4 and 5 respectively - the semantic annotation method is particularly focused on making use of the semantic schema (process descriptions languages) and notations to represent the extracted models through the metadata creation (semantic labelling) of the different attributes or relationships that the process elements share amongst themselves within the underlying knowledge-base.

SEMANTIC REASONING

One of the main benefits of the OWL ontologies is the capability to automatically compute the class hierarchies (i.e. taxonomy) by ascertaining the underlying relationships that exist amongst the different process elements (entities). This is done by making use of the *reasoner*, otherwise, referred to as the classifier. Practically, the *reasoners* (Bechhofer, 2003) are used to infer and check, for instance, if a specific class is a subClass or yet still superClass of another, or not at all within the ontology, and in so doing automatically computes the inferred class hierarchies.

More so, an additional function offered by the reasoner especially as used in the implementation of the method of this book is *consistency checking* of the process elements/parameters. Indeed, this means that based on the process description/attributes within the ontology, the reasoner is able to make use of the underlying information to *check* if it is possible for any instances (individuals) to become a member of a class. For instance, a class is classified as being inconsistent if it cannot perhaps have any instance. By definition, a reasoner is every now and then also referred to as *classifier*. According to Van der Aalst (2011), a classifier is a function that maps the attributes of an event onto a label used in the resulting process model. Therefore, in context of the ontology-based systems and analysis, a classifier (i.e. the reasoner) produces or maps the taxonomy of the defined domain process by matching the various classes as defined in the model with their associated process instances and/ or properties. In other words, the process of computing the inferred class hierarchies in an ontology is typically known as *classifying the ontology*. Henceforth, the reasoner is regarded as the *classifier* or the *inference engine* that is used in querying and manipulation of the whole ontology.

In short, the main function of the reasoner as applied in this book is summarized as follows:

- **Classifier:** Used in computing the class hierarchies i.e taxonomy
- **Consistency Checking**: For the inferred process elements, relations and parameters.

Currently, there exist different kinds of reasoners capable of classifying the different elements (entities) that can be found in an ontology. This includes the Pellet (Sirin & Parsia, 2004) which have proven to be very effective in reasoning particularly at a more conceptual level. Other kinds of reasoners have also been developed, namely: Racer (Haarslev & Möller, 2001), FaCT++ (Tsarkov & Horrocks, 2006), WSML2Reasoner (Bishop, et al., 1999; de Bruijn, et al., 2006) etc.

THEMATIC SUMMARY OF THE TOOLS AND METHODS FOR PROCESS MINING

The following table (Table 2) summarizes the various tools and methods discussed in this chapter of the book. Basically, the thematic analysis highlights and compares the main benefits, limitations, and impact of the different tools and algorithms, as well as, how are they related to the work done in this book.

CONCLUSION

In summary, the work in this chapter has considered - the main methods/components of the process mining and semantic modelling techniques, including the technologies that enable the practice and application of the technique. For the most part, the work shows that the application of the semantic-based process mining and analysis techniques (for example, as shown in earlier analysis and the thematic Table 2) must focus on feeding the semantic-based algorithms with:

- *Event Logs* or *Models* which elements have references to concepts in an ontology, and
- *Reasoners* that can be invoked to reason over the resultant models.

Table 2. Table of the various tools and algorithms used for process mining with a description of some of the main benefits, limitations, and adaptability for the research purpose

Method/ Algorithm	Proprietary Author(s)	Process Models	Main Benefits	Limitations	Are Benefits and/ or Limitations adaptable for this book purpose?
Alpha algorithm (α-algorithm)	(Van der Aalst, et al., 2004),	Petri Nets represented as Workflow nets (WF-net) (Van der Aalst & Van Hee, 2004)	Ability to discover huge amount of workflow nets that are perceived to be valid. Relatively intuitive and Simple technique that is able to deal with concurrency.	The discovered models can be structurally different, i.e, despite the similarity (trace equivalent), the resultant Workflow nets may still be unnecessarily complex (i.e. representational bias).	Yes, this book focuses on providing a method for accurate analysis of the process models which are intuitive and easy to understand.
Heuristic Miner (HM)	Weijters & Van der Aalst, 2003	Heuristic nets which makes use of representations similar to Casual nets (C-net) (Van der Aalst, 2016)	Ability to focus on frequent paths by ignoring paths which are not frequently executed within the process, thus, overcomes the problem of representational bias provided by C-nets and Petri nets. Thus, HM is less sensitive to noise and the incompleteness of logs. Moreover, the discovered models appears to be highly robust, structured, and rather sequential than most of the existing process discovery algorithms.	The results of the HM are in general relaxed sound, which for most process analysis techniques is not sufficient because the resulting models are not easy to interpret and results in low replay fitness scores, i.e, the HM trails to focus more on *precision* which comes at the cost of *generalization*.	Yes, this book makes use of the object properties assertions and relationships just like the HM which uses the likelihood of events or activities by calculating the frequencies of relations between the tasks (e.g., causal dependency, loops, etc.)
Inductive Miner (IM)	(Leemans, et al., 2013; Leemans, et al., 2014; Leemans, et al., 2014a; Leemans, et al., 2015)	Process trees, i.e., notations used to represent block structured models	Produces Sound models i.e whilst other process discovery models such as the WF-nets, Petri nets, BPMN models, EPCs, YAWL models, UML etc. might suffer from dead-locks, live-locks, and other anomalies, *process trees* discovered by the IM are sound by construction. Hence, IM produces process trees which are (i) Flexible and Scalable. (ii) Formal or Fitness guarantees. (iii) Ability to convert the resulting process trees to other notations. For example BPMN models or Petri nets etc. and (iv) Simplicity - due to its block-structure (i.e. activities are not duplicated)	One of the limitations of the IM is the fall-through which may create underfitting models in settings where there exist no process trees without silent or duplicate activities during the process of creating the observed behaviour. This is because the IM algorithms takes a constructive approach where more emphasis is put on replay fitness than on precision.	Yes, unlike the IM algorithms, the Semantic-Fuzzy mining approach in this book considers both the replay fitness and precision when discovering the process models.

continued on following page

Table 2. Continued

Method/ Algorithm	Proprietary Author(s)	Process Models	Main Benefits	Limitations	Are Benefits and/ or Limitations adaptable for this book purpose?
Genetic Process Mining	de Medeiros, 2006	Randomly distributed models or *search methods* that mimics the process of evolution.	The Genetic process mining approach tackles problems such as noise, incomplete data, non-free-choice constructs, hidden activities, concurrency, and duplicate activities which are often associated with the spaghetti-like or complex models. Moreover, unlike the α-algorithm and other techniques (e.g. the fuzzy and heuristics miner) which provides models in a deterministic and direct way, the genetic algorithms appears not to be fixed but instead depends on unsystematic (random) approach to discover new models.	On the whole, with genetic process mining, there exist the risks of discovering underfitting (*over-general*) or overfitting (*over-specific*) individual populations. This is due to the fact that the realization of the main ideas beneath the genetic mechanisms (i.e. crossovers and mutations) is not as simple as they may suggest. Usually, in many settings model repairs are often required when those crossovers and mutations are completed. Moreover, when large amount of models are being considered, it could take longer computational times to derive models which have a fitness that is satisfactory.	Yes, a combination of the genetic approaches with other techniques (e.g. the Heuristics miner) is quite meaningful and advantageous towards the provision of much more complete and precise models that demonstrates the benefit of such *mixture* or *hybrid algorithms*. Likewise, the proposed method of this book appears to be a fusion theory that pursues to integrate the fuzzy models with other tools in order to enhance the information values of such type of models by carefully integrating and tuning the semantics metrics that those models lack.
Fuzzy Miner (FM)	(Rozinat, 2010; G¨unther, 2009; (Rozinat & Gunther, 2012))	Fuzzy Models which are flexible and less-structured.	FM is one of the newer process discovery algorithms to directly address the problems of large numbers of activities and highly unstructured data and/ or behaviours. FM algorithms are applied with the goal to show understandable models for very unstructured processes by providing means to explore the complex processes in an interactive manner and/or on variable levels of abstraction. Thus FM algorithms are used to produce simplified models.	Most often the fuzzy models are relaxed in nature especially when compared with the semantics of other process modelling languages such as Petri nets or BPMN. Hence, there is no explicit distinction possible between simple choice (i.e. OR split), parallel choice (i.e. AND split), or multiple choice (i.e. XOR split) which indicates why the FM models are ambiguous and tends to lack the real descriptions (semantics) behind the event logs.	Yes, just like the work carried out in this book - FM approaches are useful especially in settings where the analyst is interested in process mining algorithms that are capable of providing simplified process models. Besides, Fuzzy models are conceived to be easily adaptable (i.e. extendible) by utilizing a mixture of clustering and abstraction techniques that are similar to the classification and abstraction (conceptual) method of analysis used in this book.

continued on following page

Table 2. Continued

Method/ Algorithm	Proprietary Author(s)	Process Models	Main Benefits	Limitations	Are Benefits and/ or Limitations adaptable for this book purpose?
Semantic LTL Checker	(deMedeiros, et al., 2008)	Semantically Annotated Models	The Semantic LTL Checker pursues to analyse event logs based on concepts by presenting the analysis of the processes in question at a more abstraction level by making use of the WSML2Reasoner to infer all the necessary associations.	The Semantic-LTL checker applies concepts in an ontology as input to parameters of a Linear Temporal Logic (LTL) formulae to formulate and answer questions about process elements (instances) which requires the systematic knowledge of how the LTL template is applied and can only be utilized for verification of properties that are defined in terms of the LTL Logics.	Yes, just like Semantic LTL checker, this book introduces the Semantic-Fuzzy miner which aims to analyse events logs based on concepts by integrating the three main building blocks - semantic annotation, ontologies, and reasoner. Besides, the Semantic-Fuzzy mining approach supports concepts as a value i.e. when a concept is selected, the algorithm will test whether an attribute is an instance of that concept (i.e. class) and concepts can only be specified for set attributes as explained in details in chapter 8 of this book.

In theory, the work demonstrates how the semantic concepts and annotations can be layered on top of extracted information asset (e.g. the events logs) to provide more enhancements to the resulting process model. This includes the automatic and further analysis of the models through the concept matching (i.e. *ontology classifications*) or *semantic reasoning* aptitudes. Besides, semantic reasoning is supported due to the formal definition of the ontological concepts and expression of the different relationships that exist between the process elements. To this end, the conceptual method of analysis and how the author of this book has designed and implemented the framework is explained in detail in the following chapter of this book.

REFERENCES

W3C. (2004). *RDF Vocabulary Description Language 1.0: RDF Schema.* MIT: W3C Recommendation.

W3C, S. W. (2012). *Web Ontology Language (OWL).* Oxford, UK: OWL Working Group.

Alkharouf, N. W., Jamison, D. C., & Matthews, B. F. (2005). Online Analytical Processing (OLAP): A Fast and Effective Data Mining Tool for Gene Expression Databases. *Journal of Biomedicine & Biotechnology, 2005*(2), 181–188. doi:10.1155/JBB.2005.181 PMID:16046824

Baader, F. (2003). *Description Logic Handbook: theory, implementation, and applications* (1st ed.). New York, NY: Cambridge University Press.

Baader, F. (2003). *Description Logic Handbook: theory, implementation, and applications* (1st ed.). New York, NY: Cambridge University Press.

Baati, K., Hamdani, T. M., Alimi, A. M., & Abraham, A. (2017). Decision quality enhancement in minimum-based possibilistic classification for numerical data. *Proceedings of the 8th International Conference on Soft Computing and Pattern Recognition (SoCPaR 2016),* 634-643.

Bechhofer, S. (2003). *OWL Reasoning Examples.* Manchester, UK: University of Manchester.

Bishop, B. (1999). WSML Reasoner, Boston, MA: IRIS Reasoner - SOA4All.

Brewster, C., & O'Hara, K. (2007). Knowledge representation with ontologies: Present challenges future possibilities. *International Journal of Human-Computer Studies, 65*(7), 563–568. doi:10.1016/j.ijhcs.2007.04.003

Buijs, J. C. A. M. (2014). *Flexible evolutionary algorithms for mining structured process models* (PhD thesis). Eindhoven, The Netherlands: Technische Universiteit Eindhoven.

Cairns, A. H. (2015). Process Mining in the Education Domain. *International Journal on Advances in Intelligent Systems, 8*(1-2).

Calvanese, D. (2009). Ontologies and databases: The DL-Lite approach. In *Proc. of RW.* Springer-Verlag.

Calvanese, D., Montali, M., Syamsiyah, A., & van der Aalst, W. M. P. (2016). Ontology-Driven Extraction of Event Logs from Relational Databases. In Lecture Notes in Business Information Processing. Cham: Business Process Management Workshops. BPM 2015. Springer. doi:10.1007/978-3-319-42887-1_12

Carmona, J., de Leoni, M., Depair, B., & Jouck, T. (2016). *Process Discovery Contest @ BPM 2016*. Rio de Janeiro: IEEE CIS Task Force on Process Mining.

Cunningham, H. (2005). *Information Extraction, Automatic*. Sheffield, UK: University of Sheffield.

de Beer, H. T. (2005). *The LTL Checker Plugins: a (reference) manual*. Eindhoven, The Netherlands: processmining.org.

De Giacomo, G. (2018). Using Ontologies for Semantic Data Integration. In S. Flesca, S. Greco, E. Masciari, & D. Saccà (Eds.), *A Comprehensive Guide Through the Italian Database Research Over the Last 25 Years. Studies in Big Data* (pp. 187–202). Cham: Springer. doi:10.1007/978-3-319-61893-7_11

De Leoni, M., & Van der Aalst, W. M. P. (2013). Data-Aware Process Mining: Discovering Decisions in Processes Using Alignments. In *ACM Symposium on Applied Computing (SAC 2013)*. Coimbra, Portugal: ACM Press. 10.1145/2480362.2480633

de Medeiros, A. K. A. (2006). *Genetic Process Mining* (PhD thesis). Eindhoven, The Netherlands: Technische Universiteit Eindhoven.

de Medeiros, A. K. A., & Van der Aalst, W. M. P. (2009). Process Mining towards Semantics. In T. Dillon, E. Chang, R. Meersman, & K. Sycara (Eds.), Lecture Notes in Computer Science: Vol. 4891. *Advances in Web Semantics I* (pp. 35–80). Berlin: Springer. doi:10.1007/978-3-540-89784-2_3

de Medeiros, A. K. A., Weijters, A. J., & van der Aalst, W. M. P. (2007). Genetic Process Mining: An Experimental Evaluation. *Data Mining and Knowledge Discovery*, *14*(2), 245–304. doi:10.100710618-006-0061-7

deMedeiros, A., van der Aalst, W. M. P. & Pedrinaci, C. (2008). *Semantic Process Mining Tools: Core Building Blocks*. Galway, Ireland: ECIS.

Dolog, P., & Nejdl, W. (2007). Semantic web technologies for the adaptive web. In The adaptive web Volume 4321 of the series Lecture Notes in Computer Science. Berlin: Springer-Verlag. doi:10.1007/978-3-540-72079-9_23

Dou, D., Wang, H., & Liu, H. (2015). Semantic Data Mining: A Survey of Ontology-based Approaches. *9th IEEE Int. Conference on Semantic Computing*, 244 – 251. 10.1109/ICOSC.2015.7050814

Fahland, D., & van der Aalst, W. M. P. (2012). Repairing Process Models to Reflect Reality. In Business Process Management. BPM 2012. Lecture Notes in Computer Science, vol 7481. Berlin: Springer. doi:10.1007/978-3-642-32885-5_19

Fensel, D. (2000). OIL in a Nutshell. *EKAW '00 Proceedings of the 12th European Workshop on Knowledge Acquisition, Modeling and Management*, 1-16. 10.1007/3-540-39967-4_1

Goedertier, S., Martens, D., Vanthienen, J., & Baesens, B. (2009). Robust Process Discovery with Artificial Negative Events. *Journal of Machine Learning Research*, *10*(1), 1305–1340.

Gruber, T. R. (1993). A translation approach to portable ontology specifications. *Knowledge Acquisition*, *5*(2), 199–220. doi:10.1006/knac.1993.1008

Gruber, T. R. (1995). Toward principles for the design of ontologies used for knowledge sharing. *International Journal of Human-Computer Studies*, *43*(5), 907–928. doi:10.1006/ijhc.1995.1081

Günther, C. (2009). *Process Mining in Flexible Environments* (PhD thesis). Eindhoven, The Netherlands: Department of Technology Management, Technical University Eindhoven.

Gunther, C. W. (2009). *OpenXES - Developer Guide*. IEEE 1849-2016 XES.

Günther, C. W., & Van der Aalst, W. M. P. (2006). A generic import framework for process event logs. In J. Eder & S. Dustdar (Eds.), *Business Process Management Workshops* (pp. 81–92). Berlin: Springer. doi:10.1007/11837862_10

Günther, C. W., & Van der Aalst, W. M. P. (2007). Fuzzy Mining – Adaptive Process Simplification Based on Multi-perspective Metrics. In Business Process Management. BPM 2007. Lecture Notes in Computer Science, vol 4714. Berlin: Springer.

Haarslev, V., & Möller, R. (2001). RACER System Description. In R. Goré, A. Leitsch, & T. Nipkow (Eds.), Lecture Notes in Computer Science: Vol. 2083. *Automated Reasoning. IJCAR 2001* (pp. 701–705). Berlin: Springer.

Han, J., Kamber, M., & Pei, J. (2011). *Data Mining: Concepts and Techniques* (3rd ed.). Burlington, MA: The Morgan Kaufmann Series in Data Management Systems, Morgan Kaufmann Publishers.

Hashim, H. (2016). Ontological structure representation in reusing ODL learning resources. *Asian Association of Open Universities Journal*, *11*(1), 2–12. doi:10.1108/AAOUJ-06-2016-0008

Heflin, J., & Hendler, J. (2000). Searching the web with SHOE. *AAAI-2000 Workshop on AI for Web Search*, 35-40. 10.21236/ADA440405

Hiroshi, S. (1997). *What is Occam's Razor,* University of California Riverside.

Horrocks, I. (2002). Daml+oil: A description logic for the semantic web. *A Quarterly Bulletin of the Computer Society of the IEEE Technical Committee on Data Engineering*, *25*(1), 4–9.

Horrocks, I. (2004). *SWRL: A Semantic Web Rule Language Combining OWL and RuleML.* Network Inference, Canada and Stanford University: W3C Member Submission - 2004 National Research Council of Canada, Network Inference, and Stanford University.

Horrocks, I. (2008). Ontologies and the semantic web. *Communications of the ACM*, *51*(12), 58–67. doi:10.1145/1409360.1409377

Horrocks, I., Patel-Schneider, P. F., McGuinness, D. L., & Welty, C. A. (2007). Owl: a description logic based ontology language for the semantic web. In *The Description Logic Handbook: Theory, Implementation, and Applications* (2nd ed., pp. 458–486). New York, NY: Cambridge University Press. doi:10.1017/CBO9780511711787.016

Horrocks, I., Patel-Schneider, P. F., & van Harmelen, F. (2003). From shiq and rdf to owl: The making of a web ontology language. *Journal of Web Semantics*, *1*(1), 7–26. doi:10.1016/j.websem.2003.07.001

Hosseini, S. A., Tawil, A.-R. H., Jahankhani, H., & Yarandi, M. (2013). Towards an ontological learners modelling approach for personalised e-learning. *International Journal of Emerging Technologies in Learning*, *8*(2), 4–10. doi:10.3991/ijet.v8i2.2476

IEEE 1849-2016, X. (2016). *OpenXES - reference implementation of the First XES standard.* Available at: http://www.xes-standard.org/openxes/start

IEEE CIS Task Force on Process Mining. (2016). *1849-2016 - IEEE Standard for eXtensible Event Stream definition.* Available at: http://www.xes-standard. org/

IEEE Standards. (2016). *IEEE Standard for eXtensible Event Stream (XES) for Achieving Interoperability in Event Logs and Event Streams.* Available at: https://ieeexplore.ieee.org/document/7740858/

Ingvaldsen, J. E. (2011). *Semantic process mining of enterprise transaction data* (PhD thesis). Norwegian University of Science and Technology.

Ingvaldsen, J. E., Gulla, J. A., Hegle, O. A., & Prange, A. (2005). Revealing the real business flows from enterprise systems transactions. *7th International Conference on Enterprise Information Systems.*

Karel, R. (2011). *Stop Trying To Put A Monetary Value On Data – It's The Wrong Path.* Cambridge, MA: Forrester Research, Inc.

Karp, P. D., Chaudhri, V. K. & Thomere, J. (1999). *Xol: An xml-based ontology exchange language.* Technical report, SRI International. Pangea Systems Inc.

Kifer, M., Lausen, G., & Wu, J. (1995). Logical foundations of object-oriented and frame-based languages. *Journal of the Association for Computing Machinery, 42*(4), 741–843. doi:10.1145/210332.210335

Kumar, A. P., Abhishek, K., & Vipin Kumar, N. (2011). Architecting and Designing of Semantic Web Based Application using the JENA and PROTÉGÉ – A Comprehensive Study. *International Journal of Computer Science and Information Technologies, 2*(3), 1279–1282.

Leemans, S. J. J., Fahland, D., & Van der Aalst, W. M. P. (2013). Discovering Block-Structured Process Models from Event Logs: A Constructive Approach. In Applications and Theory of Petri Nets 2013, Volume 7927 of LNCS. Berlin: Springer. doi:10.1007/978-3-642-38697-8_17

Leemans, S. J. J., Fahland, D., & Van der Aalst, W. M. P. (2014). Discovering Block-Structured Process Models from Event Logs Containing Infrequent Behaviour. *Business Process Management Workshops, International Workshop on Business Process Intelligence (BPI)*, 66-78. 10.1007/978-3-319-06257-0_6

Leemans, S. J. J., Fahland, D., & Van der Aalst, W. M. P. (2014a). Discovering Block-Structured Process Models from Incomplete Event Logs. Applications and Theory of Petri Nets 2014, 91-110. doi:10.1007/978-3-319-07734-5_6

Leemans, S. J. J., Fahland, D., & Van der Aalst, W. M. P. (2015). Scalable Process Discovery with Guarantees. Business-Process and Information Systems Modeling (BPMDS 2015), 85-101. doi:10.1007/978-3-319-19237-6_6

Leemans, S. J. J., Fahland, D., & Van der Aalst, W. M. P. (2015). Exploring Processes and Deviations. In F. Fournier & J. Mendling (Eds.), *Business Process Management Workshops. BPM 2014. Lecture Notes in Business Information Processing* (Vol. 202, pp. 304–316). Cham: Springer.

Lisi, F. (2008). Building Rules on Top of Ontologies for the Semantic Web with Inductive Logic Programming. *Theory and Practice of Logic Programming*, 8(3), 271–300. doi:10.1017/S1471068407003195

Lisi, F., & Esposito, F. (2007). *Building Rules on top of Ontologies? Inductive Logic Programming can help!* Bari, Italy: SWAP.

Manning, C. D., Raghavan, P., & Schütze, H. (2008). *Introduction to Information Retrieval*. Cambridge: Cambridge University Press. doi:10.1017/CBO9780511809071

M¨uller, H.-M., Kenny, E. E., & Sternberg, P. W. (2004). Textpresso: An ontology-based information retrieval and extraction system for biological literature. *PLoS Biology*, 2(11), e309. doi:10.1371/journal.pbio.0020309 PMID:15383839

Musen, M. A. (2015). The Protégé project: A look back and a look forward. AI Matters. *AI Matters*, 1(4), 4–12. doi:10.1145/2757001.2757003 PMID:27239556

Obitko, M. (2007). Knowledge Interchange Format. Prague, Czech Republic: Ontologies and Semantic Web.

Obitko, M. (2007). Web Ontology Language OWL. Prague, Czech Republic: Ontologies and Semantic Web.

Okoye, K. (2016). Using semantic-based approach to manage perspectives of process mining: Application on improving learning process domain data. *Proceedings of 2016 IEEE International Conference on Big Data (Big Data)*, 3529-3538.

Okoye, K. (2018). Semantic-based Model Analysis towards Enhancing Information Values of Process Mining: Case Study of Learning Process Domain. *Proceedings of SoCPaR 2016 Conference*, 622-633. 10.1007/978-3-319-60618-7_61

Okoye, K., Islam, S., & Naeem, U. & Sharif, S. (2020). Semantic-based Process Mining Technique for Annotation and Modelling of Domain Processes. *International Journal of Innovative Computing, Information, & Control.*

Okoye, K., Islam, S., Naeem, U., Sharif, M. S., Azam, M. A., & Karami, A. (2019). The Application of a Semantic-Based Process Mining Framework on a Learning Process Domain. In K. Arai, S. Kapoor, & R. Bhatia (Eds.), *Intelligent Systems and Applications. Advances in Intelligent Systems and Computing* (Vol. 868, pp. 1381–1403). Springer Cham. doi:10.1007/978-3-030-01054-6_96

Okoye, K., Naeem, U., & Islam, S. (2017). Semantic Fuzzy Mining: Enhancement of process models and event logs analysis from Syntactic to Conceptual Level. *International Journal of Hybrid Intelligent Systems*, *14*(1-2), 67–98. doi:10.3233/HIS-170243

Patel-Schneider, P. F., Hayes, P. & Horrocks, I. (2004). *Owl web ontology language semantics and abstract syntax.* Bell Labs Research, Lucent Technologies.

Polyvyanyy A. (2016). *Process Querying.* Available at: http://processquerying.com/

Rozinat, A. (2010). *Process Mining: Conformance and Extension* (PhD thesis). Eindhoven, The Netherlands: Technische Universiteit Eindhoven.

Rozinat, A. (2016). Data Quality Problems In Process Mining And What To Do About Them. Eidhoven, Netherlands: Fluxicon.com.

Rozinat, A. (2016). *Data Quality Problems for Process Mining.* Eindhoven, The Netherlands: Fluxicon.

Rozinat, A., & Gunther, C. (2012). Disco User Guide - Process Mining for Professionals. Eindhoven, The Netherlands: Fluxicon.com.

Seng, J. L., & Kong, I. (2009). A schema and ontology-aided intelligent information integration. *Expert Systems with Applications*, *36*(7), 10538–10550. doi:10.1016/j.eswa.2009.02.067

Sheth, A., Bertram, C., Avant, D., Hammond, B., Kochut, K., & Warke, Y. (2002). Managing semantic content for the web. *IEEE Internet Computing*, 6(4), 80–87. doi:10.1109/MIC.2002.1020330

Sirin, E., & Parsia, B. (2004). Pellet: An owl dl reasoner. *Proceedings of the 2004 International Workshop on Description Logics (DL2004)*, 104.

Sure, Y., & Domingue, J. (Eds.). (2006). Lecture Notes in Computer Science: Vol. 4011. *The Semantic Web: Research and Applications. ESWC*. Berlin: Springer.

Thorburn, W. M. (1918). The Myth of Occam's razor. *Mind*, 27(1), 345–353. doi:10.1093/mind/XXVII.3.345

Tsarkov, D., & Horrocks, I. (2006). FaCT++ Description Logic Reasoner: System Description. Lecture Notes in Computer Science, 4130, 292-297.

Turner, C. J., Tiwari, A. & Mehnen, J. (2008). A genetic programming approach to business process mining. *Proceedings of the 10th annual conference on Genetic and evolutionary computation (GECCO '08)*, 1307–1314. 10.1145/1389095.1389345

Van der Aalst, W. M. P. (2004). Business Process Management Demystified: A Tutorial on Models, Systems and Standards for workflow Management. Lectures on Concurrency and Petri Nets, 1-65.

Van der Aalst, W. M. P. (2011). *Process Mining: Discovery, Conformance and Enhancement of Business Processes* (1st ed.). Berlin: Springer. doi:10.1007/978-3-642-19345-3

Van der Aalst, W. M. P. (2016). *Process Mining: Data Science in Action* (2nd ed.). Berlin: Springer-Verlag Berlin Heildelberg. doi:10.1007/978-3-662-49851-4

Van der Aalst, W. M. P. (2019). *Process Mining Conference Series: IEEE Task Force on Process Mining*. Available at: https://icpmconference.org/2019/general-information/ieee-task-force/

Van der Aalst, W. M. P., & Van Hee, K. M. (2004). *Worflow Management: Models, Methods, and Systems* (1st ed.). Cambridge, MA: MIT Press.

Van der Aalst, W. M. P., Weijters, A. J. M. M. & Maruster, L. (2004). Workflow Mining: Discovering Process Models from Event Logs. *International Journal of IEEE Transactions on Knowledge and Data Engineering*, 16(9), 1128-1142.

Van Dongen, B., Claes, J., Burattin, A., & De Weerdt, J. (2016). *12th International Workshop on Business Process Intelligence 2016.* Available at: http://www.win.tue.nl/bpi/doku.php?id=2016:start#organizers

Verbeek, H. (2014). *Process Mining research tools and application.* Available at: http://www.processmining.org/promimport/start

Verbeek, H., Buijs, J., van Dongen, B., & van der Aalst, W. M. P. (2011). XES, XESame, and ProM 6. *Information Systems Evolution*, 60-75.

Weijters, A. J. M. M., & Ribeiro, J. T. S. (2010). *Flexible Heuristics Miner (FHM).* Eindhoven, the Netherlands: BETA Working Paper Series, WP 334, Eindhoven University of Technology.

Weijters, A. J. M. M., & Van der Aalst, W. M. P. (2003). Rediscovering Workflow Models from Event-Based Data using Little Thimb. *Integrated Computer-Aided Engineering, 10*(2), 151–162. doi:10.3233/ICA-2003-10205

Witbrock, M., Panton, K., Reed, S. L., Schneider, D., Aldag, B., & Reimers, M. (2004). Automated OWL annotation assisted by a large knowledge base. *Proceedings of 4th International Workshop on Knowledge Markup and Semantic Annotation, 3rd International Semantic Web Conference.*

Yarandi, M. (2013). *Semantic Rule-based Approach for Supporting Personalised Adaptive E-Learning* (PhD thesis). London, UK: University of East London.

Chapter 3
Main Component and Architecture of the Semantic–Based Process Mining and Analysis Framework (SPMaAF)

ABSTRACT

This chapter describes the proposed semantic-based process mining and analysis framework (SPMaAF) and the main components applied for integration and ample implementation of the method. Technically, the conceptual method of analysis and how the book has designed the framework is explained in detail. The chapter also shows that the quality augmentation of the derived process models is as a result of employing process mining techniques that encodes the envisaged system with three rudimentary building blocks, namely semantic labelling (annotation), semantic representation (ontology), and semantic reasoning (reasoner).

SEMANTIC-BASED PROCESS MINING AND ANALYSIS FRAMEWORK (SPMAAF)

The design structure of the SPMaAF is primarily constructed on the following building blocks (or phases) as shown in Figure 1.

DOI: 10.4018/978-1-7998-2668-2.ch003

Figure 1. The Semantic-based Process Mining and Analysis Framework (SPMaAF)

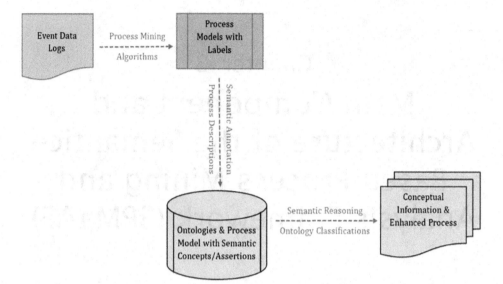

In Figure 1 the work describes the proposed framework for the semantic-based process mining and analysis method of this book (SPMaAF). Typically, the method consists of the following phases or individual components:

- **Extraction of Process Models from Event Data Logs**: Whereby the derived models are represented as a set of annotated terms that links or connects (relates) to defined terms in an ontology, and in so doing, encodes the process logs and deployed models in the formal structure of ontology (semantic modelling) for further analysis.
- **The Inferred Ontology Classifications**: Helps in association of meaning to the labels in the event logs and models by pointing to concepts (references) defined within the ontologies.
- **The Reasoner (inference engine):** Designed to perform automatic classification of the various elements or tasks, and carries out consistency checking to validate the resulting model as well as clean out inconsistent results. In turn, it presents the inferred (underlying) associations.
- **The Conceptual Referencing**: Which supports semantic reasoning over the ontologies in order to derive new information (or knowledge) about the process elements and the relationships they share amongst themselves within the knowledge base.

In short definition, the main mechanism (components) applied towards achieving an effective application of the aforementioned process was focused on connecting the mining algorithms with two key core elements:

1. Event logs or process models where the labels have references to concepts in an ontology, and
2. Reasoners which are invoked to reason over the resulting ontologies or semantic models.

To summarize the SPMaAF design framework - the work notes in Okoye et al (2019) that the development and application of such semantically-based framework has gained significant interest within the field of process mining.

On the one hand, the proposed framework (SPMaAF) focuses on making use of the semantics captured in the event logs or models (i.e. metadata) to create new techniques for process mining, or better still, support the enhancement (or in some cases, re-modification) of existing approaches to provide a more improved real-time process analysis that is closer to human understanding (e.g, a machine-understandable system). For example, methods that can be applied to assist humans in gaining a novel and more accurate results for process mining tasks. Perhaps, by being able to analyse the datasets or models at a higher level of conceptualization as opposed to the traditional process mining techniques that tend to analyse the data at the syntactic level.

On the other hand, owing to the semantic (conceptual) level of analysis, the outcome of the method (SPMaAF) can be easily understood by the process owners, process analysts, or IT experts. Besides, event logs from the different process domains usually carry domain-specific information (semantics), but quite often, the classical process mining techniques/algorithms lack the ability to interpret or make use of the underlying semantics across the different domains.

To this end, the work in this book illustrates through the instantiation of the SPMaAF framework, the formalization of the sets of semantically motivated algorithms, and the resultant semantic fuzzy mining approach - that by annotating and encoding the process models with rich semantics and application of semantic reasoning, that it is possible to specify (infer) useful domain knowledge (semantics) capable of bridging the semantic gap conveyed by the traditional process mining techniques (Dou, et al., 2015; deMedeiros, et al., 2008; Okoye et al, 2020). Interestingly, with such kind and level of analysis (i.e semantic-based process mining and analysis) useful information (semantics) about how activities depend on each other in a process domain is made possible, and essential for extracting models capable of creating newly valuable (conceptual) information.

In fact, the main difference between the SPMaAF framework described in Figure 1 and the traditional process mining framework described earlier in Chapter 1 (Figure 3) - is that whilst the traditional process mining framework (Figure 3) tends to analyse the extracted events logs (to derive some explicit and/or implicit information about the processes they support in reality) without considering the *semantic* aspects of the information that are contained in the events log, the SPMaAF framework (Figure 1) mainly focus on semantical integration and extension of the method in Figure 3 in Chapter 1 by taking into account the semantic gap that is missing with the traditional process mining technique. Moreover, the method (SPMaAF) tackles the semantic aspects by considering the extracted events log and the derived process models. In other words, whilst the traditional process mining technique trails to analyse the events log at *syntactic levels* (i.e. considering the labels or tags in the event logs), the SPMaAF focuses on extending and analyse the available input data logs and models at a more *conceptual level* (i.e based on the concepts that are well-defined within the derived models).

Therefore, the work describes in the following section of this chapter - the main architecture of the proposed SPMaAF framework. Basically, the work illustrates how it has applied the SPMaAF framework and the resultant method to support implementation of the sets of semantically motivated algorithms, as well as, the resulting semantic-based application otherwise referred to as the semantic-fuzzy miner (see: chapter 7).

ARCHITECTURE OF THE SPMaAF FRAMEWORK

The work presents in this section - the general architecture of the proposed SPMaAF framework and how it integrates the main building blocks (annotated logs/models, ontology, and semantic reasoning) for the purpose of the work done in this book. For all intents and purposes, the work summarizes in Figures 2 and 3 - the various components of the semantic-based process mining approach and the different stages of its implementation as follows:

Figure 2. Main Architecture of the SPMaAF framework with different stages of its implementation

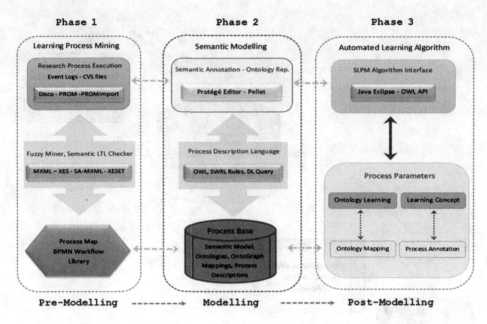

Figure 3. Practical aspects of implementing the proposed system

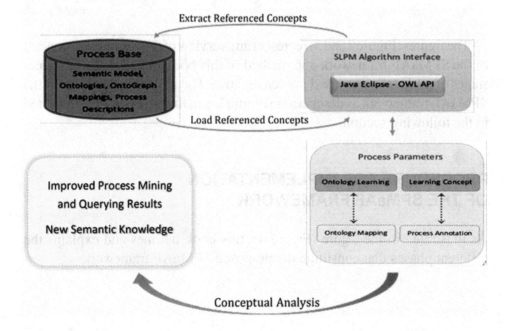

Figure 4. Incremental procedure or phases for implementation of the semantic-based process mining framework

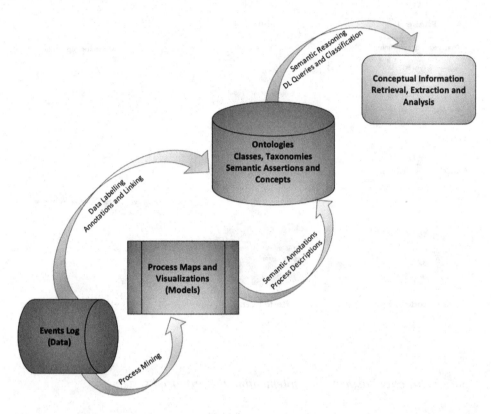

The figures (Figure 2 and 3) represent an overview of the various components of the SPMaAF framework and method of this book including the different stages of its development and implementation. Clearly, the application of the SPMaAF framework as described in Figure 2 is in three phases as represented in the following section.

PROCEDURE FOR IMPLEMENTATION OF THE SPMaAF FRAMEWORK

As illustrated in the figure (Figure 4), this book outlines and explains the different phases that constitute the proposed SPMaAF framework.

In Phase 1

The work applies the process mining techniques in order to make available the process mappings (models discovered from the events log) for the given process (e.g. case study of the learning process) and also checks its conformance with the real-time (executed) process as performed in reality. This is based on the Fuzzy Miner (Rozinat & Gunther, 2012) as illustrated in detail in chapters 5 and 7 of this book. The main purpose of the approach is that the resulting process map allows us to quickly, and interactively explore the processes into multiple directions and to determine the individual activities workflow, and then provide a mechanism for semantic annotation of the different process elements within the knowledge base. The proposed *Algorithm 1* in the following chapter (Chapter 4) describes the procedures on how the work has implemented this phase of the process.

In Phase 2

The work performs the semantic modelling of the resulting process mappings in terms of the annotated terms. Essentially, the resultant (semantic) model contains domain knowledge about the various activities that make up the process including the sequence of activities (workflows) as performed. This is achieved through the different *concepts* (assertions) defined in an ontology (which also sits at the core of the method in this book) by using process description languages such as the OWL (Horrocks, et al., 2007) and SWRL (Horrocks, et al., 2004). More so, the method also uses the Reasoner i.e. Pellet (Sirin & Parsia, 2004) to infer the different entities (process instances) and ontological representations or class hierarchies (taxonomy). The proposed *Algorithms 2* (see: chapter 4) explains the steps the work has taken to implement this stage of the process.

In Phase 3

The work carries out the manipulation (information retrieval and extraction) and automated querying of the different concepts defined within the knowledge-base. In other words, the work implements the semantic-based application (otherwise referred to as the semantic fuzzy miner) used to extract, load, and automatically query the semantic model. Practically, the work uses the java runtime environment to create the methods and interface for loading

Table 1. Different Phase of implementing the SPMaAF framework and thematic target of the proposed Algorithms

	SPMaAF Framework	Algorithm 1	Algorithm 2	Algorithm 3	Target Sections
Phase 1	X	X			Chapter 4 Algorithm 1
Phase 2	X		X	X	Chapter 4 Algorithm 2 and 3
Phase 3	X			X	Chapter 4 Algorithm 3

the parameters (i.e. the ontological concepts) and makes use of the OWL Application Programming Interface (OWL API) to extract and load the inferred concepts by linking to the well-defined ontologies. Examples of the inferred underlying concepts and application of the OWL API and the resulting ontologies are as shown in chapter 7 of this book.

CONCLUSION

We introduce in this chapter - the proposed SPMaAF framework and description of the different phases of its implementation with an ephemeral look at the main tools that enables the application of the method in real-time. The work also highlights the different procedures or phases (described in detail in the next chapter - Chapter 4) which it applies for ample implementation of the method. It is also important to note that the purpose of the entire framework (SPMaAF) is focused on improving the analysis of the events log and discovered models. Thus far, Figures 2 and 3 shows the general architecture of the different phases of implementing the semantic-based process mining method. Fundamentally, the purpose for integrating the different phases and implementation of the SPMaAF framework and the algorithms is to match the questions one would like to answer about the relationships (or attributes) the process instances share amongst themselves within the knowledge-base by linking to the inferred concepts within the well-defined ontologies. Essentially, the work recognizes that much of the effort in developing the semantic-based process mining and analysis framework relies mainly on constructing an effective system that integrates the three main building blocks, namely; annotated logs/models, ontologies, and semantic reasoner.

The following table (Table 1) is a thematic summary of the targeted goal for each of the different phases for implementing the SPMaAF framework and the subsequently proposed algorithms (see: chapter 4) in this book.

Indeed, from the descriptions in Table 1 which summarises the thematic focus of this book; the work represents the motivation behind the SPMaAF framework and its main application in real-time. Henceforth, whilst the focus of the process mining technique and semantic annotation process in Phase 1 is on describing the meaning of the labels (attributes) in the events logs and the discovered process models, the ontological description process in Phase 2 is devoted to binding together the different concepts (e.g classes and object/data properties) in ways that maximize their analysis at a more conceptual level. Consequently, the semantic reasoning aptitudes described in Phase 3 focus on allowing the abstract analysis and manipulation of the underlying ontologies (or semantic model). In other words, this chapter has looked at the main tools/components that are used to support the proposed semantic-based process mining and analysis approach, and its application in real-time. Clearly, we note that the best way to create such a machine-understandable system is to make use of tools that supports the different components particularly the ontologies which every now and then are required to maintain consistency of the process elements or individual entities that makes up the envisaged systems. Without a doubt, the use of a reasoner to compute the relationships between the various entities (process instances) is practically possible, especially when building such huge ontologies with numerous entities in them. Besides, one can argue that without an automated classification process (semantic reasoning) it may become very challenging to manage those massive ontologies. For example, in a logical and precise manner. Therefore, not only does this type of ontology-based system (SPMaAF) supports the implementation of semantic rules such as the OWL, SWRL and DL queries, etc, and/or re-use of an ontology by another ontology. But, also it minimalizes the level of human-errors which are every now and then present particularly when managing the manifold existence of entities (concepts) defined within the ontologies. Moreover, the said domain processes can now (or now) be complemented by some implicit knowledge that may also be discovered inadvertently as a result of applying the method.

Theoretically, on the one hand, the semantic-based process mining approach described in this book can be applied to analyse and enhance the discovered process models, and even more, leveraged to recommend future patterns or behaviours. On the other hand, the work assumes to have introduced the SPMaAF framework to support the development of semantic-based process mining techniques or algorithms that exhibit a high level of semantic reasoning (or capabilities) as opposed to the syntactic nature of analysis displayed by the traditional process mining techniques. In principle, the results of the method (see: chapter 8) means that the SPMaAF approach can be perceived as an ontology-based system that is able to perform information retrieval and query answering in a more efficient and effective way compared to other standard logical procedures used for process mining. Eventually, the instantiation of each phase of the SPMaAF framework is represented in terms of the proposed Algorithms 1, 2, and 3 as described in the following chapter 4 of this book.

REFERENCES

de Medeiros, A., van der Aalst, W. M. P. & Pedrinaci, C. (2008). *Semantic Process Mining Tools: Core Building Blocks*. Galway, Ireland: ECIS.

Dou, D., Wang, H., & Liu, H. (2015). Semantic Data Mining: A Survey of Ontology-based Approaches. *9th IEEE Int. Conference on Semantic Computing*, 244 – 251. 10.1109/ICOSC.2015.7050814

Horrocks, I. (2004). *SWRL: A Semantic Web Rule Language Combining OWL and RuleML*. Network Inference, Canada and Stanford University: W3C Member Submission - 2004 National Research Council of Canada, Network Inference, and Stanford University.

Horrocks, I., Patel-Schneider, P. F., McGuinness, D. L., & Welty, C. A. (2007). Owl: a description logic based ontology language for the semantic web. In *The Description Logic Handbook: Theory, Implementation, and Applications* (2nd ed., pp. 458–486). New York, NY: Cambridge University Press. doi:10.1017/CBO9780511711787.016

Okoye, K., Islam, S., & Naeem, U. & Sharif, S. (2020). Semantic-based Process Mining Technique for Annotation and Modelling of Domain Processes. *International Journal of Innovative Computing, Information, & Control*.

Okoye, K., Islam, S., Naeem, U., Sharif, M. S., Azam, M. A., & Karami, A. (2019). The Application of a Semantic-Based Process Mining Framework on a Learning Process Domain. In K. Arai, S. Kapoor, & R. Bhatia (Eds.), *Intelligent Systems and Applications. Advances in Intelligent Systems and Computing* (Vol. 868, pp. 1381–1403). Springer Cham. doi:10.1007/978-3-030-01054-6_96

Rozinat, A., & Gunther, C. (2012). Disco User Guide - Process Mining for Professionals. Eindhoven, The Netherlands: Fluxicon.com.

Sirin, E., & Parsia, B. (2004). Pellet: An owl dl reasoner. *Proceedings of the 2004 International Workshop on Description Logics (DL2004)*, 104.

Chapter 4
Proposed Algorithms and Formalizations

ABSTRACT

In this chapter, the work presents and describes the different algorithms that it proposes for ample implementation of the SPMaAF framework. The procedures outlined in the Algorithms 1, 2, and 3 illustrates the method that the work applies for developing the semantic-based process mining approach described in this book. Technically, the outlined procedures (i.e., Algorithms 1, 2, and 3) are aligned with the entire speculation of the work in this book, which are grounded on the three different phases or components of the SPMaAF Framework.

SEMANTICALLY MOTIVATED PROCESS MINING ALGORITHMS

Essentially, the following sets of algorithms are provided for the purpose of the work done in this book by considering the different phases that constitutes practical implementation of the SPMaAF framework.

Algorithm 1

The work describes in this section the proposed *Algorithm 1* and how it makes use of the method to perform the process mining and model discovery (Phase 1). Perhaps, the algorithm (Algorithm 1) is developed to show how to

DOI: 10.4018/978-1-7998-2668-2.ch004

effectively discover useful process models from the readily available events (data) logs. In principle, the process proves useful towards generation and mapping of the individual traces that makes up each of the process executions. For example, we illustrate in Chapters 5 and 7 how the proposed *algorithm 1* is implemented using process mining tools such as Disco that is based on Fuzzy Miner framework (Rozinat & Gunther, 2012) to generate and map the process models from the readily available event logs. In addition to the process models discovery, the process is also carried out for conformance checking and analysis of the individual cases (i.e. classified traces) and visualization of the several sequence(s) of activities executions.

Practically, the following *Algorithm 1* describes how the work discovers and generates the process models and individual traces from any given events data log as follows:

Algorithm 1: Discovering Fitting Process Models through Fuzzy Mining Approach

```
1: For all Recorded Events Data Log, L
2: Input:   PM - Process mining tool used to extract model, M
                L - Input Data for process Mapping/
Visualization
                e - Classifier for the event logs, L and
traces, T
3: Assign:  case_id(e)  i.e. the Case associated to event, e
within the events log, L
                act_name(e)  i.e. Activities associated to
event, e within L
                other_attributes e.g. Event ID, Timestamp,
Resources, Roles etc. related to event, e within L
4: Output: Process maps (fuzzy model), M & individuals traces,
T classifications for the events log, L
                Model or TraceFitness, TF discovery through
semantic fuzzy mining
5: Procedure: Discover Fuzzy Models, M from L for cross-
validation to determine how well M reflects the performed
activities in reality, i.e TraceFitness, TF and for further
analysis
6: Begin
7:     For all Event Data Log L
8:         Extract Process Maps, M, & Traces, T ← from Event Log
L
9:         while no more process element is left do
10:        Analyze Fuzzy Model, M and Traces, T to determine
tracesFitness, TF
```

```
11:              If T ← Null then
12:                  obtain the occurring act_name(e) sequence sets
from Log L
13:              Else If T ← 1 then
14:                  cross-validate resulting Trace, T from L with
Fuzzy Model, M
15:              If trace, T exist then
16:                      For each event Classifier, e output ←
return as True_Positive, TP i.e fits the Fuzzy Model, M
17:              Else If trace, T does not exist then
                            Return event Classifier, e output
as True_Negative, TN i.e does not fit the Fuzzy Model, M
18: Return: Classification Results of the Semantic Fuzzy Mining
approach and Process Maps
19: End If statements
20: End while
       21: End For
```

Ultimately, from the proposed *Algorithm 1*, and as earlier explained in the description of the *phase 1* of the SPMaAF framework in chapter 3, we recognize that:

- A typical process model, M consists of Traces, T (i.e. Cases)
- A Trace (Case), T, consist of events, e, such that each event relates to precisely one case.
- Events, e, within a Trace are ordered, most often in a sequential order
- Events for any process mining task must have atleast a Case identification Id (*Case_id*) and Activity Name (*Act_name*) attributes to allow for the process model discovery to follow.
- Other additional information may be required for ample implementation of process mining e.g. Event ID, Timestamp, Resources, Cost, Roles, and Places etc. (Van der Aalst, 2016)

Algorithm 2

Semantic depiction (*representation*) of processes (or models) in an ontological form (Phase 2 – see: Chapter 3) is a very important step in the work done in this paper. The method is used to ensure the ample implementation of the semantic-based process mining technique such as the SPMaAF approach. Technically, the method is aimed at unlocking the informative value of the Event Data Logs, *EDL* and the derived process Models, *M* (as described in the Algorithm 1) by way of finding useful and/or previously unknown links between the process elements and the deployed models. In fact, the main purpose for developing the algorithm 2 (as represented below) and its main implementation component is focused on augmenting the meaning (property descriptions) and conceptual analysis of the resulting models by semantically annotating the process elements with concepts they represent in the real-time settings. This is done by linking the process elements (attributes) to well-defined ontologies in order to allow for analysis of the extracted data logs and models at a more abstraction level. Moreover, the use of a *reasoner* (classifier) to automatically infer the whole process or individual process instances relies exclusively on the ability to represent such information in a formal way (ontology) to help create platform for an enhanced conceptual analysis of the domain processes in question.

To this effect, the following *algorithm (Algorithm 2)* describes how we generate ontologies from the process models and event logs:

Algorithm 2: Developing Ontology from process models and event logs

```
1: For all defined models M and event log EV
2: Input:   C - different classes for all process domain
               R - relations between classes
               I - sets of instantiated process individuals
               A -- sets of axioms which state facts
3: Output: Semantic annotated graphs/labels & an ontology-
driven search for process models and explorative analysis
4: Procedure: create semantic model with defined process
descriptions and assertions
5: Begin
6:     For all process models M and event log EV
7:        Extract Classes C ← from M and EV
8:        while no more process element is left do
9:        Analyze Classes C to obtain formal structures
10:           If C ← Null then
11:               obtain the occurring Process instances (I)
from M and EV
12:           Else If C ← 1 then
13:               create the Relations (R) between subjects
and objects // i.e between classes C and individuals (I)
14:           If relations R exist then
15:               For each class C ← semantically analyse
the extracted relationships (R) to state facts i.e Axioms (A)
16:               create the semantic schema by adding the
extracted relationships and individuals to the ontology
17: Return: taxonomy
18: End If statements
```

19: **End** while
20: **End** For

As gathered in the algorithm (Algorithm 2), the annotated logs/models (ontological representations) have shown to be useful in carrying out the semantic-based analysis of any given process domain. This is owing to the fact that at this stage, the input data for the process mining method are presented in a formal structure (taxonomies) that can connect to concepts that are referenced within the underlying ontologies (Okoye et al, 2016, 2018 & 2020). In return, as represented in the Algorithm 2, we show that ontologies (schema) can be defined as a quadruple;

$$Ont = (C, R, I, A)$$

which consists of different classes, C, and relations, R, between the classes (Gruber, 1995; Lautenbacher et al, 2009; Lautenbacher et al, 2008; Okoye et al, 2018 & 2020). Perhaps, a relation, R, trails to connect a set of class(es) with either another class, or with a fixed literal and is capable of also describing the sub assumption hierarchy (e.g. taxonomy) that exists between the various classes and their underlying relationships. In addition, the classes are instantiated with a set(s) of individuals, I, and can likewise contain a set(s) of axioms, A, which states fact. For instance, what is true and fitting within the model, or what is true and not fitting within the model? In other words, the work in this book notes that ontologies can be represented or described as connected sets of taxonomies (i.e. RDF + Axioms) or yet, structuring of the process elements in a formal way (Triple + Facts) where the subject includes the *Classes*, predicate represents the *Relations*, and the object includes the *Individuals*, in addition to the sets of *Axioms* which states facts. Thus, the definition of ontologies as a quadruple (C, R, I, A). Interestingly, Petrenko and Petrenko (2017) are even more specific about the importance of the aforementioned ontological concepts in semantic representation of real-time processes. To note, the work (Petrenko and Petrenko, 2017) states that "classes are the central item of the ontology" and further explain that a well-defined class(es) may represent all types of procedures e.g. running tasks, data transmission, data flow control, activity workflows etc.

Therefore, without a doubt, the *Algorithm 2* illustrates the need for a well-defined semantic annotation process especially when developing such an ontology-based framework (SPMaAF) that supports semantic-based process mining and analysis (Okoye et al, 2019). In practice, this is done by producing in an automatic manner the underlying taxonomies (class hierachies) and/or properties the process instances share within the semantic model or knowledge-base (Lautenbacher et al, 2009; Okoye et al, 2017). Henceforth, the semantic annotation process is deemed necessary for concrete implementation of the SPMaAF approach including the further steps of enhancing the discovered process models (Okoye et al, 2017 & 2020). In theory, a semantically annotated graph is described as follows (Lautenbacher et al, 2009):

SemAn:: $N \cup E \rightarrow COnts$

where: SemAn describes all kinds of annotations which can be input, output, meta-model annotation etc. Also, it is important to note that semantic annotations could be carried out either manually, or automatically computed bearing in mind the similarity of words (Born, et al., 2007) to generalize the individual entities (process instances) within the domain ontologies or processes in question. Therefore, a *semantic annotated graph* (described in detail in Chapters 5 and 6) which forms part of the semantic model that have been developed in this book (see Chapter 7) is defined as follows:

Gsem = (Nsem, Esem, Onts) with *Nsem = {(n, SemAn(n))|n ∈ N}* and *Esem = {(nsem, n_sem)|nsem = (n, SemAn(n))∧n_sem = (n_, SemAn(n_))∧(n, n_) ∈ E}*. (Lautenbacher, et al., 2009).

In general, the works in Okoye et al (2018 & 2019) notes that the semantical planning of any ontology-based system (such as the SPMaAF framework) must take into account the relationships that exist amongst the individual process instances that constitutes the underlying ontologies and must consist of various kinds of metadata descriptions (semantic annotation). Moreover, according to the definition in Lautenbacher et al (2009): if we Let A be the set(s) of all process actions. A process action $a \in A$ is characterized by a set(s) of input parameters *Ina* $\in P$, which are required for the execution of a and a set of output parameters *Outa* $\subseteq P$, which are provided by a after execution. Besides, all elements $a \in A$ are stored as a triple (*namea, Ina, Outa*) within a process library *libA*.

To do this, at first, the extracted logs/models from the standard process mining techniques are represented as a set of annotated terms which links or relates to defined terms within an ontology as illustrated in detail in the following figure (Figure 1). Indeed, the method makes it straightforward to represent the extracted information in an easy and yet accurate manner.

Secondly, the resulting ontologies provide means to represent the annotated terms or described process in a formal and structured way by defining the associations (relationships) that exist between the different process elements as observed (inferred) in the model. Perhaps, the method also ensures that the various range of tasks (activities) conforms naturally to the event logs or executed process as well as the model representations. Perhaps, this is achieved by encoding the deployed models in a formal structure of ontologies (i.e. through the semantic modelling process), and even more, supports further expansion (or improvement) of the existing model.

Finally, the Reasoner (or the inference engine) is designed to perform semantic reasoning and ontological classification of the different process elements in order to validate the resulting model and clean out inconsistent outputs, and consequently, presents the inferred (underlying) semantic associations in a structured manner that can be easily grasped by the search/ queries initiator (e.g process analysts).

Consequently, given the definition of ontologies as a quadruple and the stated formal representations means that *semantic annotation* (Algorithm 2) is another essential component in realizing such an approach (SPMaAF) that supports the semantic-based process mining by automatically conveying the formal semantics of the derived process models and/or extracted input logs (Lautenbacher, et al., 2009; Lautenbacher, et al., 2008). In other words, the annotated process models or logs are necessary for the semantic-based analysis and model enhancement to follow.

Thus far, in order to achieve this importance step in the work done in this book, we show in the following figure (Figure 1) the incremental procedure the work applies in order to achieve the different defined steps in the algorithm (Algorithm 2).

Technically, the defined procedure as explicated in the figure (Figure 1) are aligned with the entire speculation of the proposals and analysis carried out in this book - which is focused on provision of an effective method and suitable practice towards the development and application of the semantic-based process mining techniques.

Algorithm 3

Accordingly, another essential component in realizing the SPMaAF framework and its application for real-time processing is the capability of performing automated reasoning through the use of a (semantic) reasoner to classify, and

Figure 1. Incremental procedure (stages) for implementation of the algorithm (Algorithm 2)

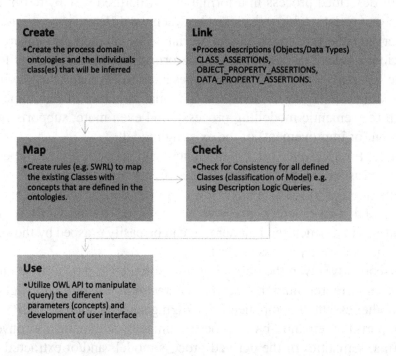

even more, check for consistency for all defined classes and/or relationships that exist within the (semantic) model. This implies that given the metadata or process descriptions (i.e. object/data properties assertions within the domain ontology) the reasoner is able to use the underlying information to check for consistency within the process knowledge-base (semantic model). For instance, the method may be applied to determine if it is possible for any process instances (individuals) to become a member of a class, and to establish (produce) the necessary results or associations as requested or queried by te users based on the executed information retrieval and extraction process (see: chapter 7).

To this effect, the following *Algorithm 3* describes how we make use of the reasoner to produce the necessary outputs by automatically classifying (infer) the associations that exist within the semantic model or knowledge-base.

Algorithm 3: Reasoning over Ontologies, Classification of Parameters and
   Outputs

```
1: For all defined Ontology models OntM
2: Input:  classifier e.g. Pellet Reasoner
3:                    Output: classified classes, process
instances and attributes
4:                        Procedure: automatically generate
process instance, their individual classes and Learning
concepts
5: Begin
6:              For all defined object properties (OP) and
datatype properties (DP) assertions in the model (OntM)
7:       Run reasoner
8:       while no more process and property description is left
do
9:       Input the semantic search queries SQ or set parameter
P to retrieve data from OntM
10       Execute queries
11:            If SQ or P ← Null then
12:                re-input query or set the parameter concepts
13:            Else If SQ or P ← 1 then
14:                            infer the necessary
associations and provide resulting outputs
15: Return: classified Concepts
16: End If statements
17: End while
18: End For
```

Clearly, as described in the algorithm (Algorithm 3), *semantic reasoning* otherwise referred to as the *ontological classifications* process helps to infer and associate meanings to the attributes (entities) within the defined ontologies by referring to the different concepts (i.e. Classes, Individuals, Objects and Datatype properties) assertions and/or set(s) of rules/expressions that are defined within the said ontologies. Perhaps, the resultant method is used to answer and produce meaningful information, and even in many cases, new knowledge about the process instances and the relationships they share amongst themselves within the knowledge base.

Therefore, in short description, the work in this book demonstrates that any process mining technique or data analytical method that integrates the different sets of algorithm (Algorithms 1, 2 and 3) as introduced in this cahpter can be used to lift the process mining and analysis from the syntactic to a more conceptual level. In theory, the work shows that the use of ontologies and understanding (inference) of the relations that exist between the concepts in the ontologies can be utilized to collectively combine tasks and/or compute the various entities within the process models in a hierarchical form (taxonomy) including several levels of abstraction analysis (Gruber, 1993; Wimalasuriya & Dou, 2010; deMedeiros, et al., 2008; Okoye, et al., 2016 & 2020). Perhaps, the main idea is that for any semantic-based process mining approach (such as the SPMaAF), those aspects of aggregating the task or computing the hierarchy of the process models should not only be *machine-readable*, but also *machine-understandable*. This means that the process models are either semantically annotated, or already in a form which allows a computer (i.e. the reasoner) to infer new facts by making use of the underlying ontologies. Therefore, without a doubt, we can say that the presented method for semantic-based process mining and analysis (SPMaAF) focuses on information about resources hidden within the process knowledge-base, and how they are related (Jareevongpiboon & Janecek, 2013; Okoye, et al., 2016 & 2020; deMedeiros, et al., 2008). Moreover, reasoning on the ontological knowledge plays an important role in the semantic representation of the various process elements (Calvanese, et al., 2017) by allowing for extraction and conversion of the explicit information (that makes up the given processes in question) into some implicit information as illustrated in the Algorithms 1, 2 and 3.

Thus, the main components as noted (incorporated) in the algorithms (Algorithm 1, 2 and 3) namely: Annotated logs/models, Ontologies, and Semantic Reasoning - are the foundation upon which the SPMaAF framework is developed.

CONCLUSION

To summarize the work in this chapter, the different steps or procedures outlined in Algorithms 1, 2 and 3 illustrates the method which we apply for ample implementation of the semantic-based process mining approach in this book. A description of the different notations as used in the algorithms are presented in the table of notations (Table 1) below.

At first, the work applies the process mining, *PM*, technique (Algorithm 1) to make available the process mappings, *M*, for the events log, *L*, based on the Fuzzy Miner (Rozinat and Gunther, 2012) as described in detail in the following Chapter 5 and Chapter 7. The main purpose of the process mining (mapping) method is that the resulting process map (fuzzy model) allows us to quickly, and interactively explore the processes into multiple directions and to visualize the individual activities workflow, otherwise known as the traces, T, and then provide a platform for semantical annotation of the different process elements.

Secondly, the work performs the semantic annotation, and consequently, ontological representation (modelling) of the fuzzy model in terms of the annotated terms (Algorithm 2). Henceforth, the resultant semantic model represents the domain knowledge about the various activities and sequence workflows i.e. the individual traces, T, as concepts defined in an ontology. This is done by making use of the process descriptions and querying languages such as the OWL (Bechhofer et al, 2004; Motik et al, 2012), SWRL (Horrocks et al, 2004), and DL queries (Baader et al, 2003).

In the end, we make use of the Reasoner i.e. Pellet (Sirin and Parsia, 2004) to classify, e, and infer the different relationships (taxonomies) about the process instances that can be found within the model (Algorithm 3). Again, this is done in order to automatically determine the TraceFitness, TF, for the different traces, T, discovered from the model, M. For instance, the True_Positives (TP) or True_Negatives (TN) values or traces are being determined.

Accordingly, the work describes in details in the next chapter (Chapter 5); the method for semantical annotation of the process models (using example of the learning process domain) that its uses to demonstrate the proposed semantic-based approach throughout this book including the experimental design (setup) and practical implementation of the different algorithms (Algorithm 1, 2 and 3) and the SPMaAF method in general.

Table 1. Table of Notations for the different algorithms (Algorithm 1, 2 and 3)

Notation	Description
M	Discovered process Model
PM	Process Mining tool used to discover M
L	Input Data or Event Logs used for PM
T	Individual Traces or a collection of Events
e	Events in the log, L
e	Classifier for the events log, L and traces, T
TF	Trace Fitness for the models, M
C	Classes
R	Relations
I	Individuals
A	Axioms
EV	Events Log
$OntM$	Ontological Model
OP	Object Properties
DP	Data Properties
SQ	Semantic Queries or search
P	Parameter or set of concepts

REFERENCES

Baader, F. (2003). *Description Logic Handbook: theory, implementation, and applications* (1st ed.). New York, NY: Cambridge University Press.

Bechhofer, S. (2004). *OWL Web Ontology Language Reference*. Manchester, UK: Technical report W3C Proposed Recommendation.

Born, M., Dörr, F., & Weber, I. (2007). User-Friendly Semantic Annotation in Business Process Modeling. In M. Weske, M. Hacid, & C. Godart (Eds.), Lecture Notes in Computer Science: Vol. 4832. *Web Information Systems Engineering – WISE 2007 Workshops. WISE 2007* (pp. 260–271). Berlin: Springer. doi:10.1007/978-3-540-77010-7_25

Calvanese, D., Kalayci, T. E., Montali, M., & Tinella, S. (2017). Ontology-based Data Access for Extracting Event Logs from Legacy Data: The onprom Tool and Methodology. *Proceedings of 20th International Conference on Business Information Systems 2017*, 220-236. 10.1007/978-3-319-59336-4_16

de Medeiros, A., van der Aalst, W. M. P. & Pedrinaci, C. (2008). *Semantic Process Mining Tools: Core Building Blocks*. Galway, Ireland: ECIS.

Gruber, T. R. (1993). A translation approach to portable ontology specifications. *Knowledge Acquisition, 5*(2), 199–220. doi:10.1006/knac.1993.1008

Gruber, T. R. (1995). Toward principles for the design of ontologies used for knowledge sharing. *International Journal of Human-Computer Studies, 43*(5), 907–928. doi:10.1006/ijhc.1995.1081

Horrocks, I. (2004). *SWRL: A Semantic Web Rule Language Combining OWL and RuleML*. Network Inference, Canada and Stanford University: W3C Member Submission - 2004 National Research Council of Canada, Network Inference, and Stanford University.

Jareevongpiboon, W., & Janecek, P. (2013). Ontological approach to enhance results of business process mining and analysis. *Journal of Business Process Management, 19*(3), 459–476. doi:10.1108/14637151311319905

Lautenbacher, F., Bauer, B., & Forg, S. (2009). Process Mining for Semantic Business Process Modeling. *13th Enterprise Distributed Object Computing Conference Workshops*, 45-53. 10.1109/EDOCW.2009.5332017

Lautenbacher, F., Bauer, B., & Seitz, C. (2008). *Semantic Business Process Modeling - Benefits and Capability.* AAAI Spring Symposium: AI Meets Business Rules and Process Management, Stanford University.

Motik, B., Patel-Schneider, P. F., Parsia, B., Bock, C., Fokoue, A., Haase, P., . . . Smith, M. (2012). *OWL 2 Web Ontology Language Structural Specification and Functional-Style Syntax* (2nd ed.). W3C Recommendation 11 Dec. 2012. Available at: https://www.w3.org/TR/owl2-syntax/

Okoye, K. (2016). Using semantic-based approach to manage perspectives of process mining: Application on improving learning process domain data. *Proceedings of 2016 IEEE International Conference on Big Data (Big Data),* 3529-3538.

Okoye, K. (2018). Semantic-based Model Analysis towards Enhancing Information Values of Process Mining: Case Study of Learning Process Domain. *Proceedings of SoCPaR 2016 Conference,* 622-633. 10.1007/978-3-319-60618-7_61

Okoye, K., Islam, S., & Naeem, U. & Sharif, S. (2020). Semantic-based Process Mining Technique for Annotation and Modelling of Domain Processes. *International Journal of Innovative Computing, Information, & Control.*

Okoye, K., Islam, S., Naeem, U., Sharif, M. S., Azam, M. A., & Karami, A. (2019). The Application of a Semantic-Based Process Mining Framework on a Learning Process Domain. In K. Arai, S. Kapoor, & R. Bhatia (Eds.), *Intelligent Systems and Applications. Advances in Intelligent Systems and Computing* (Vol. 868, pp. 1381–1403). Springer Cham. doi:10.1007/978-3-030-01054-6_96

Okoye, K., Naeem, U., & Islam, S. (2017). Semantic Fuzzy Mining: Enhancement of process models and event logs analysis from Syntactic to Conceptual Level. *International Journal of Hybrid Intelligent Systems, 14*(1-2), 67–98. doi:10.3233/HIS-170243

Okoye, K., Tawil, A. R. H., Naeem, U. & Lamine, E. (2016). Discovery and Enhancement of Learning Model Analysis through Semantic Process Mining. *International Journal of Computer Information Systems and Industrial Management Applications, 8*(2016), 93-114.

Petrenko, O. O., & Petrenko, A. I. (2017). A Model-driven Ontology Approach for Developing Service System Applications. *Journal Computer Science Application Information Technology*, 2(4), 1–7. doi:10.15226/2474-9257/2/4/00122

Rozinat, A., & Gunther, C. (2012). Disco User Guide - Process Mining for Professionals. Eindhoven, The Netherlands: Fluxicon.com.

Sirin, E., & Parsia, B. (2004). Pellet: An owl dl reasoner. *Proceedings of the 2004 International Workshop on Description Logics (DL2004)*, 104.

Van der Aalst, W. M. P. (2016). *Process Mining: Data Science in Action* (2nd ed.). Springer-Verlag Berlin Heildelberg. doi:10.1007/978-3-662-49851-4

Wimalasuriya, D. C., & Dou, D. (2010). Ontology-based information extraction: An introduction and a survey of current approaches. *Journal of Information Science*, 36(3), 306–323. doi:10.1177/0165551509360123

Chapter 5
Method for Semantic Annotation and Lifting of Process Models

ABSTRACT

The work done in this chapter demonstrates how the main components of the SPMaAF framework and sets of algorithms described earlier in Chapters 3 and 4, respectively, fit and rely on each other in achieving the semantic enhancement of the discovered process models. This is done by representing the models discovered through the standard process mining techniques as a set of annotated terms that links to or references the concepts defined within ontologies. It permits the process analysts to formally represent and analyse the several information in the underlying knowledge-bases in a more efficient and yet accurate manner. Henceforth, the conceptualisation method or tactics is allied to semantic lifting of the process models.

INTRODUCTION

A semantic-based process mining approach should present the discovered models or patterns in a formal and structured manner. Clearly, the primary aim must be on how best to interpret the mining results to provide domain knowledge (semantics) that can help improve or extend the derived process models. Thus, such type of *conceptualization* tactics is referred to as *semantic lifting of process models*.

DOI: 10.4018/978-1-7998-2668-2.ch005

The work done in this book demonstrates how the main components and algorithms described in the earlier Chapters 3 and 4 fit and rely on each other to carry out the semantic enhancement of the discovered models. For example, the extracted logs/models from the standard process mining techniques can be represented as a set of annotated terms that links or relates to defined terms within the ontologies. Thereby, making it straightforward to formally represent the information that underlies the knowledge-bases in an easy and yet accurate manner. Perhaps, *ontolog*ies has shown to be one of the many existing tools that have the capability to provide means to represent the models (annotated terms) in a formal and structured way. This is done by defining the associations (relationships) that exist between the different process elements in the model, and also in ensuring that the various range of tasks (activities) conforms naturally to the event logs/model representations as executed in reality. In other words, by encoding the deployed models in the *formal structure of ontology* (semantic modelling), one can then further expand the existing models.

Besides, the *Reasoner* (inference engine) is designed to perform the (semantic) reasoning and ontological classifications (taxonomies) in order to validate the resulting models and clean out inconsistent outputs, and consequently, presents the inferred (underlying) semantic associations in a structured (formal) manner. Over the next sections of this chapter, we look at suitable techniques that can be applied to represent the events logs and models in the formal way of ontologies, as well as, technologies that enable the different metadata creation and automated computation. We do this using the case study of the learning process as described in Okoye et al (2016).

ANNOTATION OF FUZZY LEARNING MODEL

Indeed, the first step towards achieving the semantic annotation of any given model should be aimed at making use of process description languages/ assertions to link elements in the models with concepts that they represent in a well-defined ontology. Using the learning process model as a case study, we demonstrate that the main purpose of the semantic annotation method must be to seek the equivalence between *the concepts of the process models (e.g fuzzy models)* derived by applying the fuzzy miner algorithm on the learning process logs and the *concepts of the defined (learning) process domain ontolog*ies. Apparently, this is done by making use of the process descriptions languages and/or notations (semantic annotation) to represent the extracted models.

To this end, in order to perform the semantic annotation of the learning process models which this work uses to illustrate the method throughout this book, and the application of the semantic reasoning - the work applies the following process mining technique especially as a way to achieve the target objectives defined in Phase 1 of the SPMaAF framework or *yet Algorithm 1* (see: Chapter 4) as follows:

First, we analyse the extracted events log for the Learning process (Okoye et al, 2016) using the fuzzy miner (Günther & Van der Aalst, 2007). The outcome or result of applying the fuzzy miner algorithm is as shown in the following Figure 1a and 1b. Fundamentally, the method involves the extraction and automated modelling of the process history data (see: Figures 2 to 6) by submitting the resulting event streams format to the process mining environment in Disco (Rozinat & Gunther, 2012) to help in discovery (mapping) of the fuzzy model represented in Figures 1a and 1b.

In turn, the method provides us with reliable and extendible results and/or insights about the readily available datasets in order to further create a model that describes the individual traces (or sequence workflows) learned from the different activities based on the proven framework of the Fuzzy Miner (Gu¨nther & Van der Aalst, 2006).

Consequently, suitable learning patterns were determined (or discovered) which enables the automatic creation of the learning process mapping as shown in Figures 1a and 1b. Basically, the main logic we applied in this case is - by applying the fuzzy miner algorithm, the method allows us to see in detail how the processes have been performed by revealing the underlying process mappings (i.e. the activities workflows as performed in reality). Moreover, the method also provides us with the opportunity to focus on the streams and/or frequency of the learning patterns or behaviours as well as visualize the paths they follow in the process.

Accordingly, the process mapping (visualizations) enables us to establish a direct connection between the discovered models and the actual low-level event data about the learning process by allowing for visualizing the process elements from different perspectives or viewpoints. Henceforth, the process mapping step was necessary especially when our aim is to make the *semantical* information about the learning process data available for further steps of mining and analysis at a more abstraction level.

Figure 1a. The Events input Data log for the Research Learning process with mapped processes in real-time

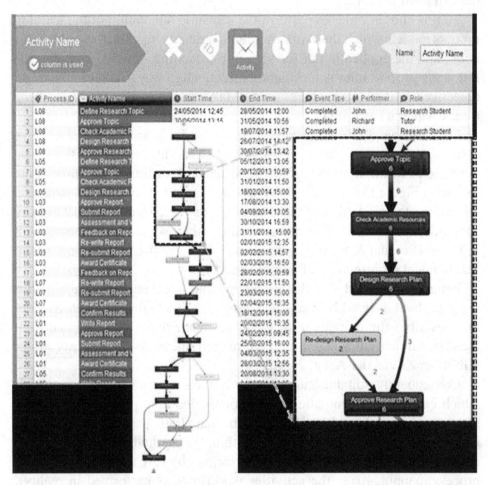

To this effect, the next step for the semantic-based planning is to define an effective means for annotation of the fuzzy models (as shown in Figures 1a and 1b). In fact, the semantic-based modelling approach is based on a comparable representation between the attributes found within the logs (or the different activities executed in reality) and the derived model. Thus, in view of the resulting fuzzy model, the work designs and develop further a BPMN model (Van der Aalst, 2016) to help make available the metadata (semantics) for each element in the fuzzy model including the individual activity paths (or sequence of activities workflow) as performed during the process executions. To achieve the stated objectives, it was necessary

Figure 1b. Fuzzy Model derived from mining the Research Learning process event data logs

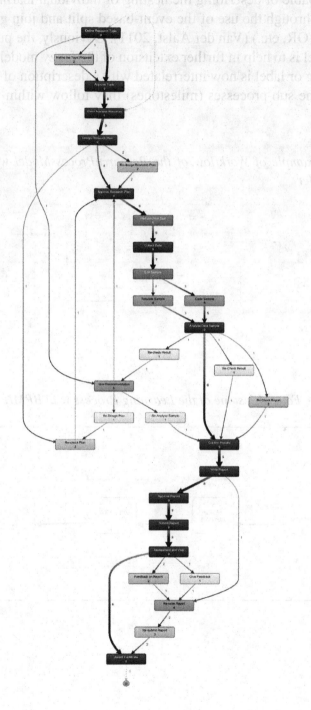

to construct the BPMN model as shown in Figures 2a to 2c with notational elements capable of describing the nesting of individual learning activities (workflow) through the use of the event-based split and join gateways (i.e. AND, XOR, OR, etc.) (Van der Aalst, 2011). Obviously, the purpose of the BPMN model is to help in further extension of the fuzzy model, where each annotated log or label is now interrelated with a description of the paths, or better still, the sub-processes (milestones) they follow within the resulting model.

Figure 2a. Example of Workflow of the ResearchProcessModel with BPMN in Bizagi Modeller

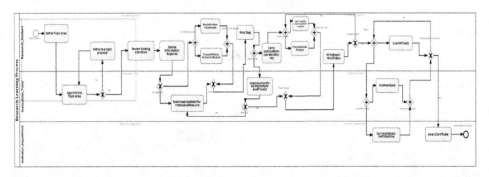

Figure 2b. The Four Milestone of the Learning Process with BPMN

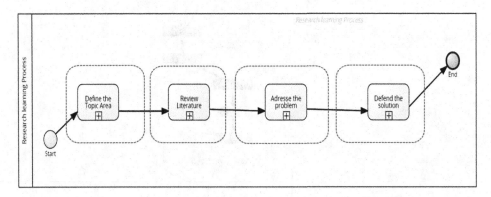

Figure 2c. The BPMN model for the Learning Process with a description of the defined milestones

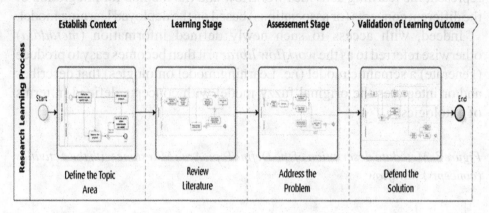

Consequently, on the one hand, in order to allow for the semantic-based analysis of the resulting models (Figures 1 and 2), it was necessary to construct process transitions (metadata information) about the mapped processes or the sequence(s) of learning activities. On the other hand, this work has based the subsequent analysis of this book on the outcome of the BPMN learning model workflow, as illustrated in Figures 2a to 2c by considering the four milestones (or sub-processes), namely: *Establish Context → Learning Stage → Assessment Stage → Validation of Learning Outcome.* Essentially, this is done with the primary aim to determine a classification (grouping) set for the learning activities. In turn, the classification tasks help in the contextual understanding of the different learning activities or groups (i.e. milestones), and even more, it helps to provide a consistency check during the design and computation (semantic reasoning) of the resulting learning model and application of the semantic fuzzy mining approach described in this book (see: chapter 7)

For all intents and purposes, this work defines and represents the BPMN model (see: Figures 2a to 2c) and its activities workflow with some set of annotations to describe the links (relationships) between each one of the concepts. This is done in order to provide (or generate) a workflow library (meta-model) that describes the concepts in the resulting learning model ontology that is developed for the purpose of the work in this book. Perhaps, the purpose of performing such task (annotation) is to allow for the semantical representation of the Workflow Activity Patterns (WAPS) (Van der Aalst, et al., 2004), i.e., creation of the meta-model, based on the sequences (control-flow) of the individual learning activities that constitutes the underlying knowledge-base.

To this end, the following Figures 3 to 6 show how we semantically represent the learning activities workflow and the method for integration of the different concepts (or associations) based on the deployed learning model.

Indeed, with access to such newly defined information (*metadata*) otherwise referred to as the *workflow library*, it then becomes easy to produce (generate) a semantic model (i.e. Learning model ontologies) that describes and/or integrates the original fuzzy model with concepts defined in terms of ontologies.

Figure 3. Metadata description of the DefineTopicArea Milestone with the Activities (concepts) workflow

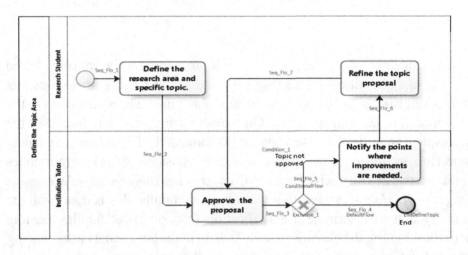

Figure 4. Metadata description for the ReviewLiterature Milestone with the Activities (concepts) workflow

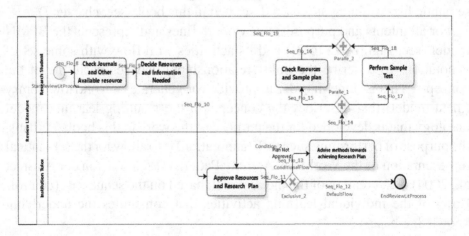

Figure 5. Metadata description for AddresstheProblem Milestone with the Activities (concepts) workflow

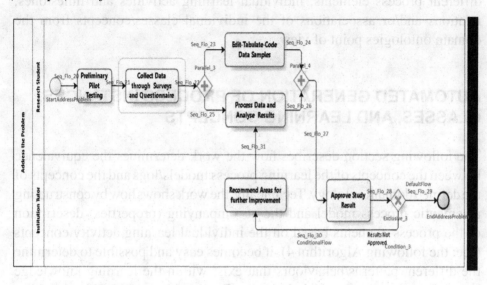

Figure 6. Metadata description of the DefendtheSolution Milestone with Activities (concepts) workflow

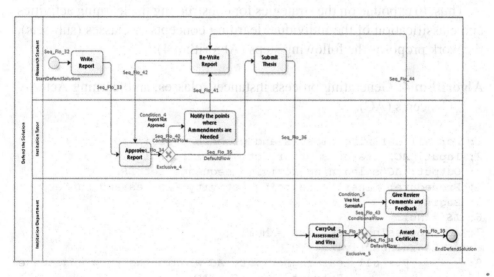

Moreover, given the newly discovered information or knowledge about the Learning model, the work presents in the next section how it makes use of the ontological concepts and schema to support the integration of the different process elements (instances) or activities that makes up the learning model.

Thus, we show the semantical modelling and automated generation of the different process elements, individual learning activities and milestones, relations and/or associations of the individual classes/concepts from the domain ontologies point of view.

AUTOMATED GENERATION OF PROCESS INSTANCES, CLASSES, AND LEARNING CONCEPTS

The following section describes how the work determines the equivalence between the concepts of the learning process models/logs and the concepts of the defined domain ontology. Technically, the work shows how by constructing a semantic process model and the accompanying (properties) description of the process elements based on the individual learning activity concepts (see: the following Algorithm 4), it becomes easy and possible to determine the different patterns/behaviours that exist within the learning knowledge base. Moreover, the Semantic Learning Process Mining (SLPM) algorithm (Algorithm 5) explains the basis for the semantical modelling, integration, and analysis of the learning process case study in real-time.

Thus, to expound on the strategies for constructing the learning activities and classification of the individual learning concepts or classes (sub-sets), the work proposes the following steps (Algorithm 4):

Algorithm 4: Generating process instances, classes, and learning Activity Concepts (AC).

```
1: For all definite classes and process descriptions
2: Input: AC, learners prior activity list ACL_List
3: Output: AC's learning activity sequence set LS
4: Procedure: Generate Learning Activity Classes and SubSets
5: Begin
6: LS = Null
7: AC_ProcessInstance_List = Null
8: AC_LearningActivity = 0
9:        For all LearningActivity_AC within the knowledge-base
10:              Extract LS ← LS + AC
11:          while no more AC is left do
12:                  For each Ci ∈ LS
13:                      Ci_Precondition_List ← Get_
Precondition (OWL_xml_Ci)
14:                  For each Cj ∈ Ci_Precondition_List
15:                      Cj_CorrespondingSubSet_List =
```

```
Null
16:                              Cj_ProcessInstance_List = Null
17:                                  If Cj ∉ ACL_List AND Cj ∉LS
then
18:                                      LS ← LS + Cj
19:                                          Cj_
CorrespondingSubclassSet_List ← Cj_ CorrespondingSubclassSet_
List + Ci
20:                                          Cj_ProcessInstance_
List ← Cj_ProcessInstance_List + Ci + Ci_ProcessInstance_List
21:                                      Cj_LearningActivity =
Ci_LearningActivity + 1
22:                                  Else If Cj ∉ACL_List AND
Cj ∉ LS AND Cj ∉ Ci_ProcessInstance_List then
23:                                          Cj_
CorrespondingSubclassSet_List ← Cj_ CorrespondingSubclassSet_
List + Ci
24:                                              Cj_
ProcessInstance_List ← Cj_ProcessInstance_List + Ci + Ci_
ProcessInstance_List
25:                                      If Cj_
LearningActivity < Ci_LearningActivity + 1
26:                                          For each
Ck ∈ LS_SubsequentTo_Cj
27:                                          Ck_LearningActivity
= All (Ck_CorrespondingSubclassSet_LearningActivity) + 1
28: Return LS
29: End For
30: End If
31: End For
32: End For
33: End while
34: End For
```

Accordingly, it is important to note - from the use case example of the Learning Process (Okoye et al, 2016) as represented in Figures 1a and 1b - that this work refers to the learning process as a *workflow* (e.g. sequence of steps) or set(s) of activities through which the learners have to perform in order to complete the research process. To this effect, it was necessary to provide pre-defined activity concepts, Ci, (e.g. classes, object properties or assertions) to be able to identify and/or monitor the entire process flow, and in turn, help in generation (through the classification method) of the sets of individuals entities (process instances) that make up the defined class(es).

Therefore, the learning activity concepts and class generation (*Algorithm 4*) outlines the procedures that takes place when generating the lists of process instances and/or the defined concepts, *Ci,* within the learning knowledge-base. Henceforth, for each concept (or class) *Ci,* within the knowledge-base, we first extract the precondition (prerequisite) list from its OWL file definition *OWL_xml_Ci* as shown in line 13. Then for each concept *Cj* within the class list (e.g the individual process instances), *if* it does not belong to an activity list and the corresponding subclass sts, add it into the learning activity sets and revise the *Cj*'s corresponding SubclassSet list, process instance list, and number of steps to the targeted learning concepts as described in lines 14 to 21 of the *algorithm 4*. Moreover, *If Cj* already exists in the learning class list, but does not belong to the activity list and the individual (process instance) list of *Ci*, *End* the process, but also update its corresponding subclass list, process instance list, and number of steps to the target learning concepts as described in lines 22 to 27 of the *algorithm 4*.

Furthermore, *if* we use the following standard notation, *R,* to refer to the Research Learning process, and *a, b, c, d* for the activity concepts as described in the following Algo*rithm 5 which* we develop to show how to perform the semantical analysis of the resulting learning model.

Then *a, b, c, d* $\in$ *R* is a function with domain *R* and the different learning process milestones *a, b, c, d*.Where:

Domain *R* is a SuperClass of the SubClasses *a, b, c, d*.

Algorithm 5: Semantic Learning Process Mining (SLPM) and Analysis Procedure

```
1: For all defined Classes or Subsets
2: Input: L - process log for Person, P, over Researchprocess,
                a - DefineTopicArea Milestone or SubClass
                b - ReviewLiterature Milestone or SubClass
                c - AddressProblem Milestone or SubClass
                d - DefendSolution Milestone or SubClass
 3: Output: Structured organisation (i.e superClass -> subClass
hierarchies) for representation of the Research process
information
4: Procedure: create the sequence set of activities that make
up the Research process, R
5: Begin
6:     For all Learning Activity concepts a, b, c, d ∈ R
7:     If    P … n is a measure of the number of times a, b, c,
d occurs in R for Person, P, then
                P … n = |n ⊆ L ∈R | where, P … n = |n ⊆
La| ± |n ⊆ Lb | ± |n ⊆ Lc | ± |n ⊆ Ld |
8:     while no more process element is left do
9:     Run Reasoner to infer anonymous classes and obtain
```

146

```
formal structures
10:      If PSL = |SL ⊆ L ∈R | where, PSL = |SL ⊆ La| + |SL ⊆ Lb
| + |SL ⊆ Lc | + |SL ⊆ Ld | then
11:                     Person P, is SuccessfulLearner
12:        Else If PUL = |UL ⊆ L ∈R-1| where, PUL = |UL ⊆ L
∈ R-a| or |UL ⊆ L ∈ R-b | or |UL ⊆ L ∈R-c | or |UL ⊆ L ∈ R-d |
then
13:                     Person P, is UnCompleteLearner
14     For each Learner class or Subsets
15:     update the semantic schema (taxonomy) by adding the
extracted relationships and individuals to the ontology
16: Return: taxonomy
17: End If statements
18: End while
    19: End For
23:            If Cj_LearningActivity < Ci_LearningActivity + 1
then
24:                  For each Ck ∈ LS_Subsequently_Cj
25:             Ck_LearningActivity = All (Ck_
CorrespondingSubclassSet_LearningActivity) + 1
26: Return LS
27: End If
28: End For
```

Perhaps, *it is important to **note** that the Subclasses (also referred to as Subsets) is a **set(s)** where each of the individual Learning Activities occurs and sometimes *may occur* multiple times.*

For example, [*a*1, *a*2, *a*3, *a*4, *a*2, *a*5] could be seen as a sequence set of learning activities for a Person, *P* … *n* over *a* (i.e. the DefineTopicArea Milestone).

Thus,

P… (*a*) = l*n* ⊆ Λ*a*l. (Line 7)
So therefore,

If
    *a*1 = Define Topic
    *a*2 = Approval Activity
    *a*3 = Topic decline
    *a*4 = Refine Topic
    *a*5 = End Topic Proposal

Then

The sequence set of activities for $P...n$ (a) = {Define Topic, Approval Activity, Topic Decline, Refine Topic, Approval Activity, End Topic Proposal}.

In theory, considering the focus of the *real-time example of a learning problem which this book trails to resolve (as outlined in Algorithm 5) – which* is on computing the set(s) of individual process instances that has completed (successful learners) or not completed (un*complete le*aners) the research learning process, R. We then note as described in line 7 (Algorithm 5*) that to complete* a research process, *R (i.e. the SuperC*lass) one must complete a set(s) *of* given milestones (i.e. the SubClasses a, b, c, d) and must perform the set(s) or perhaps a subset(s) of the activities that comprise it. Moreover, given the fact that for transition *purp*oses, a process instance does not move on to the succeeding activities or milestone without completing a distinctive sequence set(s) of learning activities that makes up the sub-process(es) or preceding learning activities (concepts).

So for this reason, we note that the sum or difference in the Logs, $\mathscr{L}$, for any named person, P, is defined in a straightforward way:

$$P...n = |n \subseteq \mathscr{L}a| \pm |n \subseteq \mathscr{L}b| \pm |n \subseteq \mathscr{L}c| \pm |n \subseteq \mathscr{L}d|.$$

Thus, $P...n$ is a finite set $|n \subseteq \mathscr{L} \in R|$. (Line 7)

For example, the work determines based on the definitions provided in the Algorithm 5 that "Every Person, P, that hasCompleteMilestone a DefineTopicArea (a) and that hasCompleteMilestone a ReviewLiterature (b) and that hasComp*leteMilesto*ne an AddressProblem *(*c) and that hasCompleteMilestone a DefendSoluti*on* (d) is a SuccessfulLearner".

Henceforth, the defi*n*ition of the Class - SuccessfulLearners, PSL, is th*e* sum of the set(s) of the activity log, $\mathscr{L}$, that a *l*earner has completed for each of the individual learning activities milestones a, and b, and c, and d.

Thus,

If

PSL is the Class that consists of the set $|SL \subseteq \Lambda a| + |SL \subseteq \Lambda b| + |SL \subseteq \Lambda c| + |SL \subseteq \Lambda d|$

Then

PSL is the set $|SL \subseteq \Lambda \in R|$. (Lines 10 and 11)

Likewise, the work also establishes from the algorithm (Algorithm 5) that "Every Person, P, that hasOnlyCompleteMilestone a DefineTopicArea (a) or that hasOnlyCompleteMilestone a ReviewLiterature (b) or that hasOnlyCompleteMilestone *an Addr*essProblem (c) is an U*n*completeLearner".

Thus far, the definition of the U*n*complete Learners class, **PUL**, is the class of Leaners *w*here some set(s) of activities for the milestone *a*, or *b*, or *c*, or *d* is missing over a finite set |*n* ⊆ Λ ∈*R* |.

Hence,

If

PUL is a Class that consists of the set |*UL* ⊆ Λ ∈ *R*−*a* | *or* |*UL* ⊆ Λ ∈ *R*−*b* | *or* |*UL* ⊆ Λ ∈*R*−*c* | *or* |*UL* ⊆ Λ ∈ *R*−*d* |,

Then

PUL is the set |*UL* ⊆ Λ ∈*R*−1|. (Lines 12 and 13)

Over the remaining sections of this chapter, the work describes the main tools and/or semantic schema which it uses to implement and apply in practical sense the proposed algorithms and formalizations as described earlier in chapter 4 and expanded in this chapter. Here, we look in detail the different technologies particularly ontologies with its enabling technologies and its main functions that allows the definition and modelling of the different classes and object/data properties. This includes the method we use to classify and query the resulting models, as well as the different sets of (semantic) rules that enable the correlation (or integration) of the different formal expressions and assertions within the knowledge-base.

MAIN COMPONENTS OF THE LEARNING DOMAIN ONTOLOGIES

The work describes in this section - how the main functions and descriptive properties of the ontology are used for the implementation of the proposed method (SPMaAF) in this book. Indeed, the ontological concepts such as the OWL - make use of the semantic technologies or components as noted earlier in Chapter 2 to provide additional (new) functions that allow for formal descriptions and/or structuring of the process elements for any given domain of interest. For instance, the Learning process domain that is considered in this book. From the definitions in Chapter 2 we describe the main components and/or features of the OWL ontologies namely: (i) Classes, (ii) Properties, (iii) Process Instances or individuals, and (iv) Reasoner.

Moreover, in order to define and use the ontological schema in the context of the work done in this book, we introduce OWL as it concerns protégé (Musen, et al., 2015). Currently, there are two main mechanisms or ways of modeling ontologies in protégé. This includes the (i) Frame-based, or (ii) OWL ontologies. Each one of those modelling techniques has its own user interface and features, presented as follows:

- **Protege Frames editor:** Which allows users to build and populate ontologies that are frame-based in accordance with the Open Knowledge Base Connectivity Protocol (OKBC).
    ◦ Classes
    ◦ Slots for properties and relationships, and
    ◦ Instances for class
- **Protege OWL editor:** Which allows users to *build an o*ntology for the Semantic Web, specifically with OWL schema
    ◦ Classes
    ◦ Properties
    ◦ Instances
    ◦ Reasoning

Typically, just like protégé, the OWL schema supports additional new facilities (the reasoner e.g. Hermit, Fact++, Pellet) that makes it possible to logically describe and infer the concepts for any domain of interest as utilized in this book to describe the learning process.

Learning Model: Classes

The OWL classes are referred to as a set(s) that contains the individuals by formally stating the actual (precise) requirement for any individual to become a member of a class. In fact, the classes a*re an e*xplicit representatio*n of co*ncept(s), and every *now and the*n in literature, the term concept is used in place of class. It is also important to note that OWL classes can be structured (ordered) into a superClass → subClass hierarchy which are most often referred to as "taxono*mies" (*Semantic Web Primer, 2012) in the literature.

For example, a *typical exa*mple of a class as utilized in the context of this book is the "SuccesfulLearners" class defined in the Learning model (this is explained in detail in the use case scenario of the learning process in the following Chapter 6). Basically, in the defined model, the SuccessfulLearners class is represented to consist of all the individuals that are classified as successful within the Learning process. Superlatively, we assume that the subClasses are unified (i.e subsumed) by their superClasses. For instance, if we *look at the* following examples of a class "LearnerCategory", and "SuccessfulLearners" (see Figure 7) which forms part of the semantic model that has been developed in this book.

As gathered in Figure 7, it is clear that a SuccesfulLearner is a subClass of LearnerCategory. This also means that inversely the LearnerCategory class is a superClass of the SuccessfulLearner. Henceforth, all SuccesfulLearners are *classed as a kin*d of Learner. Ther*efore, every me*mber of the class SuccessfulLearners a*re also members* of the class Learners, but no*t all kind of Lea*rners are necessar*ily members of th*e class SuccessfulLearners. *Moreo*ver, being classed (classified) as a S*uccessfulLearner i*mplies that the referenced enti*ty (i.e.* the individual or pro*cess ins*tance) is also a participant of the s*uperClass LearnerCa*tegory. This is owing to the fact that "Succ*essfulLearner" is* subsumed by "LearnerCategory". Indeed, this is how taxonomies (i.e. class-hierarchies) are defined in OWL ontologies *as shown in Fig*ure 7.

In summary, a good practice when designing the OWL Classes especially in semantic modelling tools such as the protégé is to note that the:

- *Necessary* and *sufficient* conditions are used to describe the p*re-Defined Classes*.
- Defined Classes are also called *equivalent classes*.
- Equivalent classes can be defined using the u*niversal restriction properties*
- Universal class restrictions are denoted using the word "*only*" value.
- Any *individual* must fulfill all the universal class (object/datatype properties) restrictions to become a member of the specified class.

On the other hand,

- *Necessary* conditions are only used to describe the *Primitive Classes*.
- Primitive Classes are called *Superclasses* in OWL ontologies.
- Primitive classes are defined using *existential restrictions*.

Figure 7. Example of class hierarchies (taxonomy) defined within the learning process domain ontology

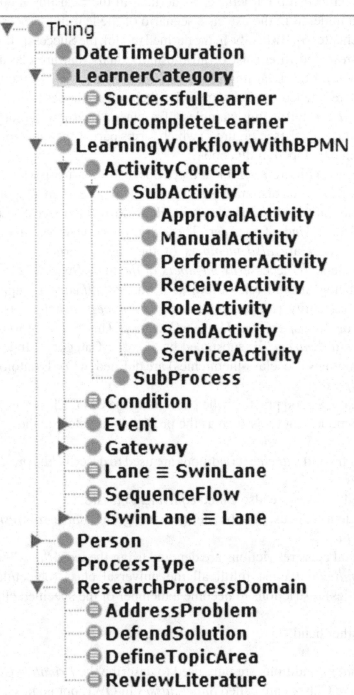

- Existential class restrictions are denoted using the word "*some*" value
- Any *individual* only needs to fulfill the existential class (object/datatype properties) restrictions to become a member of the specified class.

Learning Model: Individuals

OWL In*dividuals* (also referred to as the process instances in most settings) represents the different objects that are found within the domain ontologies. The OWL Individuals are considered to be "instances of class*es*" *(Semantic Web* Primer, 2012). Conceivably, an important practice when developing the OWL ontologies is to explicitly in*dicate if a* particular set(s) of *individuals are the sa*me as each other or dissimilar to each other. Else, the reasoner might consider them (the specified individuals in view) to be the same as each other, or on the contrary, different to each other.

For example, the following definitions "\DefineTopicArea" and "\ DefineTopic" might all refer to the same set(s) of individual, except explicitly stated that these are two different expressions (assertions) with different individuals.

The following Figure 8 is an example of an OWL ontology graph for the sets of individuals within the Learning model ontologies designed for the purpose of the work in this book. Notably, as described in the graph, individuals are represented as diamonds in modelling tools such as the protégé editor.

Learning Model: Properties

OWL properties are used to provide the different process descriptions (i.e. the logica*l expres*sions, relations or assertions) for all the Object and Data types that constitu*te the dom*ain ontologies. Most of the time, the properties restrictions are used to allow for the logical reasoning and/or querying of *the process mo*dels to follow.

Object Properties

The Owl properties restriction (such as the object properties) are used to create the Relations (R) between the subjects and objects within the domain processes (e.g between classes and individuals) (Semantic Web Primer, 2012). Thus, the object properties could be referred to as *binary* relati*ons on*

Figure 8. Example of OWL individuals within the defined learning process domain ontology

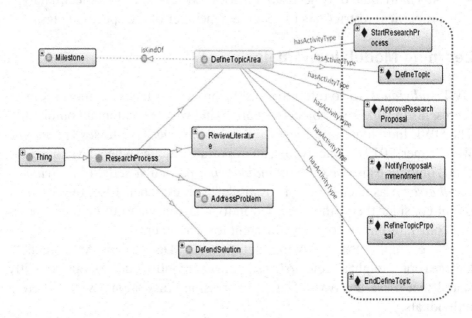

individuals and/or classes which provides the link between two individuals, or two classes, or class and *individual together*, etc.

For example, in Figure 9, we can ga*ther that t*he "Indi*viduals*" from StartResearchProcess to EndDefineTopic are linked to the class DefineTopicArea through the "hasActivityType" object property.

Also, it is important to note that the *Owl properties may a*lso *have an inver*se property for each and e*very defined p*roperty. For instance, the inverse property of "hasActivityType" as described in Figure 9 could perhaps be defined as "isActivityTypeOf". Hence, the following logical expressions can be defined or established:

"DefineTopicArea hasActivityType StartResearchProcess to EndDefineTopic"

Inversely, the

"StartResearchProcess to EndDefineTopic isActivityTypeOf DefineTopicArea"

Figure 9. Example of object properties restriction within the learning model ontology

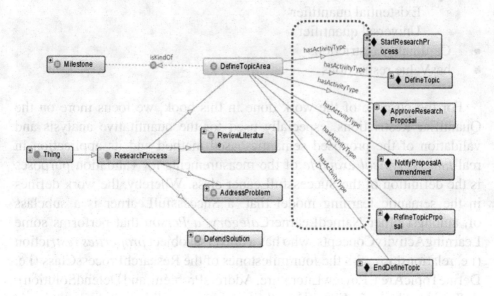

Data Properties

OWL properties can also be restricted to have a single value (i.e. FunctionalProperty), or one or the other *symmetric or trans*itive properties. So far, we have only looked at the "Object properties" (i.e. relationships between individuals and/or classes). Here, we di*scuss the* OWL *"Datatype* properties". Basically, the Owl Datatype proper*ties (restrictions)* are used to link a set(s) of individuals to RDF literal values or XML Schema Data*types. In other words,* Owl datatype properties describes the relations between an individual(s) and data-values. Henceforth, the Datatype properties restriction can be utilized to link an individual to explicit data values which can be untyped or inputted. Moreover, the Owl Datatype properties are also useful to measure numerical or literal values within the ontologies.

In summary, Owl properties restriction (be it either object or datatype properties) are used to provide assertions to help define, restrict, and/or identify a particular *set(s) of individuals that* belongs to a specific class. Predominantly, there are 3 main types of restrictions (Bechhofer, et al., 2004; Schreiber, 2005; Kumar, et al., 2011) that can be performed using the Owl schema namely:

- Quantifier restrictions
  - ◦ Existential quantifier
  - ◦ Universal quantifier
- Cardinality restrictions
- hasValue restrictions

For the purpose of the work done in this book, we focus more on the Quantifier Restrictions, especially used for the quantitative analysis and validation of the proposed semantic-based method and its application in real-*time. A typical example* of the measurements for validation purposes is the definition of the SuccessfulLeaner class. Whereby, the work defines in the semantic learning model that: a SuccessfulLearner is a subclass of, amongst other NamedLearner*Category, a Perso*n that performs some LearningActivityConcepts, who has a universal object *properties restr*iction (i.e. relationship) with the four milestones of the ResearchProcessClass (i.e. DefineTopicArea, ReviewLiterature, AddressProblem, and DefendSolution).

Thus, as shown in Figure 10 - the necessary condition is: if something is a Successful Learner, it is necessary for it to be a participant of the Learning ActivityConcept class (existen*tial restriction)* and necessary for it to have a kind of sufficiently *defined* condition (universal restriction) and relationship with the four *classes or milestones of* the *Learning p*rocess model: DefineTopicArea, ReviewLiterature, AddressP*roblem, and DefendSolu*tion.

Interestingly, one of the important characteristics of the Owl (properties) restrictions is that they are mainly used to describe anonymous classes (i.e. previously undefined classes). Whereby, on the one hand, the existential restrictions (as shown in the example Figure 10) are *used to define t*he class of individual(s) that participates in at least one link (as*sociation) alongside an* individual properties which is necessarily required for any individual to become a member of the specified class. On the other hand, universal restrictions are used to define the class of individual(s) which for a specifically defined property must only allow individuals that fulfi*ll the stated conditio*n to become part of the class. Besides, in Owl supported tools such as the Protégé (Musen, et al., 2015) the word `some' is used to signify existential restriction, whereas the words `only' or "equivalent to" are used to define universal restrictions, etc.

Figure 10. Example of OWL properties restriction

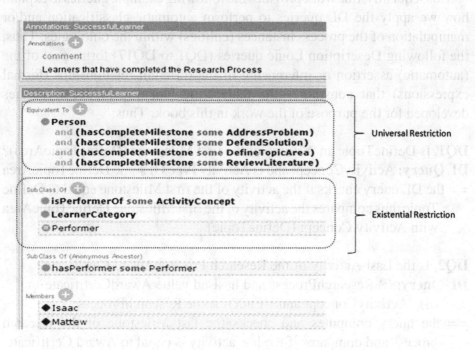

DESCRIPTION LOGIC QUERIES AND REASONING

The Description Logic (DL) (Baader, *et* al., *2003) queries* are a kind of process *description language* or syntax that can be used to check for consistency for all defined elements (entities) within the ontological models. Practically, the DL queries make use of the Reasoner (discussed earlier in chapter 2) to perform automatic classification (or assertion) of the various relationships (associations) that are d*escribed* or exist within the ontologies.

Accordingly, the work in this book makes use of the DL queries to compute and ascertain (infer) the different entities (classes, individual, relations, axioms, etc) that can be found within the learning domain ontologies. Fundamentally, the DL queries are implemented in order to check that all the parameters (process descriptions or expressions) within the defined classes are true and at least falls within the validity of the object/data properties restriction by definition, and that there are no inconsistency of data or repeatable contradicting discoveries.

Consequently, this work provides the following example queries to explain how we apply the DL queries to perform automatic classification and/or manipulation of the process instances (entities) within the ontologies. Thus, the following Description Logic queries (DQ1 to DQ17) forms part of the (automatic) assertion or inferencing of the different relationships (formal expressions) that constitutes the under**lying lear**ning model ontologies developed for the purpose of the work in this book. Thus:

DQ1. Is DefineTopic an Activity of the first Milestone (DefineTopicArea)?
DL Query: ActivityConcept and is ActivityType Of some DefineTopicArea
== the DL query checks if the activity of the first Milestone equal to Define Topic thus compares the activity of the first Milestone DefineTopicArea with Activity Concept (DefineTopic).

DQ2. Is the Last Activity of the Research Process Award Certificate?
DL Query: (i) ResearchProcess and hasEnd value AwardCertificate
   (ii)   **Activ**ityConcept and isEndOf some ResearchProcess
== the query computes and checks the last Milestone of the research process and compares if the last activity is equal to Award Certificate. Hence, compares the activity of the last Milestone DefendSolution with AwardCertificate

DQ3. What is the Start Activity of the second Milestone Review Literature?
DL Query: ActivityConcept and isStartProcessOf some ReviewLiterature
== computes and checks the start event of the second Milestone ReviewLiterature, and thus compares the activity of the second milestone with the result StartReviewLitProcess. Hence, Every Review Literature hasStartOfProcess StartReviewLitProcess.

DQ4. Is CollectData an Activity of the Third Milestone Address Problem?
DL Query: ActivityConcept and isActivityTypeOf some AddressProblem
== computes and check the activities of the Third Milestone AddressProblem, thus compare if the result is equal to the Activity Concept CollectData

DQ5. Does Person P Activity A?
   Example: Does Person (Richard) Activity Approve Research Proposal?
DL Query: Person and hasActivityType value ApproveResearchProposal

== the query computes and check for persons related to the Approve Research Proposal and then compares if person (Richard) does the activity ApproveResearchProposal.

DQ6. Does person P activity of activity A and B?
  Example: Which Persons does Activity RecheckSamplePlan and ReWriteReport?
DL Query: Person and hasActivityType some {RecheckSamplePlan, ReWriteReport}
== computes and check which persons in the model does activity RecheckSamplePlan and ReWriteReport.

DQ7. Does Person P activity A and then B and then C?
  Example: Does person Paul activity of type CollectData and then Edit_**Code**_Data Sample and then Analyse_Process_Data Sample?
DL Query: Person and hasActivityType some {CollectData, Edit_Code_Data Sample, Analyse_Process_Data Sample}
== the query computes and check if person Paul does the activity {Collect Data, Edit_Code_Data Sample, Analyse_Process_Data Sample}

DQ8. Does Person P have Activity at least value of 3?
  Example: Does Person (Danny) Activity at least three?
DL Query: Person and hasActivity Type min 3
== computes the Persons in the Model with a minimum of three Activities and compare if the result is equal to Person Danny

DQ9. Who performs Learning Task T?
  Example: What are the different category of performers of a Learning Task in the **Mod**el?
DL Query: Performer and isPerformerOf some ActivityConcept
  Or simply execute Role because of the SWRL description (**as exp**lained in the next section)
  Role (?x) -> Lane (?x) which describes that if there exists a Role then it is also a Lane.
== the executed query and SWRL rule compute and checks for various category of Persons in the Model that performs a Learning task. Performer has been described also as a Person by the SWRL Rule: Performer (?x) -> Person (?x)

DQ10. Does Person P perform Learning Task T?

Example: Which Persons Performs a role as Institution Tutor?

DL Query: Person and hasRole value InstitutionTutor

== computes the persons in the model that has a role as an Institution Tutor

DQ11. Does person P the first Milestone?

Example: Does person Clare the first Milestone (Define Topic Area)?

DL Query: Person and hasActivityType some DefineTopicArea

== compares the Persons of the First Milestone DefineTopicArea for the individual Clare i.e., checks if the persons of the first Milestone equals Clare thus if an activity of the first Milestone is done by person Clare.

DQ12. Does Person P the second Milestone?

Example: Does person Ben the Second Milestone (Review Literature)?

DL Query: Person and hasActivityType some ReviewLiterature

== checks if the persons of the second Milestone equals Ben, i.e., compares the Persons of the second Milestone ReviewLiterature with Ben, thus if an activity of the second Milestone (Review Literature) is done by person Ben.

DQ13. Does person P the Third Milestone?

Example: Does Paul the Third Milestone (Address Problem)?

DL Query: Person and hasActivityType some AddressProblem

== compares the Persons of the Third Milestone with Paul i.e., Checks if the persons of the Third Milestone equals Paul, thus if an activity of the Third Milestone DefendSolution is done by person Paul?

DQ14. Does person P the Last Milestone?

Example: Does person Danny the Last Milestone (Defend Solution)?

DL Query: Person and hasActivityType some DefendSolution

== computes and check if the result of Persons in the Last Milestone DefendSolution is equal to person Danny i.e., compares the Persons of the Last Milestone with Danny, thus if an activity of the Last Milestone (Defend Solution) is performed by person Danny?

DQ15. For all Activities always Event E implies eventually Event F?

Example: For all Activities always Event (End) implies eventually Event (Start)

DL Query: Event and hasSuccessor some Start

== describes and computes that - Hold for **all activi**ties that if event End occurs, then eventually event Start occurs too. We use this to define the Start and End of each Milestone in the Model e.g., we define that = Every DefineTopicArea is a ResearchProcess that isKindOf a Milestone and hasEndOfProcess EndDefineTopic and hasStartOfProcess StartResearchProcess.

It is possible to then ask: Does the End of a Milestone eventually means the Start of the next Milestone too?

The following Question 16 below answers this query

DQ16. Eventually Event E and then F?

Example: Eventually EndDefineTopic and then **StartReviewLitProcess?**
DL Query: Event and hasSuccessor value StartReviewLitProcess
== checks and compa**res that** the End of the DefineTopicArea during the research process execution process means the Start of the next milestone ReviewLiterature.

DQ17. Finally Person P?
Example: List all the Persons that performs an Activity **in t**he Research Process?
DL Query: Person and hasActivityType some ResearchProcess
== computes any Pe**rson P th**at is a performer of a Learning Task within the Model. This can also be described using the SWRL rule as explained in the next section of this chapter:
Person (?Performer), hasActivityType (?Perfomer, ?ActivityConcept), isPerformerOf (?ActivityConcept, ?Role) -> isPartOfResearch Process (?Performer, ?Role)
== the SWRL rule describes that any person that performs a Learning Activity is then automatically part of the Research Process.

SEMANTIC WEB RULE LANGUAGE (SWRL)

The Semantic Web Rule Language (SWRL) (Horrocks, et al., 2004; Bechhofer, et al., 2004) extends the Owl Description Logics (DL) with "rules" whilst supporting the existing semantics or sentence structures (syntax) in the predefined ontologies. According to Horrocks et al (2004), SWRL combines

Owl DL ontologies with Rule Markup Language (RML). Moreover, Yarandi (2013) also notes that:

- **Semantically:** SWRL rules derive formal meanings through the extension of the Owl DL model-theoretic semantics, and
- **Syntactically:** SWRL is based on the Owl XML representation syntax (Horrocks et al. 2004).

In theory, we note that the semantic web rule language (SWRL) format trails to add new set(s) of axiom to the Owl DL ontologies which includes a horn-like rule (i.e. First order logic) (Wang & Kim, 2006) or better *still an* Association Rule Learning (Han, et al., 2011; Okoye, et al., 2016; Ok*oye, et al., 2014) syntax* or arrangement that tends to throw more light or broaden the semantics and formal structures of ontologies.

In practice, the SWRL rules are useful to increases the expressiveness of Owl ontologies (Yarandi, 2013; Bechhofer, et al., 2004). Moreover, Vassileva & Bontchev (2009) notes that many selections of rule-engines could be utilized when applying the SWRL rules. This is owing to the fact that SWRL rules do not forcefully state (i.e. restrictions) on how the reasoning process has to be executed. For instance, the universalClass or equivalentClass that can be applied to determine if an expression within the ontology is true or false, but nevertheless, this is where the SWRL function is of paramount as it does not decide how such restrictions should be performed, but rather extends the axioms (facts) by adding rules to the already pre-defined assertions within the ontologies.

For all intents and purposes, this work assumes that a SWRL enriched ontology model comprises of a mixture of Owl concepts and rules, for instance, as described in the developed learning model in this book.

1) ResearchProcess(?x) -> LearningWorkflowWithBPMN(?x)
2) Performer(?x) -> Person(?x)
3) Person(?Performer), hasActivityType(?Performer, ?ActivityConcept), isPerformerOf(?ActivityConcept, ?Role) -> isPartOfResearchProcess (?Performer, ?Role)
4) ProcessType(?x) -> PerformerActivity(?x)
5) Start(?start) -> DateTimeDuration(?start)
6) End(?end) -> DateTimeDuration(?end)
7) isActivityTypeOf(?x, ?y), isRoleOf(?y, ?z) -> isSubProcessOf(?x, ?y)

8) hasDefaultFlow(?Exclusive, ?SequenceFlow) ->
   hasSuccessor(?Exclusive, ?SequenceFlow)
9) hasConditionalFlow(?Exclusive, ?SequenceFlow) ->
   hasSuccessor(?Exclusive, ?SequenceFlow)
10) Exclusive(?x) -> Condition(?x)
11) Role(?x) -> Lane(?x)
12) LearningWorkflowWithBPMN(?x) -> Pool(?x)
13) hasActivityType(?x, ?y), hasRole(?Role, ?z) -> belongToPool(?Role, ?z)

As demonstrated in the examples of SWRL rules 1 to 13: the SWRL syntax are of the form:

Antecedent | Consequent (written as a1 ^ a2 ^::: ^ an)

This is otherwise also referred to as the horn-like rule; where the Antecedent represents the *body and* the Consequent *represents* the head.

Thus, *a* typical SW*RL Syntax is as follows:*

atom ^ atom .... → atom ^atom

Perhaps, the Antecedent and Consequent can consist of multipl*e atoms or* stil*l be empty.*

Technically, atoms are syntactically expressed in the following form (Yarandi, 2013):

- C(x) where C is an OWL description and x is an OWL individual variable or a data value.
- P(x; y) where P is an OWL object property and x and y are OWL individual variables or data values.
- Q(x; y) where Q is an OWL data property and x and y are OWL individual variables or data values.
- B(x1; x2;:::) where B is a built-in relation and x1; x2;::: are OWL individual variables or data values.
- sameAs(x, y), differentFrom(x, y) where x, y are OWL individual variables or data values.

In general, the informal meaning of any rule (rule of thumb) e.g. the SWRL rule states that: whenever a condition defined in the Antec*edent hol*ds, then all condition(s) *stated in t*he Conse*quen*t must also hold. Apparently, su*ch conditi*ons (or set of rules) are similar to the Association Rule Learning (Han, et al., 2011; Okoye, et al., 2014) also used to describe event logs and/or data mining methods to perform a contextual process analysis (mining). Therefore:

IF (X) THEN (Y)

Where:

X = Antecedent (e.g. learning pattern) and Y = Consequent (e.g. the pattern extension)

In turn, the following rule expressions SQ1 to SQ6 are some example of the SWRL rule and syntax that are defined within the learning model ontologies used in this book. Apparently, we create and provde the SWRL rules to associate the existing domain ontologies and/or underlying entities (classes and individuals) with the right concepts. This is done in order to automatically infer the whole ontology. Thus, from the definitions in the SWRL rules (SQ1 to SQ6), this work describes some of the capabilities and functionalities of the SWRL rules (implemented in the resultant semantic model) as follows:

SQ1. Person (?Performer), hasActivityType (?Perfomer, ?ActivityConcept), isPerformerOf (?ActivityConcept, ?Role) -> isPartOfResearch Process (?Performer, ?Role)
== this Rule describes that any person that performs a Learning Activity classified as a Role is then automatically part of the Research Process.

SQ2. hasDefaultFlow (?Exclusive, ?SequenceFlow) -> hasSuccessor (?Exclusive, ?Sequence Flow)
== describes that if there exists a Default flow for an Exclusive gateway then this flow is also a Successor i.e. If X hasDefaultFlows Y then Y is DefaultFlowOf s X.

SQ3. Research Process (?x) -> Learning Workflow With BPMN (?x)
== describes that if there exists a Research process then it is automatically a Learning Workflow

SQ4. LearningWorkflowWithBPMN **(?x)** -> Pool (?x)
== describes that if there exists a Learning Workflow then it is also a Pool

SQ5. Role (?x) -> Lane (?x)
== describes that if there exists a Role then it is also a Lane

SQ6. hasActivityType (?x, ?ActivityConcept), hasRole (?ActivityConcept, ?Role) -> belongToPool (?x, ?Role)
== describes that if there exists a learning activity which is performed under a particular Role, then this activity belongs to the pool of that Role. The role has also been described as a Lane.

CONCLUSION

The work presents in this chapter, the technique for annotation of the process models discovered as a result of applying the process mining technique on the readily available datasets. At first, the chapter looks at how it determines the equivalence between the concepts of the learning process models (or events logs) and the concepts of the defined domain ontologies. This is followed by an introduction of the main functions and descriptive properties of the ontological concepts as utilized for the work in this book. Perhaps, ontologies make use of process descriptions languages to provide additional new functions that allow for the semantic reasoning, otherwise referred to as the automated classification of the process elements to follow. We note that without an automated classification process (semantic reasoning) it may become logically challenging to manage the different ontologies that make up the semantic models, especially when managing the manifold existence of entities and concepts defined within the ontologies (see: chapter 2). The Description Logic queries are also presented in this chapter as one of the many process description languages that can be used to check for consistency for all defined entities or associations within the ontologies (semantic model). In addition, the work also describes in detail the SWRL rules and syntax which are necessarily used to increases the expressiveness and formal meaning of the ontologies. In a nutshell, the work has described in this chapter how the main components of the SPMaAF approach and algorithms as described earlier in Chapters 3 and 4 fit and rely on each other in carrying out the semantic enhancement of the discovered process models. This includes a description of the different tools and technologies that enable its implementation for real-time processing or analysis.

REFERENCES

Baader, F. (2003). Description Logic H*andbook: theory, implementation, and applications (1st ed.). New York*, NY: Cambridge University Press.

Bechhofer, S. (2004). OWL Web Ontology *Language Reference. Manchester, UK*: Technical report W3C Proposed Recommendation.

Gu"nther, C. W., & Van der Aalst, W. M. P. (2006). A generic import framework for process event logs. In J. Eder & S. Dustdar (Eds.), Business Pro*cess Management Workshops (pp. 81–92).* Berlin: Springer. doi:10.1007/11837862_10

Günther, C. W., & Van der Aalst, W. M. P. (2007). Fuzzy Mining – Adaptive Process Simplification Based on Multi-perspective Metrics. Business Process Management. BPM 2007, 328-343.

Han, J., Kamber, M., & Pei, J. (2011). Data Mi*ning: Concepts and Techniques (3rd* ed.). Burlington, MA: The Morgan Kaufmann Series in Data Management Systems, Morgan Kaufmann Publishers.

Horrocks, I. (2004). SWRL*: A Semantic Web Rule Language Combining OWL and RuleML. Net*work Inference, Canada and Stanford University: W3C Member Submission - 2004 National Research Council of Canada, Network Inference, and Stanford University.

Kumar, A. P., Abhishek, K., & Vipin Kumar, N. (2011). Architecting and Designing of Semantic Web Based Application using the JENA and PROTÉGÉ – A Comprehensive Study. *International Journal of Computer Science and Information Technologies, 2*(3), 1279–1282.

Musen, M. A. (2015). The Protégé project: A look back and a look forward. AI Matters. *AI Matters, 1*(4), 4–12. doi:10.1145/2757001.2757003 PMID:27239556

Okoye, K. (2016). Using semantic-based approach to manage perspectives of process mining: Application on improving learning process domain data. *Proceedings of 2016 IEEE International Conference on Big Data (Big Data)*, 3529-3538.

Okoye, K., Tawil, A. R. H., Naeem, U., & Lamine, E. (2014). A Semantic Rule-based Approach Supported by Process Mining for Personalised Adaptive Learning. *Procedia Computer Science*, *37*(C), 203–210. doi:10.1016/j.procs.2014.08.031

Okoye, K., Tawil, A. R. H., Naeem, U. & Lamine, E. (2016). Discovery and Enhancement of Learning Model Analysis through Semantic Process Mining. *International Journal of Computer Information Systems and Industrial Management Applications, 8*(2016), 93-114.

Rozinat, A., & Gunther, C. (2012). Disco User Guide - Process Mining for Professionals. Eindhoven, The Netherlands: Fluxicon.com.

Schreiber, G. (2005). *OWL restrictions*. Amsterdam: Department of Computer Science, VU University.

Semantic Web Primer. (2012). Introducing RDFS & OWL. Cambridge, UK: Linked Data Tools.

Van der Aalst, W. M. P. (2011). *Process Mining: Discovery, Conformance and Enhancement of Business Processes* (1st ed.). Berlin: Springer. doi:10.1007/978-3-642-19345-3

Van der Aalst, W. M. P. (2016). *Process Mining: Data Science in Action* (2nd ed.). Springer-Verlag Berlin Heildelberg. doi:10.1007/978-3-662-49851-4

Van der Aalst, W. M. P., Weijters, A. J. M. M. & Maruster, L. (2004). Workflow Mining: Discovering Process Models from Event Logs. *International Journal of IEEE transactions on Knowledge and Data Engineering, 16*(9), 1128-1142.

Vassileva, D., & Bontchev, B. (2009). Adaptation engine construction based on formal rules. *Proceedings of the First International Conference on Computer Supported Education*, 1, 326-331.

Wang, E., & Kim, Y. S. (2006). A Teaching Strategies Engine Using Translation from SWRL to Jess. *Proceedings of the 8th international conference on Intelligent Tutoring Systems, ITS'06*, 51-60. 10.1007/11774303_6

Yarandi, M. (2013). *Semantic Rule-based Approach for Supporting Personalised Adaptive E-Learning* (PhD thesis). London, UK: University of East London.

Chapter 6
Experimental Setup and Case Study Example

ABSTRACT

This chapter represents as a practical follow-up or implementation of the main components of the SPMaAF described in Chapter 5. In the experimental setup, the chapter demonstrates by using the case study of the learning process: the development and application of the semantic-based process mining. Essentially, the chapter looks at how the proposed semantic-based process mining and analysis framework (SPMaAF) is applied to answer real-time questions about any given process domain, as well as the classification of the individual process instances or elements that constitutes process models. This includes the semantic representations and modelling of the learning process in order to allow for an abstraction analysis of the resultant models. The chapter finalizes with a conceptual description of the resultant semantic fuzzy mining approach which is discussed in detail in the next chapter.

USE CASE SCENARIO OF THE LEARNING PROCESS

The case study utilized in this book is based on the running example of the Research Learning Process domain (introduced earlier in the examples given in chapters 2, 3, 4 and 5 – particularly in the beginning of chapter 5). Technically, the work makes use of the events log about the research learning process to demonstrate the real-time application and modelling of the learning

DOI: 10.4018/978-1-7998-2668-2.ch006

process. This included the method applied to resolve the different learning questions/analysis problems, as well as, used in validation of the experiments.

Typically, in the case study example, the work shows that the first step to conducting a *research* is to decide on what to investigate (i.e. developing the research topic) and then go about finding answers to the research questions. At the end of the research process, the researcher is expected to be awarded a certificate. In theory, this process(es) involves the workflow of the journey from choosing the research topic to being awarded a certificate, and comprises of a sequence of practical steps or set(s) of activities through which must be performed in order to find answers to the research questions.

Indeed, the workflow for those steps are not static, it changes as the researcher travels along the research process. Besides, at each phase or milestone of the process, the researcher(s) is required to complete a variety of learning activities which are intended to help and/or directed towards achieving the research goal. Moreover, when considering the available process logs and/or from the process mining perspective; the derived process models may not disclose (or in some cases inadvertently disclose) to the process analysts some of the valuable information at the abstraction (semantic) levels, despite all of the visualizations (process mappings) from mining the said process(es). For instance, the process maps may not disclose how the individual process instances that make up the resultant model interact or differ from each other, and/or which attributes they share amongst themselves within the knowledge base, or the activities the instances perform together or differently. As a result, questions like - who are the individuals that have successfully completed the research process? may not be established. For this reason, this book shows that by adding semantic knowledge to the deployed models that it then becomes possible to determine and address the identified learning questions or problem.

To explicate such tactics, we assume that for a research process to be classified as *successful*, it is necessary that the researcher must complete a given set(s) of milestones (ranging from Defining the Topic Area –to- Review Literature –and- Addressing the Problem –and then- Defending the Solution) in order to be awarded the degree or certificate (Okoye et al, 2016), as demonstrated in the Figures 2 to 6 in Chapter 5. However, in any case, whereby the researcher has not completed the set(s) of milestones that are necessary to ensure the research outcome, the learner(s) can be classified as *incomplete*. Therefore, given such a method, it becomes possible to logically ascertain which set(s)of individuals that have successfully completed the research process or not.

In summary, the case study of this book focuses on the use case scenario of the *successful* and *uncomplete* learners to demonstrate the capability of the proposed SPMaAF framework, the different sets of semantically motivated algorithms, and the resultant semantic fuzzy mining approach. Essentially, the case study example is used to show how to perform analysis of the different learning activities log based on concepts rather than the event tags or labels about the processes in question. In turn, presenting the process mining results at a more conceptual level. The method used for the representations and/ or conceptual analysis of the process models is explained in detail in the following section.

SEMANTIC REPRESENTATIONS AND MODELLING OF THE LEARNING PROCESS DOMAIN

In this section, the work applies semantic representations to determine the different patterns or behaviours that describes/distinguishes certain entities within the learning knowledge base from another. Thus, the method is used to recognize (determine) what attributes/paths the learners (i.e. process instances) have in common or follow, or what attributes distinguish the successful learners from the uncomplete ones.

Indeed, the purpose of the semantic representations is not only to answer the specified questions by making use the ontologies or semantic modelling approaches but to show how by referring to the attributes (concepts) and the application of semantic reasoning, it becomes easy to refer to particular cases (e.g. certain group of learners) within the underlying knowledge-base. For instance, the analysis of this book which is focused on the use case scenario of the *Successful* and *Uncomplete* learners.

Accordingly, we note that the workflow of the research process from the definition of the research topic to being awarded a certificate; consists of different learning steps that a researcher has to or partly perform in order to complete the research process. To this end, the work provides the following milestones; Establish Context → Learning Stage → Assessment Stage → Validation of Learning Outcome (see: Chapter 5) in order to establish and explain the steps taken during the research process. In other words, from

Defining the Topic Area –to- Review Literature –and- Addressing the Problem –then- Defending the Solution.

Technically, the following steps (or milestones) consists of different set(s) or sequence of activities, and we also note that the order in which the individual learning activities are carried out has the capability of determining the research outcome. Henceforth, as represented in the following figure (Figure 1) the work shows the Learning Activities concepts that are defined within the learning model created for the purpose of this work, and how they are mapped to the various milestones of the Research Process. Perhaps, this is done in order to ensure the sequence of transitions during the entire learning process.

Accordingly, the following figures (Figures 1 to 5) represents the different four milestones of the research process as defined within the learning model (ontologies), and the resulting activity concepts and relations mapping (OntoGraph) between the process instances (entities) that can be found within the resultant semantic model.

Ultimately, as represented in the figures (Figures 1 to 5), the drive for the semantically-focused mapping of the learning activities concepts is that the method allows the meaning of the learning objects and properties to be enhanced through the use of property description languages (e.g OWL and

Figure 1. The Research Learning Process Domain with a description of the Learning activity concepts (milestones)

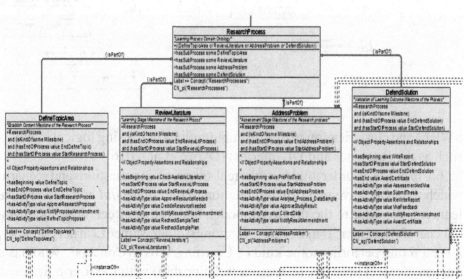

Figure 2. Learning ActivityConcept mapping (Ontograph) for the DefineTopicArea Milestone

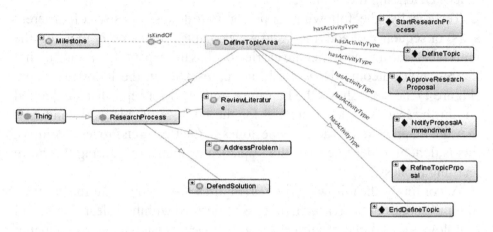

Figure 3. Learning ActivityConcept mapping (Ontograph) for the ReviewLiterature Milestone

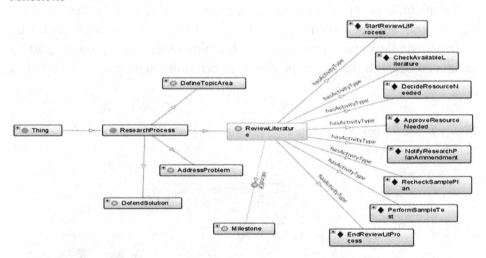

SWRL) and classification of discoverable entities (e.g. using logical methods such as the Reasoner and DL queries) (Okoye et al, 2016).

For instance, in order to address the real-time learning questions and scenario which the work have identified in relation to the *successful* and *uncomplete* learners. We refer to the deployed model, and to this effect, describe that a "Successful Learner" is a subclass of, amongst other NamedLearnerCategory, a Person that performs some kind of LearningActivityConcepts, who has a universal object property restriction (relationship) with the four milestones

Figure 4. Learning ActivityConcept mapping (Ontograph) for the AddressProblem Milestone

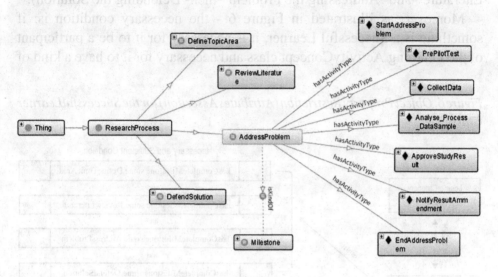

Figure 5. Learning ActivityConcept mapping (Ontograph) for the DefendSolution Milestone

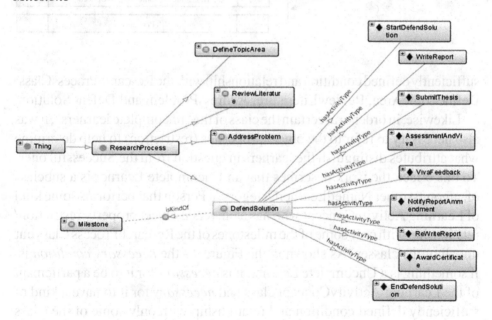

of the ResearchProcessClass (i.e. from Defining the Topic Area –to– Review Literature –and– Addressing the Problem –then– Defending the Solution).

Moreover, as illustrated in Figure 6 - the necessary condition is: if something is a Successful Learner, it is necessary for it to be a participant of the Learning ActivityConcept class and necessary for it to have a kind of

Figure 6. Object Property Restriction (Attributes Assertion) for the SuccessfulLearner Class

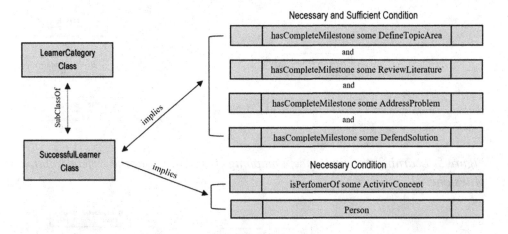

sufficiently defined condition and relationship with the ResearchProcessClass: DefineTopicArea, ReviewLiterature, AddressProblem and DefendSolution.

Likewise, in order to ascertain the class of the "uncomplete learners", it was also necessary to refer to the object properties (restriction) to help determine what attributes distinguish the learners in question from the Successful ones. To this effect, the work describes that an Uncomplete Learner is a subclass of, amongst other NamedLearnerCategory, a Person that performs some kind of Learning ActivityConcept who has a universal object property restriction/relationship with only some of the milestones of the ResearchProcess Class but not all of the classes. As shown in the Figure 7 - the *necessary condition* is: if something is a Uncomplete Learner, it is *necessary* for it to be a participant of the Learning ActivityConcept class and *necessary* for it to have a kind of sufficiently defined condition and relationship with only some of the Class e.g. DefineTopicArea, ReviewLiterature, AddressProblem but not all of the four classes.

Ideally, as gathered in the figures (Figures 6 and 7) we note that the *Object* and/or *Data Property Restrictions* are used to infer anonymous classes that contain all of the individuals that logically satisfy the restriction. In essence, all of the individuals who have the necessary characteristics or association rule description (Okoye et al, 2016) required to be a participant or member of a specific class. For instance, the definitions (or assertions) used to express the *successful* and *uncomplete* learner classes. Perhaps, the consequence is the *necessary* and *sufficient* condition which makes it possible to implement in a logical manner the different taxonomies (i.e. class hierarchies) and to check for consistency within the underlying model. In other words, it means that it is necessary to fulfill the condition of the *universal* or *existential* restrictions by definition for any individual to become a member of the specified class.

Figure 7. Object Property Restriction (Attributes Assertion) for the UncompleteLearner Class

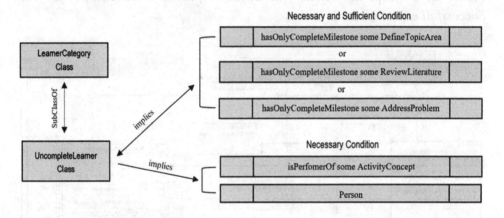

For example, as this work has used to define the characteristics (properties) of the Successful and Uncomplete learners class in this section of the book.

In fact, it is important to note that the *properties restrictions* as referred to in this book - are used to provide a structured organization (taxonomies) and to support the semantic labelling (annotation) process for the discovered models. Indeed, the method serves as a good practice for representation of the learning process information by providing a formal way of determining the individual process instances that constitutes the process knowledge base.

For example, the following Figure 8 and 9 are a typical description of the implemented *concepts* and the resultant *axioms* as defined within the learning model ontology. Thus, the definitions in Figure 8 including the associated

OWL XML file syntax used to ascertain the "successful learners" class is as follows:

SuccessfulLearner Class:

1: **ontology** ResearchProcess
2: **concept** SuccessfulLearner
3: hascompleteMilestone **ofType** {DefineTopicArea, ReviewLiterature, AddressProblem, DefendSolution}
4: isPerformerOf **some** LearningActivity
5: is **ofType** Person
6: hasInstance **members** {Mattew, Isaac}
7: **axiom** DefinitionOfSuccessfulLearner

Figure 8. Concept assertions (the different formal relationships) for the SuccessfulLearner Class

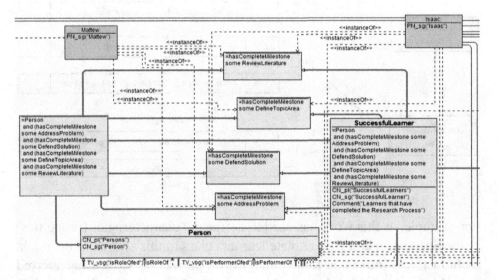

```
<EquivalentClasses>
        <Annotation>
                <AnnotationProperty IRI="http://attempto.ifi.uzh.
ch/acetext#acetext"/>
                <Literal datatypeIRI="&xsd;string">Every
SuccessfulLearner is a Person that hasMilestones an
AddressProblem and that hasMilestones a DefendSolution and
that hasMilestones a DefineTopicArea and that hasMilestones
a ReviewLiterature. Every Person that hasMilestones an
```

```
AddressProblem and that hasMilestones a DefendSolution and
that hasMilestones a DefineTopicArea and that hasMilestones a
ReviewLiterature is a SuccessfulLearner.</Literal>
        </Annotation>
        <Annotation>
            <AnnotationProperty IRI="http://purl.org/dc/
elements/1.1/date"/>
            <Literal datatypeIRI="&xsd;string">2016-04-1
13:40:36</Literal>
        </Annotation>
        <Class IRI="#SuccessfulLearner"/>
        <ObjectIntersectionOf>
            <Class IRI="#Person"/>
            <ObjectSomeValuesFrom>
                <ObjectProperty IRI="#hasCompleteMilestone"/>
                <Class IRI="#AddressProblem"/>
            </ObjectSomeValuesFrom>
            <ObjectSomeValuesFrom>
                <ObjectProperty IRI="#hasCompleteMilestone"/>
                <Class IRI="#DefendSolution"/>
            </ObjectSomeValuesFrom>
            <ObjectSomeValuesFrom>
                <ObjectProperty IRI="#hasCompleteMilestone"/>
                <Class IRI="#DefineTopicArea"/>
            </ObjectSomeValuesFrom>
            <ObjectSomeValuesFrom>
                <ObjectProperty IRI="#hasCompleteMilestone"/>
                <Class IRI="#ReviewLiterature"/>
            </ObjectSomeValuesFrom>
        </ObjectIntersectionOf>
    </EquivalentClasses>
```

On the other hand, the work provides an example description of the implemented *concepts* and *axioms* for the "uncomplete learner class" within the learning model ontology. Thus, the following definitions in Figure 9 including the associated OWL XML file syntax is used to ascertain the uncomplete learners class as follows:

Uncomplete Learner Class:
 1:   **ontology** ResearchProcess
 2:   **concept** UncompleteLearner
 3:   hasOnlycompleteMilestone **ofType** {DefineTopicArea, Or ReviewLiterature, Or AddressProblem, Not DefendSolution}
 4:   isPerformerOf **some** LearningActivity
 5:   is **ofType** Person

177

6:   hasInstance **members** {Paul, Danny, Mark, Gregory, John}
7:   **axiom** DefinitionOfUncompleteLearner

Figure 9. Concept assertions (the different formal relationships) for the UncompleteLearner Class

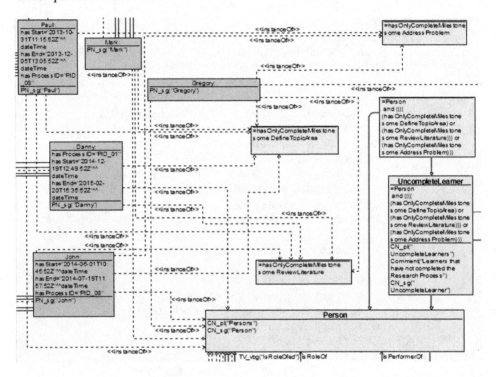

```
<EquivalentClasses>
      <Annotation>
            <AnnotationProperty IRI="http://attempto.ifi.uzh.
ch/acetext#acetext"/>
            <Literal datatypeIRI="&xsd;string">Every
UncompleteLearner is a Person that onlyHaveMilestones an
AddressProblem or that onlyHaveMilestones a DefineTopicArea or
that onlyHaveMilestones a ReviewLiterature. Every Person that
onlyHaveMilestones an AddressProblem or that onlyHaveMilestones
a DefineTopicArea or that onlyHaveMilestones a ReviewLiterature
is an UncompleteLearner.</Literal>
      </Annotation>
      <Annotation>
            <AnnotationProperty IRI="http://purl.org/dc/
elements/1.1/date"/>
```

```
            <Literal datatypeIRI="&xsd;string">2016-04-19
13:40:23</Literal>
        </Annotation>
        <Annotation>
            <AnnotationProperty abbreviatedIRI="rdfs:comment"/>
            <IRI>#UncompleteLearner</IRI>
        </Annotation>
        <Class IRI="#UncompleteLearner"/>
        <ObjectIntersectionOf>
            <Class IRI="#Person"/>
            <ObjectUnionOf>
                <ObjectUnionOf>
                    <ObjectSomeValuesFrom>
                        <ObjectProperty IRI="#hasOnlyCompleteMi
lestone"/>
                        <Class IRI="#DefineTopicArea"/>
                    </ObjectSomeValuesFrom>
                    <ObjectSomeValuesFrom>
                        <ObjectProperty IRI="#hasOnlyCompleteMi
lestone"/>
                        <Class IRI="#ReviewLiterature"/>
                    </ObjectSomeValuesFrom>
                </ObjectUnionOf>
                <ObjectSomeValuesFrom>
                    <ObjectProperty IRI="#hasOnlyCompleteMiles
tone"/>
                    <Class IRI="#AddressProblem"/>
                </ObjectSomeValuesFrom>
            </ObjectUnionOf>
        </ObjectIntersectionOf>
    </EquivalentClasses>
```

CONCLUSION

The work represents in this chapter, the case study example of the Learning process which it uses to implement the semantic-based process mining approach (SPMaAF) proposed in this book. Typically, the chapter describes the various concepts (e.g. the learning activities) that makes up the learning process, as well as, demonstrate how the classification of the individual process instances (or traces) that constitute the event logs and/or the discovered process models is done. Consequently, to show the real-time application of the method, the work refers to the use case scenario of the Successful and Uncomplete learners class (see: Figures 8 and 9) that can be found within the learning model ontologies or process knowledge-base. Technically, the process is performed (i.e. the definition of the different process instances) through the use of ontological representation and modelling of the learning process using the semantic schema and/or technologies such as the OWL (see: chapter 5). Over the next chapter (Chapter 7), the work looks at the application of the (semantic-based) process mining approach in real-time. The experimental analysis is carried out not only to show how the method of this book is applied in different settings for process mining, but also, to show how we apply the method for the implementation of the semantic fuzzy mining approach introduced in this book.

REFERENCES

Okoye, K. (2016). Using semantic-based approach to manage perspectives of process mining: Application on improving learning process domain data. *Proceedings of 2016 IEEE International Conference on Big Data (Big Data)*, 3529-3538.

Okoye, K., Tawil, A. R. H., Naeem, U., & Lamine, E. (2016). A Semantic Reasoning Method Towards Ontological Model for Automated Learning Analysis. *Proceedings of NaBIC Conference*, 49-60. 10.1007/978-3-319-27400-3_5

Chapter 7
Process Mining With Semantics:
Real–Time Processing and Application

ABSTRACT

This chapter contains the application of the semantic process mining approach in real-time. This includes the series of analysis that were performed not only to show how the method is applied in different scenarios or settings for process mining purposes, but also how to technically apply the method for semantic process mining tasks. In the first section, the work shows how the authors practically apply the current tools that supports the process mining through its participation in the Process Discovery Contest organised by the IEEE CIS Task Force on Process Mining. In the second section, the chapter shows how it expounds the results and amalgamation of the two process mining techniques, namely fuzzy miner and business process modelling notation (BPMN) approach, in order to demonstrate the capability of the proposed semantic-based fuzzy miner being able to perform a more conceptual and accurate classification of the individual traces within the process or input models.

DOI: 10.4018/978-1-7998-2668-2.ch007

FUZZY-BPMN MINING APPROACH

In this section, the work shows how we practically apply the current tools that support the process mining through participation in the First Process Discovery Contest (Carmona, et al., 2016) organized by the IEEE CIS Task Force on Process Mining (IEEE CIS Task Force on Process Mining, 2016; Van der Aalst, et al., 2012). In theory, the IEEE group has introduced the contest to foster scientific research within the area of process mining with the primary aim of promoting the techniques and its main applications in real-world settings. According to Carmona, et al (2016) the process mining contest is dedicated to the assessment of tools and methods that discover business process models from the event logs. Accordingly, a number of event logs were provided for the purpose of the different analysis by the group (Carmona, et al., 2016). Typically, the provided events log were generated from business process models that show different behavioral characteristics. The main objective is to compare the efficiency of the different techniques that can discover fitting process models, that in turn, are capable of providing a proper balance between "overfitting" and "underfitting" models. In other words, the discovered models are seen as *overfitting* (the event log) if it is too restrictive by disallowing behaviours which are part of the underlying process. On the other hand, the model is considered as *underfitting* (the reality) if it is not restrictive enough by allowing behaviours which are not part of the underlying process. Thus:

- Given a trace (t) representing real process behaviour, the process model (m) classifies it as allowed, or
- Given a trace (t) representing a behaviour not related to the process, the process model (m) classifies it as disallowed (Carmona, et al., 2016)

Moreover, each of the test event logs precisely ((*test_log_april_1* to *test_log_april_10*) and (*test_log_may_1* to *test_log_may_10*)) which can be found in (Carmona, et al., 2016) represents part of the original model that was not initially revealed for the purpose of the analysis. Also, the *test logs* with a complete total of 20 traces for each log are considered to consist of 10 traces which are replayable (*allowed*) and another 10 traces which are not replayable (*disallowed*) by the model. Therefore, the total number of traces for the test logs is distributed as follows:

10 test logs x 20 traces which equals to a total of = 200 Traces for each of the *April log* and *May log* respectively

The aim of the resultant analysis as represented in this section is to carry out a classification task to determine the individual traces that make up the two test event logs, as well as, establish their fitness within the original model as follows:

To do this, firstly, the work discovers the set of 10 process models from the *training sets* (Carmona, et al., 2016) using the Fuzzy miner (G¨unther, 2009; Günther & Van der Aalst, 2007; Rozinat & Gunther, 2012) and then second, make use of the Business Process Modelling Notations (BPMN) (Van der Aalst, 2016) to analyse and provide the replaying semantics for each of the process models. The details about the 10 different process models that are discovered using the method is described in Okoye et al (2016 & 2017) and are provided in the Appendix A section of this book.

Furthermore, the work performs a classification task for the *test set* (Carmona, et al., 2016), to generate the various cases (traces) that make up each of the process executions. Again, the work summarises in this section how it generates the 20 individual traces for each of the test logs including the sequence of the activity executions for each of the individual traces. Further details about the classification method and the results are also provided in Okoye et al (2016 & 2017).

It is important to note that the *data set* that has been provided for the process discovery contest (Carmona, et al., 2016) contains the typical information needed to perform the implementation of the Fuzzy-BPMN miner as well as the proposed Semantic-Fuzzy mining approach in this book. Basically, we presume that each of the events log are set(s) of data that are related to a single process. Perhaps, a single process refers to some trace (*Case*) and can be related to some *Activity*. Likewise, the events log in question contains two attributes *case_id* and *act_name* which precisely specify the minimal requirements that are required (or allows) for implementing the Fuzzy-BPMN approach following the definition 4.1 in Van der Aalst (2011). To this end, this work assumes the following standard:

- #*case_id*(e) is the identifier or case associated with an event *e*.
- #*act_name*(e) is the activity associated to event *e*.

Indeed, the standard definitions above were necessary because, for the employed approach (Fuzzy-BPMN), the activities play an important role in terms of the discovered models and thus tend to correspond to the individual cases within the discovered fuzzy models. Moreover, as there are multiple *events* that refer to similar *Activities*, we support the filtering of the 200 individual traces that make up the test event logs with a *classifier* (Van der Aalst, 2016).

Therefore, if we make use of the notation *e* to refer to the different event within the logs, then the classifier for any event in the given log is represented as follows:

$e \in \mathcal{E}$, where *e* is the name of the event in view

Accordingly, since the events are solely recognized by the corresponding activities name (*act_name*), we then formerly assume that:

$e = \#act\_name(e)$

Hence, *if* we apply the classification conversion of the event logs provided in Carmona et al (2016), i.e., Simple Event Log which are explained in detail in Definition 4.4 of (Van der Aalst, 2011) to obtain the Log.

Then, the described events log definition: Let A be a set of *act_name* implies that a single trace σ is a sequence of activities, i.e., $\sigma \in A^*$. Where the simple event Log *L* is a multiset of traces over some set A.

Thus, $L \in \mathbb{B}(A^*)$.

Equally, for the *training log*, there are 1000 cases (traces) that define the log. However, the research focus is to identify the sets of traces (i.e. 200 for *April* and 200 for *May* logs) that characterize the *test events log* for use in validation of the discovered models (i.e. training log).

Perhaps, *if* we Let $L \subseteq C$ be the event logs for the test log, and assuming that the classifier $e \in \mathcal{E}$, is applied to the sets of activities, then the results are a representation of the standard definition 4.5 in (Van der Aalst, 2011)

$$\langle e1, e2, \ldots, en \rangle = \langle e1, e2, \ldots, en \rangle$$

where $L = [(\hat{c}) | c \in L]$ is the simple event log corresponding to the *test log*.

Accordingly, all the Cases (traces) in the *test log* are converted into sequences of the activities (*act_name*) using the classifier. Thus in overall;

- A Case $c \in L$, is an identifier from the case C.
- $\hat{c} = \#trace(c) = e1, e2, ..., en \in \mathcal{E}^*$ is the sequence of events executed for c
- $(\hat{c}) = e1, e2, ..., en$ maps these events onto the activity names (*act_name*) using the classifier.

For instance, from the described classification method ($e = \#act\_name(e)$), we obtain from the logs containing the sequence sets of 200 traces for the test event log (*test_log_april_1* to *test_log_april_10*), i.e., 20 *traces* for each log as follows:

L (test_log_april_1) =
    [⟨*b,g,e,q,h,i,l,r,m,o,d,f,p*⟩,
    ⟨*b,b,c,n,h,e,i,q,r,l,m,f,o,d,p*⟩,
    ⟨*g,h,i,q,q,m,r,o,e,d,p*⟩,
    ⟨*j,a,k,b,b,g,e,h,q,l,r,i,m,d,f,o,p*⟩,
    ⟨*b,g,h,i,q,i,m,o,d,p,f*⟩,
    ⟨*e,e,e,q,h,r,d,o,r,p*⟩,
    ⟨*g,h,e,i,i,q,l,m,o,f,p,d*⟩,
    ⟨*b,a,j,k,g,e,q,h,l,i,r,m,o,f,d,p*⟩,
    ⟨*g,i,e,r,l,i,m,d,o,p,d,p*⟩,
    ⟨*b,b,g,e,l,l,h,q,r,r,r,d,o,o,p,f*⟩,
    ⟨*b,g,e,h,i,q,l,r,m,d,p,o,f*⟩,
    ⟨*b,q,g,h,i,m,m,r,p,f*⟩,
    ⟨*h,g,h,e,r,l,q,i,f,f,p*⟩,
    ⟨*b,j,a,k,g,q,e,i,h,l,r,f,d,o,p*⟩,
    ⟨*c,n,q,e,i,h,r,d,m,o,p,f,p*⟩,
    ⟨*b,g,h,i,e,q,r,l,m,d,o,p,f*⟩,
    ⟨*g,i,h,e,r,q,m,l,o,d,f,p*⟩,
    ⟨*k,b,n,m,c,h,h,e,q,l,q,r,r,i,m,f,f,i,p*⟩,
    ⟨*b,b,b,g,q,i,h,e,r,l,m,f,o,d,p*⟩,
    ⟨*b,b,g,q,e,h,i,r,m,l,d,o,p,f*⟩]

The Log *L* (test_log_april_1) is an example of the set of 20 traces which we obtained for the *test_log_april_1*. Further details of all the classified traces for the complete test logs can be found in Okoye et al (2016 & 2017).

Furthermore, having classified the test event logs using the method described above. The test logs were then imported into Disco (Rozinat & Gunther, 2012) to see in details how the processes have been performed (i.e. process mappings), and more importantly to determine the individual Cases (traces) that makes up the process, as well as, to check if in reality it conforms (i.e. corresponds) with the classified traces. In turn, the results are fuzzy models (see: Appendix A) that represents the various *cases* and *activities sequence* mappings as shown in the example Figure 1.

Figure 1. Case view for the test_log_april_1 showing the 20 cases with an example of case 1 (trace) with 13 events and table showing the set of Activities for trace 1

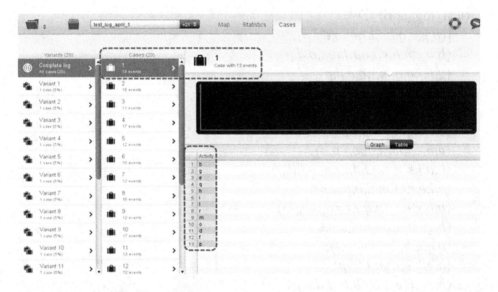

Indeed, the method described here is what the work used to check the results of the classification tasks to see if they conform (test of fitness) to the given event logs. For example, the activities for the first *case* 1 highlighted in the figure (Figure 1) corresponds to the first trace discovered by the classifier, i.e.

L (test_log_april_1) =
$[\langle b,g,e,q,h,i,,l,r,m,o,d,f,p \rangle$, etc.

Accordingly, in view of the trace classifications, the work applies the Fuzzy-BPMN approach to determine the *fitness* (replaying semantics) of the individual traces for the test event logs by cross-validating the classified traces (as represented in the above example) against the discovered process models from the *training logs* (see: Appendix A).

To achieve the set objective (Fuzzy-BPMN approach), it was necessary to construct BPMN models with notational elements (Figure 2) as shown in the example Figure 3 capable of describing the nesting of individual activities (also referred to as *tasks*) by using the event-based split and join gateways - i.e. *AND, XOR,* and *OR* etc. Technically, the BPMN models are an extension of the Fuzzy models. The main purpose is that since our target is to classify as correctly as possible the traces which are allowed and the traces which are not allowed in the original process model, the work makes use of the BPMN event-based gateways to replay the different trace fitness alongside the derived models from the training log. In so doing, we identify which traces that are fitting or not fitting the original model.

Figure 2. BPMN Gateway with Notational elements (Van der Aalst, 2011)

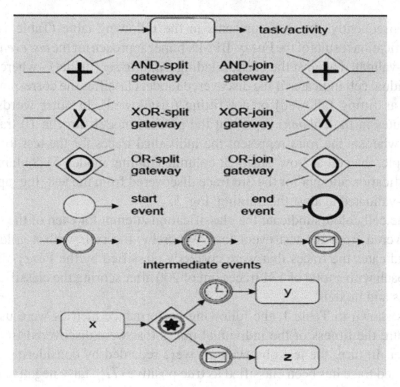

Clearly, an event within the BPMN model may be compared to a place in a Petri-net, and just like Petri nets, are token-based semantics that can be used to replay a particular trace within the discovered process models (Van der Aalst, 2011; Van der Aalst, 2016). For this purpose, the work utilizes the *Convert Petri net to BPMN* plugin in ProM (Verbeek, et al., 2011) to discover the BPMN models for the training logs. Figure 3 is an example of the discovered BPMN Diagram for the *training_log_1*. Further details about the 10 different BPMN models that were discovered using the approach can be found in Okoye et al (2016 & 2017) and are included in the Appendix section (Appendix B) of this book.

Figure 3. Example of the BPMN model discovered for the training_log_1

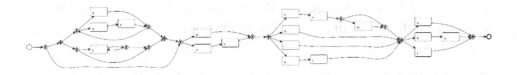

Consequently, the work presents in the following table (Table 1.) the classification results of the Fuzzy-BPMN miner approach for the *test event logs* cross-validated against the corresponding *training set* (model) - where each individual cell indicates if the discovered model classifies the corresponding trace as fitting (allowed) or not fitting (disallowed). In other words, the attributes in the *columns* represent the process models for the 10 training logs, whereas the *rows* represent the individual traces for the test log. For example, the cell at (row Trace_3; column Training model_5) contains the classification attempt for the 3rd trace discovered from the test_log_april_5 cross-validated against the training_log_5.

The cell colours indicate the classification attempt for each of the traces discovered from the test event logs. Whereby, the cells with a gold sign (*) indicates the traces that were correctly classified by the Fuzzy-BPMN approach with a total of 171 traces out of 200 after scoring the classification results and models.

As shown in Table 1, the following performance metrics were used to measure the fitness of the individual traces that were discovered from the dataset. In turn, the test observations were recorded by considering if the specified trace has been classified as true positive (*TP*), false negative (*FN*),

Table 1. Trace Fitness and Classification Table for the Test Event Logs and Models using the Fuzzy-BPMN Miner

	Model 1	Model 2	Model 3	Model 4	Model 5	Model 6	Model 7	Model 8	Model 9	Model 10
Trace_1	TP *	TN *	TP *	FP	TN *	FP	TP *	TP *	TP *	TP *
Trace_2	TN *	TN *	TP *	TP *	TP *	TP *	TP *	TN *	TP *	TP *
Trace_3	TP *	TP *	TP *	TN *	TN *	FP	FP	TP *	TP *	TN *
Trace_4	TP *	TP *	FP	TP *	TN *	TP *	TN *	TP *	TP *	FP
Trace_5	TN *	FP	FP	TP *	TN *	TP *	TN *	TP *	TP *	TN *
Trace_6	TP *	FP	FP	TP *	TN *	TP *	TP *	TN *	TN *	TP *
Trace_7	TN *	TP *	TP *	TN *	TN *	TP *	TN *	TP *	TN *	TN *
Trace_8	TN *	TP *	TP *	FN	TN *	FP	TP *	TP *	TP *	TP *
Trace_9	TP *	TN *	TP *	TN *	TP *	FP	TP *	TP *	TN *	TP *
Trace_10	TP *	FP	TP *	TN *	TN *	FP	TP *	TP *	TP *	TP *
Trace_11	TN *	TP *	TP *	FN	TP *	TN *	TN *	FP	TN *	TP *
Trace_12	TP *	FP	FP	TP *	TP *	TP *	TP *	FP	TP *	TN *
Trace_13	TP *	TP *	FP	TN *	TP *	FP	TN *	TN *	TN *	TP *
Trace_14	TN *	TP *	TN *	TN *	TN *	FP	TN *	TP *	TN *	TP *
Trace_15	TP *	TN *	TN *	TN *	TP *	TP *	TN *	TN *	TN *	TN *
Trace_16	TN *	TN *	FP	TP *	TP *	FP	TN *	FP	TP *	TN *
Trace_17	TP *	TP *	TP *	TP *	TP *	TP *	TP *	TN *	TN *	TP *
Trace_18	TN *	TP *	FP	TN *	TP *	TP *	TP *	TN *	TN *	TN *
Trace_19	TN *	TP *	TP *	TP *	TN *	TP *	TP *	TP *	TN *	TN *
Trace_20	TN *	TN *	FP	TN *	TP *	FP	TN *	TN *	TP *	TN *
True Positive (TP):	10	10	10	8	10	10	10	10	10	10
False Positive (FP):	0	4	8	1	0	9	1	3	0	1
True Negative (TN):	10	6	2	9	10	1	9	7	10	9
False Negative (FN):	0	0	0	2	0	0	0	0	0	0
NO. of traces correctly classified	20	16	12	17	20	11	19	17	20	19

false positive (*FP*), or true negative (*TN*) (Van der Aalst, 2011; Van der Aalst, 2016). Thus:

- *TP* denotes the true positive values i.e. the traces that were correctly classified as positive.
- *FN* signifies the false negatives i.e. the traces that are predicted to be negative but ought to have been classified as positive.
- *FP* denotes the false positive values i.e. the traces that are predicted to be positive but ought to have been classified as negative.
- *TN* signifies the true negatives i.e. the traces that were correctly classified as negative.

The IEEE CIS Task Force on Process Mining committee publish on the website (Carmona, et al., 2016) (a) 10 test logs, each of which contains 20 traces that were used to score the submissions, and (b) 10 reference process models in BPMN format generated from the original event logs which were not previously revealed. Consequently, the final result after scoring by the committee (panel of judges) shows that the Fuzzy-BPMN miner approach has correctly classified 171 out of 200 (85.5%) traces in the original process model.

Presently, the only other contests related to the process mining is the annual Business Process Intelligence Challenge (BPIC) (van Dongen, et al., 2016) which makes use of real-life datasets but without an objective evaluation criteria, and the recently introduced Conformance Checking Challenge 2019 (Munoz-Gama et al, 2019). On the one hand, whereas the BPIC contest focuses more on the observed values of the process mining and analysis techniques, and as such does not limit its submissions to the process discovery methods (e.g. the contest also looks at some performance analysis techniques, conformance checking, etc.). And, the Conformance Checking Challenge provides the participants with artifacts stemmed from a real process and invites them to analyze the conformance between the observed (events log) and expected behaviours (model) of the process, in an effort to provide the process owners with interpretable and understandable conformance results. Although, the submissions are also being assessed by a panel of judges. On the other hand, the BPM Process Discovery Contest (Carmona, et al., 2016) is quite different from the BPIC and Conformance Checking Challenge because it focuses more on the process discovery techniques. In essence, datasets that are synthetic in nature are used to have an objectified "proper" answer to real-life process mining problems. Thus, the process discovery is turned into a classification task with a training set and a test set, where a discovered process model needs to decide whether the classified 'traces' are fitting or not as represented in this section of the book.

SEMANTIC-FUZZY MINING APPROACH

Furthermore, in this section, the work makes use of the same event logs (Carmona, et al., 2016) to describe how the work expounds the results and amalgamation of the two process mining techniques namely: Fuzzy miner and Business Process Modelling Notation (BPMN) approach in order to demonstrate the capability of the proposed Semantic-based Fuzzy miner being able to perform a more accurate classification of the individual traces within the process base (dataset). This includes the capability to integrate the semantic technologies (ontological concepts or schema) and perform an automated classification (semantic reasoning) that is capable of discovering fitting and accurate models given the datasets (with *the training set* and a *test set*) for the cross-validation experiments. Henceforth, the sematic-based fuzzy mining and analysis allows the meaning of the process elements to be enhanced through the use of property characteristics and classification of discoverable entities. Indeed, the method is introduced in order to generate inference (semantic) knowledge that is used to determine useful patterns (traces) in an easy way and predict accurately to a significant degree the future outcomes or process instances/behaviours. Moreover, such type of conceptualization method allows for analysis of the process elements at a more abstraction level.

Perhaps, as explained earlier in the proposed sets of algorithms in Chapter 4, *ontology* is one of such methods that can be used to connect the set(s) of discoverable entities in the models with either another class or with a fixed literal. Besides, the ontologies can also describe the sub assumption hierarchies (i.e. taxonomy) that exist between the various classes and their relationships with the other classes. Moreover, the classes are instantiated with a set(s) of individuals, *I*, and can likewise contain a set(s) of axioms, *A*, which states. For example, what is true and fitting? (true positives) or what is true and not fitting? (true negatives) etc. within the process base. In view of that, as illustrated in Figures 4 and 5, the work makes use of the "*hasTraceFitness*" object property it has created for the purpose of the work in this book to reference the class used to represent the test events logs that have a "*TrueTrace_Classification_(TP)*" or "*FalseTrace_Classification_(TN)*"

Figure 4. Example of the Object Property Assertion (annotation) for the True trace classifications

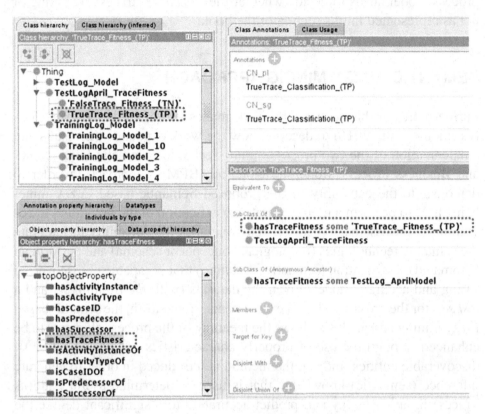

Thus far, as described earlier in Chapter 5, if we Let A be the set of all process executions or the individual classification tasks that can be performed within the semantic model. A process action $a \in A$ is characterized by a set of input parameters $Ina \in P$, which is required for the execution of a and a set of output parameters $Outa \subseteq P$, that is produced by a after execution. For example, the work executes the DL (Baader, et al., 2003) queries below as a set of input parameters to the different set of traces for the example "TestLog_Apri_1" (Figure 5) within the model in order to output the traces that has been classified or has 'TrueTrace_Fitness_(TP)' and 'FalseTrace_Fitness_(TN)' respectively. Thus:

"TestLog_April_1 and hasTraceFitness some 'TrueTrace_Fitness_(TP)'"
"TestLog_April_1 and hasTraceFitness some 'FalseTrace_Fitness_(TN)'"

Figure 5. Example of OntoGraph for the TestLog_April_1 class with a description of some of the semantic annotation

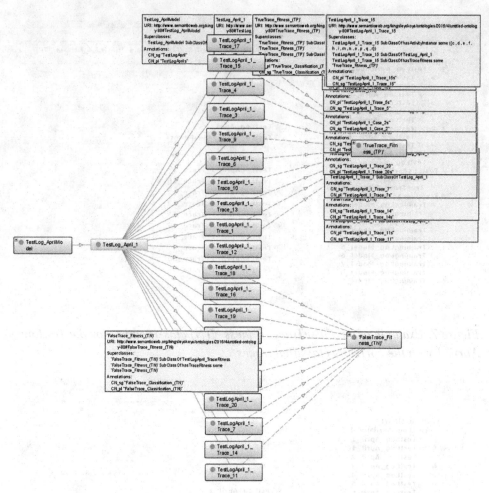

The results of computing the queries (input and output parameters) are as shown in Figure 6 and 7 respectively.

Accordingly, for the purpose of integration and application of the semantic-fuzzy mining approach, the work implements a user interface used to support the extraction and automated mining of the process parameters, especially useful in loading the concepts defined within the ontologies. Technically, the work applies the Web Ontology Language Application Programming Interface (OWL API) (Clark & Parsia, et al., 2017) in java runtime environment in order to extract and load the inferred concepts ascertained (defined) within the ontologies (i.e. the semantic model). Moreover, the purpose for creating

Figure 6. Example of the TrueTrace_Fitness_(TP) classification for the TestLog_ April_1 with the correctly classified traces

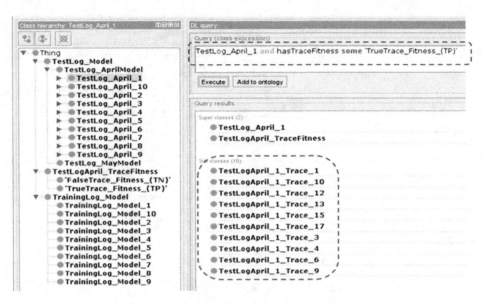

Figure 7. Example of the FalseTrace_Fitness_(TN) classification for the TestLog_ April_1 with the correctly classified traces

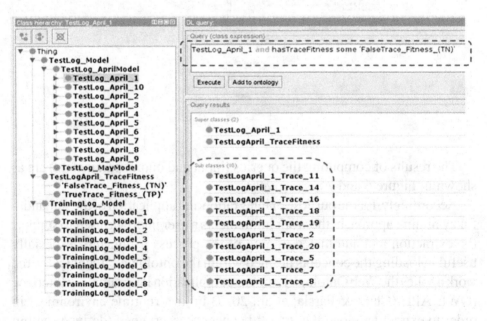

the interface is to match the questions one would like to answer, for instance, about the attributes and relationships the process elements share amongst themselves within the learning model (see: Chapter 5 and 6) by linking to the referenced concepts (classes) within the model. Thus, figures 8 and 9 shows the application interface and the methods the work has developed for automated querying (reasoning) of the datasets or concepts (input and output variables) within the defined ontologies (semantic model).

Indeed, the semantic fuzzy mining approach and its main application (e.g. as shown in Figures 4 to 9) references a number of different OWL ontologies. For instance, the training model ontology, test set ontology, traceFitness Classification ontology, etc. which were all created for the experimentations. Clearly, for each ontology, all concepts in their turn were considered by the reasoner (Pellet) (Sirin & Parsia, 2004) and are checked for consistency by referencing the process parameters. Perhaps, based on the behavioural characteristics of the provided datasets (Carmona, et al., 2016) which contain in each test log 10 traces that are considered allowed (true positives) and 10

Figure 8. Application Interface for the semantic-fuzzy miner (SFM) in the java runtime environment

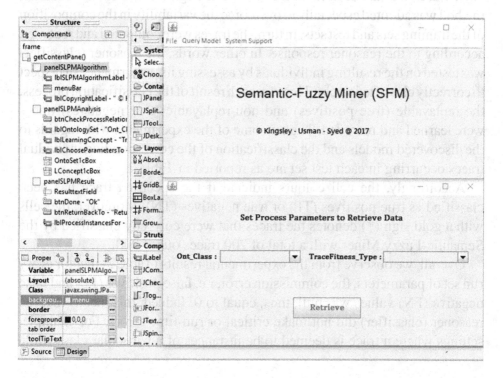

Figure 9. Concepts Reasoning using the OWL API

other traces that are seen as disallowed (true negatives), a cross-validation method was adopted especially to overcome the variability in the composition of the training sets and test sets. In turn, the traces were computed and recorded according to the reasoner response. In other words, the reasoner (classifier) was tested on the resulting individuals by assessing its performance in respect to correctly classified traces. Thus, for each result of the classification process, the replayable (true positives) and non-replayable (true negatives) traces were learned and recorded. The outcome of the experiments with regards to the discovered models and the classification of the corresponding individual traces occurring in each test set are as reported in Table 2.

Accordingly, the cell colours indicate if the specified trace has been classified as true positives (TP) or true negatives (TN). Moreover, the cells with a gold sign (*) denotes the traces that were correctly classified by the Semantic-Fuzzy Miner with a total of 200 traces out of 200.

Overall, we observe from the experimental results (Table 2) that for every run set of parameters, the commission error, i.e. false positives (FP) and false negative (FN) values was null, thus, equal to 0. Indeed, this means that the reasoner (classifier) did not make critical or run-time errors. For example, settings where a trace is deemed to be instances of a particular class while

Table 2. Trace Fitness and Classification results for the events log (Carmona, et al., 2016) using the Semantic-Fuzzy mining approach

	Model 1	Model 2	Model 3	Model 4	Model 5	Model 6	Model 7	Model 8	Model 9	Model 10
Trace_1	TP *	TN *	TP *	TN *	TN *	TN *	TP *	TP *	TP *	TP *
Trace_2	TN *	TN *	TP *	TP *	TP *	TP *	TP *	TN *	TP *	TP *
Trace_3	TP *	TP *	TP *	TN *	TN *	TN *	TN *	TP *	TP *	TN *
Trace_4	TP *	TP *	TN *	TP *	TN *	TP *	TN *	TP *	TP *	TN *
Trace_5	TN *	TN *	TN *	TP *	TN *	TP *	TN *	TP *	TP *	TN *
Trace_6	TP *	TN *	TN *	TP *	TN *	TP *	TP *	TN *	TN *	TP *
Trace_7	TN *	TP *	TP *	TN *	TN *	TP *	TN *	TP *	TN *	TN *
Trace_8	TN *	TP *	TP *	TP *	TN *	TN *	TP *	TP *	TP *	TP *
Trace_9	TP *	TN *	TP *	TN *	TP *	TN *	TP *	TP *	TN *	TP *
Trace_10	TP *	TN *	TP *	TN *	TN *	TN *	TP *	TP *	TP *	TP *
Trace_11	TN *	TP *	TP *	TP *	TP *	TN *	TN *	TN *	TN *	TP *
Trace_12	TP *	TN *	TN *	TP *	TP *	TP *	TP *	TN *	TP *	TN *
Trace_13	TP *	TP *	TN *	TN *	TP *	TN *	TN *	TN *	TN *	TP *
Trace_14	TN *	TP *	TN *	TN *	TN *	TN *	TN *	TP *	TN *	TP *
Trace_15	TP *	TN *	TN *	TN *	TP *	TP *	TN *	TN *	TN *	TN *
Trace_16	TN *	TN *	TN *	TP *	TP *	TN *	TN *	TN *	TP *	TN *
Trace_17	TP *	TP *	TP *	TP *	TP *	TP *	TP *	TN *	TN *	TP *
Trace_18	TN *	TP *	TN *	TN *	TP *	TP *	TP *	TN *	TN *	TN *
Trace_19	TN *	TP *	TP *	TP *	TN *	TP *	TP *	TP *	TN *	TN *
Trace_20	TN *	TN *	TN *	TN *	TP *	TN *	TN *	TN *	TP *	TN *
True Positive (TP):	10	10	10	10	10	10	10	10	10	10
False Positive (FP):	0	0	0	0	0	0	0	0	0	0
True Negative (TN):	10	10	10	10	10	10	10	10	10	10
False Negative (FN):	0	0	0	0	0	0	0	0	0	0
Number of traces correctly classified	20	20	20	20	20	20	20	20	20	20

it really is an instance of another class. Moreover, the results show that the individual trace accuracy rate was very high i.e. for the true positive (TP) and true negative (TN) values and was consistently observed for all the test sets. In short, the result of the experiment shows that the semantic fuzzy mining approach exhibits a high level of accuracy when classifying the various traces as evaluated and presented in detail in the next chapter (Chapter 8) of this book.

CONCLUSION

The work in this chapter has shown how the process mining techniques are applied to answer real-time questions about the different process domains. The chapter also outlines the implication of the annotations and classification of the individual process elements that can be found within the models through the semantic process mining approach. This includes the integration of the main tools (see: Table 3) that supports the semantic-based fuzzy mining approach and the sets of semantically motivated algorithms described earlier in chapter 4. Practically, the method is illustrated through the use case study of the learning process and data about the real-time business process represented in this chapter of the book.

In principle, the following Table 3 shows the thematic summary of all the implementation components and main tools utilized for the purpose of the work done in this book as follows:

Table 3. Main tools and implementation components of the proposed semantic-based approach and case studies in the thesis.

	Business Process (IEEE CIS Task Force on Process Mining)	Learning Process (Research Process Domain)	Main Tools
Events Log	X	X	Learning Activity Log, Training Log, Test Log
Process Models	X	X	Fuzzy Models, BPMN Models, OntoGraph
Semantic Annotation		X	Process Description Languages, SWRL Rules
OWL Ontology		X	Protégé Editor, OWLGriD
Reasoner		X	Pellet
Fuzzy-BPMN Notation	X		PROM, Disco
Semantic Model and Conceptual Analysis		X	DL Queries, OWL API

As gathered in the table (Table 3) and practical implementation of the process mining approach in this chapter; such method for classification and/ or conceptual model analysis can be applied to any given process domain provided there is an available event data from the processes in question, and the captured events log contains the minimum requirement (i.e. a Case id and Activity name) required for any process mining tasks. Moreover, the integration of the stated tools and methods can be utilized by the process analysts or IT experts as a way of performing information retrieval and/or query answering in a more efficient, yet effective way compared to other standard logical procedures.

In summary, the practical implementations in this chapter show that the classification performance of the semantic-based fuzzy mining approach is not only comparable to the outcome of just a reasoner, but also represents as an automated method (classifier) that is able to induce new knowledge based on previously unobserved behaviours. Indeed, the predictive mechanism and/or accuracy of the semantic fuzzy mining approach were achieved through the semantic annotations and conceptual method of analysis. In essence, the semantic-based method can be exploited in any form of data analysis procedures for prediction and/or suggestion of missing information (metadata) about the different process elements. Besides, the method can be regarded to be most effective especially when completing large ontology-based systems. In addition, the newly discovered information or knowledge (semantic assertions) could be used by the process owners, process analysts or IT experts to address and answer real-time questions about the different processes, as well as, used for process-related decision-making purposes.

REFERENCES

Baader, F. (2003). *Description Logic Handbook: theory, implementation, and applications* (1st ed.). New York, NY: Cambridge University Press.

Carmona, J., de Leoni, M., Depair, B., & Jouck, T. (2016). *Process Discovery Contest @ BPM 2016*. Rio de Janeiro: IEEE CIS Task Force on Process Mining.

Clark & Parsia. (2017). The OWL API. Manchester, UK: Sourceforge.net - original version API for OWL 1.0 developed as part of the WonderWeb Project.

G¨unther, C. (2009). *Process Mining in Flexible Environments* (PhD thesis). Eindhoven, The Netherlands: Department of Technology Management, Technical University.

Günther, C. W., & Van der Aalst, W. M. P. (2007). Fuzzy Mining – Adaptive Process Simplification Based on Multi-perspective Metrics. Business Process Management, 328-343.

IEEE CIS Task Force on Process Mining. (2016). *1849-2016 - IEEE Standard for eXtensible Event Stream definition.* Available at: http://www.xes-standard.org/

Munoz-Gama, J., de la Fuente, R., Sepúlveda, M., Fuentes, R. (2019). *Conformance Checking Challenge 2019.* 4TU. Centre for Research Data. doi:10.4121/uuid:c923af09-ce93-44c3-ace0-c5508cf103ad

Okoye, K., Naeem, U., Islam, S., Tawil, A. R. H., & Lamine, E. (2017). Process Models Discovery and Traces Classification: a Fuzzy-BPMN Mining Approach. *Journal of International Technology and Information Management, 26*(4), 1-50.

Okoye, K., Tawil, A. R. H., Naeem, U., & Lamine, E. (2016). Fuzzy-BPMN miner approach - Process Discovery Contest @ BPM 2016. Rio de Janeiro: Technical Report Submission, IEEE CIS Task Force on Process Mining discovery contest [1st Edition] in BPI workshop at BPM 2016 Conference.

Rozinat, A., & Gunther, C. (2012). Disco User Guide - Process Mining for Professionals. Eindhoven, The Netherlands: Fluxicon.com.

Sirin, E., & Parsia, B. (2004). Pellet: An owl dl reasoner. *Proceedings of the 2004 International Workshop on Description Logics (DL2004),* 104.

Van der Aalst, W. M. P. (2011). *Process Mining: Discovery, Conformance and Enhancement of Business Processes* (1st ed.). Berlin: Springer. doi:10.1007/978-3-642-19345-3

Van der Aalst, W. M. P. (2016). *Process Mining: Data Science in Action* (2nd ed.). Berlin: Springer-Verlag Berlin Heildelberg. doi:10.1007/978-3-662-49851-4

Van der Aalst, W. M. P., Adriansyah, A., & de Medeiros, A. K. A. (2012). Process Mining Manifesto. *Business Process Management Workshops, 99,* 169-194.

Van Dongen, B., Claes, J., Burattin, A., & De Weerdt, J. (2016). *12th International Workshop on Business Process Intelligence 2016.* Available at: http://www.win.tue.nl/bpi/doku.php?id=2016:start#organizers

Verbeek, H., Buijs, J., van Dongen, B., & van der Aalst, W. M. P. (2011). XES, XESame, and ProM 6. In *Information Systems Evolution.* Springer.

APPENDIX A

In this section of the book, the work encloses all supplementary documents as pertinent to the work done in this book particularly examples of the discovered process models used for the purpose of its experimentations, results analysis, and outcomes.

Discovered Process Models for the Event Logs

Fuzzy Models and Petri nets

Figure 10. Fuzzy Model for training_log_1

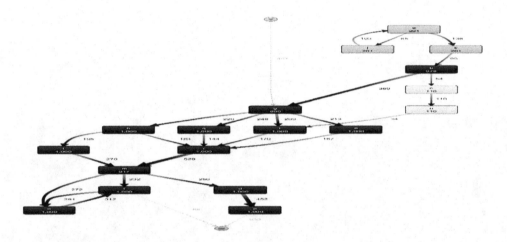

Figure 11. Petri net Model for training_log_1

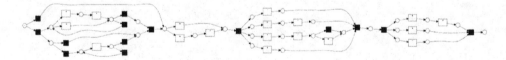

Figure 12. Fuzzy Model for training_log_2

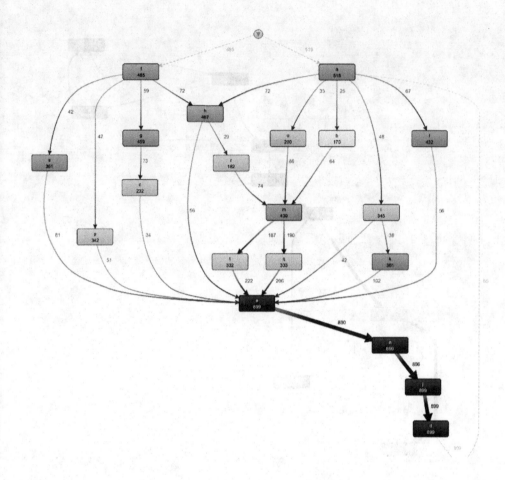

Figure 13. Petri net Model for training_log_2

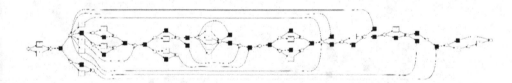

Figure 14. Fuzzy Model for training_log_3

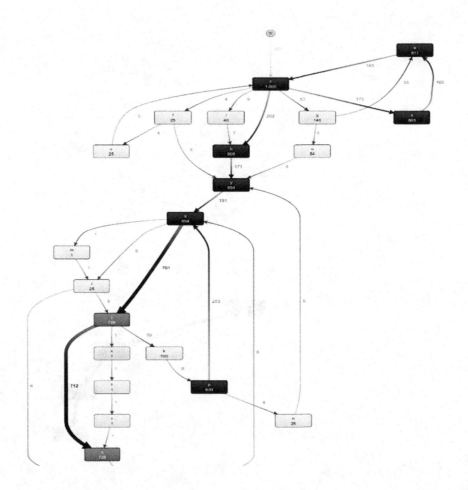

Figure 15. Petri net Model for training_log_3

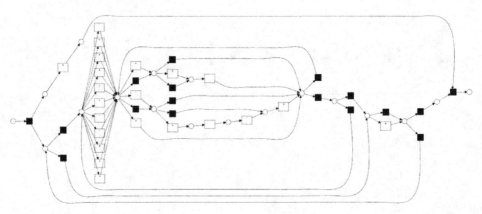

Figure 16. Fuzzy Model for training_log_4

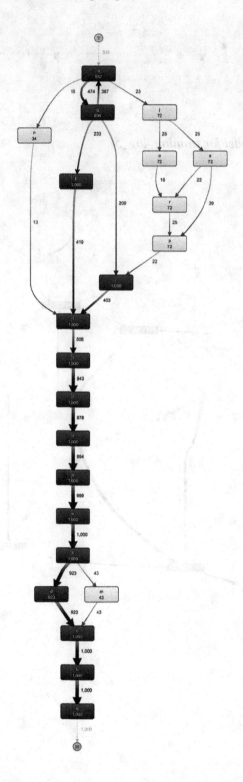

Figure 17. Petri net Model for training_log_4

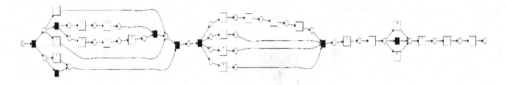

Figure 18. Fuzzy Model for training_log_5

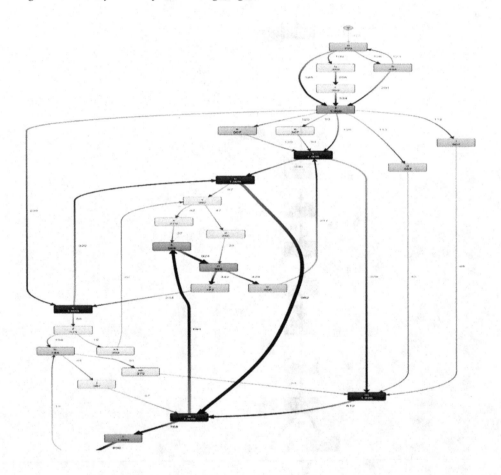

Figure 19. Petri net Model for training_log_5

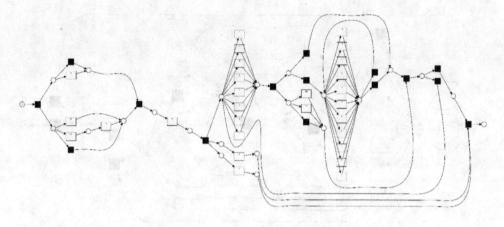

Figure 20. Fuzzy Model for training_log_6

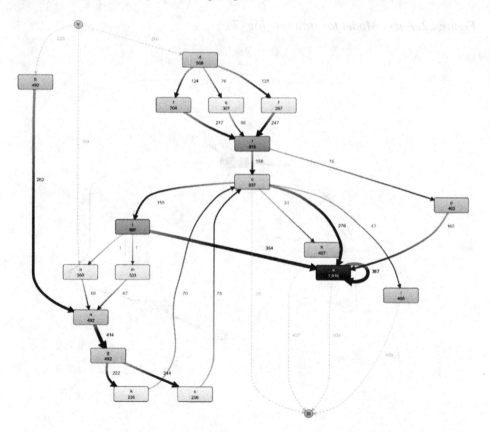

Figure 21. Petri net Model for training_log_6

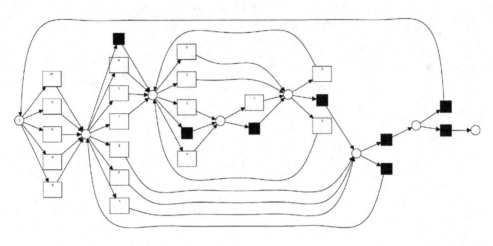

Figure 22. Fuzzy Model for training_log_7

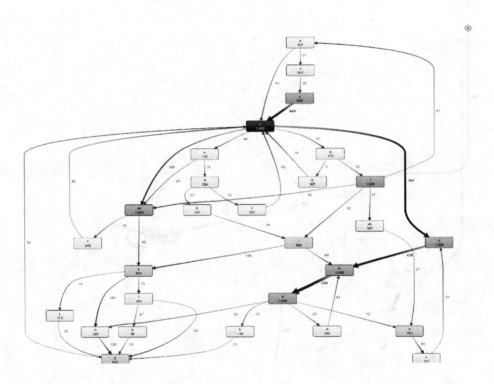

Figure 23. Petri net Model for training_log_7

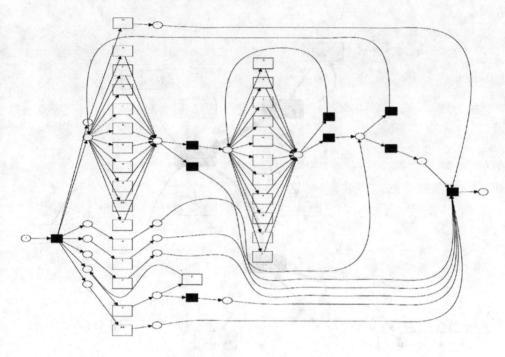

Figure 24. Fuzzy Model for training_log_8

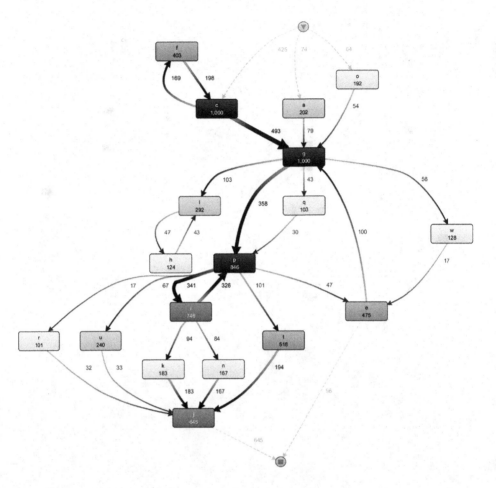

Figure 25. Petri net Model for training_log_8

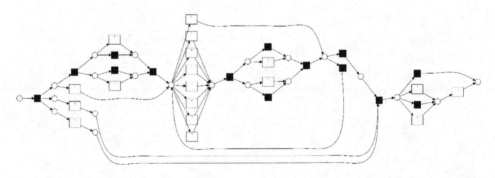

Figure 26. Fuzzy Model for training_log_9

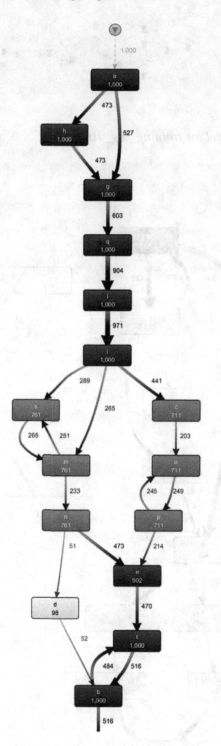

Figure 27. Petri net Model for training_log_9

Figure 28. Fuzzy Model for training_log_10

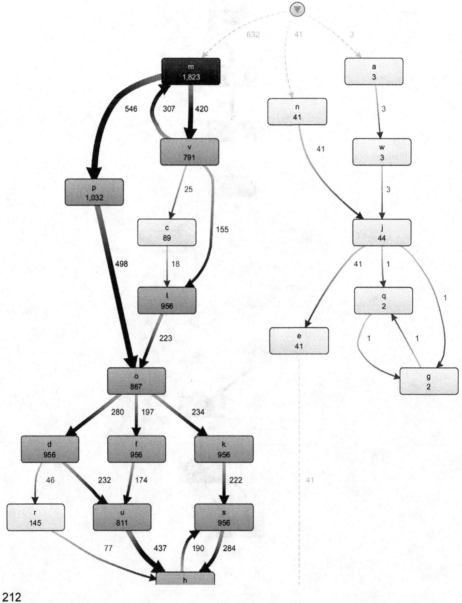

Figure 29. Petri net Model for training_log_10

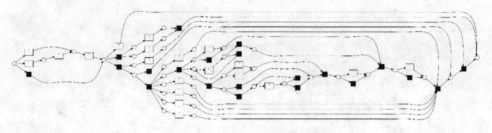

APPENDIX B

BPMN Models for the Training Logs

Figure 30. BPMN model for training_log_1

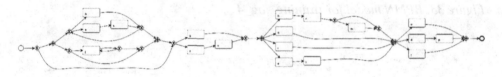

Figure 31. BPMN model for training_log_2

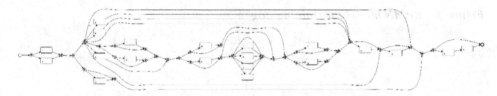

Figure 32. BPMN model for training_log_3

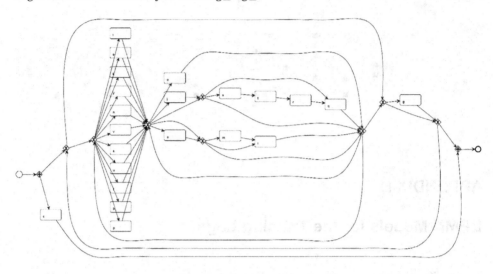

Figure 33. BPMN model for training_log_4

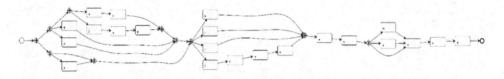

Figure 34. BPMN model for training_log_5

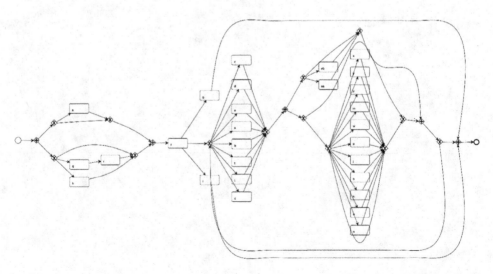

Figure 35. BPMN model for training_log_6

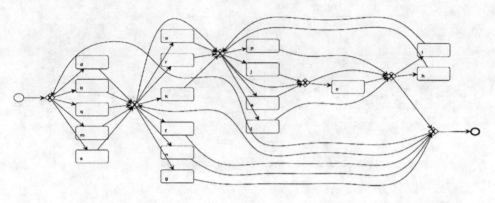

Figure 36. BPMN model for training_log_7

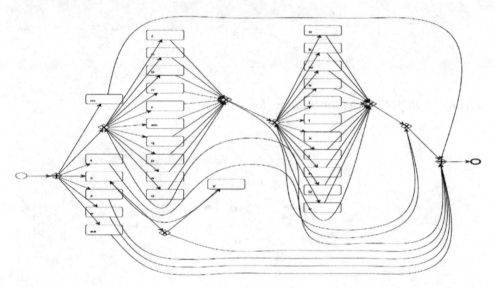

Figure 37. BPMN model for training_log_8

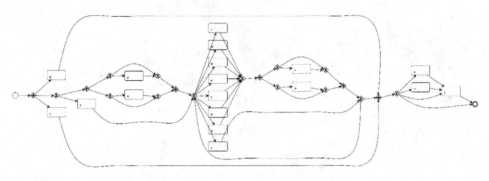

Figure 38. BPMN model for training_log_9

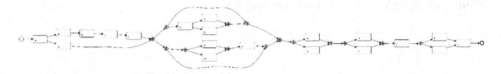

Figure 39. BPMN model for training_log_10

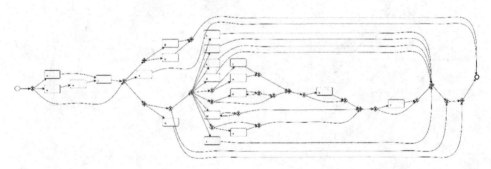

Chapter 8
Measuring the Impact of the Semantic–Based Process Mining Approach

ABSTRACT

This chapter looks at the extent to which the semantic-based process mining approach of this book supports the conceptual analysis of the events logs and resultant models. Qualitatively, the chapter leverages the use case study of the research learning process domain to determine how the proposed method support the discovery, monitoring, and enhancement of the real-time processes through the abstraction levels of analysis. Also, the chapter quantitatively assesses the level of accuracy of the classification process to predict behaviours of unobserved instances within the underlying knowledge base. Overall, the work looks at the implications of the semantic-based approach, validation of the classification results, and their influence compared to other existing benchmark techniques/algorithms used for process mining.

QUALITATIVE EVALUATION OF THE SEMANTIC-BASED PROCESS MINING APPROACH

Evidence from the design framework (SPMaAF), algorithms and experimentations show that the semantic-based approach sparks methods that highly influence and support:

DOI: 10.4018/978-1-7998-2668-2.ch008

- the application of process mining techniques to the various domain processes, and
- provision of real-time semantic knowledge and understanding about the different domain processes (e.g. the case study of learning process in this book) that proves useful towards the development of process mining algorithms that are intelligent with high level of effective conceptual reasoning capabilities.

In the experimentations and implementation of the semantic-based approach (see: Chapters 6 and 7), we observe that ontologies help in harmonizing the various process elements that are found within the process models and/or knowledge-bases. Besides, the semantically-based annotations and reasoning aptitudes help to extract and add useful conceptual knowledge to the mining process and the resulting outcomes.

Accordingly, the work qualitatively applies the case study of the learning process to address the series of real-time learning questions as previously explained in chapters 5 and 6. Typically, the work resolves the learning problems in order to show in detail how the semantic-based process mining and its application in real-time has shown to be relevant to support a contextual (concepts) method for process mining and performing of abstract analysis. Therefore, the main technical development and application mechanisms or components realized as a result of implementing the semantic-based process mining approach (which included the SPMaAF framework and semantically motivated algorithms described in chapters 3 and 4 respectively) are summarised as follows:

- **Event Logs**: Used to show how the process mining techniques can be applied to improve the informative value of real-time business processes and data.
- **Process Models**: Describes how improved models can be derived from the large volumes of events (data) logs that are found within the domain processes e.g. the learning process.
- **Annotation**: Describe how semantic descriptions and representation of the deployed models can help enrich the result of the process mining and outcomes through further analysis and/or discovering of new knowledge about the different process elements.
- **Ontology**: Describes how to make use of the semantic technologies and schema (particularly an effective semantic reasoning aptitudes) to

   lift the process mining analysis from the syntactic level to a much more
   conceptual level.

- **Semantic-based Process Mining and Algorithms**: Reveals how
  references to ontologies and effective raising of the process analysis
  from the syntactic to semantic level enable real-time viewpoints on
  the derived process models. In turn, the method helps to address the
  problem of analyzing the different domain processes and data based
  on concepts rather than the events tags or labels about the process.
  Overall, the method is used to answer questions about relationships
  the different process elements (instances) share amongst themselves
  within the knowledge-base.

   In principle, we utilized the case study of the learning process and case
scenario of the *successful* and *uncomplete* learners to pilot the structure of
the event logs and process models to describe the semantic viewpoints (e.g
metadata) about how the processes have been performed in reality. This
includes the discovering of the actual process workflows (as performed
within the executing environment) and relationships that exist amidst the
process instances within the knowledge-base. Besides, the semantic-based
modelling and analysis approach; provides us with the opportunity to develop
algorithms or methods that are capable of analysing the process models
and/or event logs through an explicit specification of conceptualization (i.e
conceptual analysis). Truly, the resulting technique proves useful in identifying
appropriate domain semantics and/or relationships amongst the different
process elements. In short, the use case example or scenario of the *successful*
and *uncomplete* learners were focused on identifying useful information
that describes the different behaviours/patterns that can be found within the
deployed model, and performing of abstraction levels of analysis based on the
semantic reasoning aptitudes. Fundamentally, the integration of the different
ontologies within the conceptual reference models, and a logical (semantic)
reasoner enables the definition of a more universal (concept-based) analysis
questions, and then, trails to find answers for those questions in an automated
(computerized) manner.

   Nonetheless, owing to the fact that the said analysis is carried out at a
more abstraction level (i.e. conceptualization), for instance, as illustrated in
the analysis performed earlier in chapters 6 and 7 - the results of the method
can be easily understood (i.e. closer to human comprehension) and the process
of adding new concepts to the ontologies or yet changes (modifications) to
the attributes (e.g the different labels or tags) do not necessarily entail or

requires updating the analysis questions or applied queries. Therefore, we assume to have introduced a machine-understandable system in this regard. For example, we can refer to the method which the work used to determine the process instances (learners) that have successfully completed the research process. To this end, one can easily integrate further (more) activities or concepts (attributes) without requiring updating the actual question. In order words, the learning problem or questions remain the same and applicable to the class of individual that fulfills the universal and/or existential restrictions by way of definition (i.e object/data properties assertions or descriptions). Without a doubt, such characteristics or feature of the proposed method proves to bring much-added tractability and flexibility to the entire process, and most importantly, supports the analysis of the derived process models at a more conceptual level.

From all evidence and the analysis of this book (see: chapters 6 and 7), the semantic-based approach (SPMaAF) is a significant contribution to the current literature or state of the art, where many existing process mining techniques require some form of reconstruction to bring the process analysis to a more conceptual level, or yet in many cases, lack the ability to identify and/or make use of the semantic information or concepts across the different process domains. Moreover, to the best of my knowledge as of the time of writing this book, this form of conceptualization method has not been previously applied within the area of the learning process domain to determine the characteristics (properties) that links or distinguishes a certain group of learners from the other. Although, a number of works have been done within the educational process mining domain in recent years, perhaps, over the past few decades.

Consequently, the series of experimentations in this book shows that a system which is formally encoded with semantic labelling (annotation), semantic representations (ontologies), and semantic reasoning (reasoner) capabilities (as connoted in the design framework (SPMaAF), algorithms, and implementations of this book) has the capacity not only to improve the process mining tasks but also allows for a more conceptual analysis of the different process elements.

Therefore, as gathered in Table 1, the work has carefully analysed the level of influence of the proposed semantic fuzzy mining approach compared to other existing benchmark algorithm used for semantic process mining. Perhaps, as described in this book (see: chapters 2 and 7) and the resulting analysis in Table 1; the use of ontologies, semantic annotation and reasoning (i.e. references to labels within the event logs and process models) makes it possible to define a more intelligent and yet accurate way to analyse and automatically find answers to the real-time questions about the different process elements, as well as, the relationships they share between themselves within the knowledge-base (see: Figures 4 to 9 in chapter 7).

Clearly, the resulting semantic-fuzzy mining approach introduced in this book differs as well as combine interesting properties with existing, if not the only, semantic process mining algorithm (the Semantic LTL Checker) (de Medeiros, et al., 2008) currently in literature as presented in Table 1.

Table 1. The Semantic-Fuzzy miner and its development properties evaluated against existing benchmark algorithm for process mining

	Semantic LTL Checker	**Semantic-Fuzzy Miner**
Data Input	Takes event Logs concepts as input to parameters of Linear Temporal Logic (LTL) formulae	Takes process models derived from fuzzy mining of the event log as input to learn and reason about the domain process
Ontology	Ontologies are defined in WSML format	Ontologies are defined in OWL and SWRL format
Reasoning	Integrated using the WSML2Reasoner (W2RF)	Integrated using the Pellet Reasoner
Functionality	Uses LTL properties or formulae defined in LTL Template files (i.e. contains the specification of properties written in the special LTL language)	Uses process description properties (*CLASS_ASSERTIONS; OBJECT_ PROPERTY ASSERTIONS* and *DATA_ PROPERTY ASSERTIONS*) defined using OWL and SWRL Language/schema.
GUI*	There is option to select *concepts* for the parameter values	There is option to select *concepts* for the parameter values
Support*	Supports *concepts* as a value (i.e. when a concept is selected, the algorithm will test whether the attribute is an *instance of* that concept, and concepts can only be specified for set attributes).	Supports *concepts* as a value (i.e. when a concept is selected, the algorithm will test whether the attribute is an instance of that concept, and concepts can only be specified for set attributes).

As gathered in the table (Table 1), in order to describe the distinctive features and implication of the semantic fuzzy mining approach; First, the method based on the stated distinctive properties (Table 1) proves to be a more robust and accurate way of conceptually analysing the events log and models in comparison to other standard methods for process mining and analysis. Perhaps, this is owing to the fact that the semantic fuzzy mining approach also takes into account the semantic information or perspectives of the event logs and models. Moreover, as opposed to the existing semantic LTL checker that only considers and takes event logs concept as input to parameters of a Linear Temporal Logic (LTL) formula to analyse the process, the semantic fuzzy mining approach also takes the process models as an input. Besides, because those models are automatically created from the actual event logs about the process domains (e.g. the events log about the research learning process domain in this book), the system tends not to unnecessarily leave out useful information or missing data about the variables/parameters.

Secondly, although both methods (see: Table 1) makes use of ontologies, a major difference between the existing semantic LTL checker algorithm and the proposed Semantic-Fuzzy Miner is the fact that ontologies are defined in Web Service Modelling Language (WSML) (de Bruijn, et al., 2006) format with the semantic LTL checker. Whereas in this book, ontologies are defined using the OWL (W3C, 2012; Horrocks, et al., 2007) and SWRL (Horrocks, et al., 2004) format. Interestingly, whilst there are limitations with WSML ontologies concerning the exchange of syntax over the web, OWL ontologies focuses on bringing the expressive and reasoning power of description logic (DL) to the semantic web. Moreover, the OWL schemas have been accepted as the state of the art *logical layer* upon which semantic architectures (such as the SPMaAF framework) are currently built in the literature (Lisi, 2008). In fact, OWL ontologies (as described in chapter 2 and implemented in chapter 7 of this book) allows one to specify far more about the *different object/data properties* and individual *class hierarchies* (taxonomies) that are well-defined within the underlying knowledge-bases. In other words, OWL as utilized in the method of this book is designed to represent rich and complex knowledge about the different process domains by referring to *things* (superClass), *groups of things* (subClasses) and *relations between things* (i.e. relationships between the classes and individuals). Consequently, the ontologies (OWL) are developed not just for representing the sets of information in formats that can be easily understood by humans, but also for building applications that trail to inclusively process the pieces of information that they contain or supports. In essence, the method supports *machine-understandable* systems rather than just *a machine-readable* system.

Thirdly, from the automated *reasoning* or *classification* (classifier) point of view, whilst the semantic LTL checker, on the one hand, makes use of the WSML2Reasoner (Bishop, et al., 1999; de Bruijn, et al., 2006) to perform a more complex inferences that are past subsumption reasoning by only benefiting from the inclusion of semantic annotations. The semantic fuzzy mining approach, on the other hand, is integrated with Pellet reasoner (Sirin & Parsia, 2004) which typically in addition to semantic annotations has been proven to incorporate optimizations for nominals, conjunctive rules and query answering, including incremental reasoning capabilities that support the process descriptions and logic. For instance, the different class(es) and object/data properties assertions that are without a doubt shown to be very effective in reasoning particularly at a more conceptual level (see: chapters 5 and 7).

In general, the semantic LTL checker and the Semantic Fuzzy miner both have the option to select concepts for the parameter values, and fundamentally, supports concepts as a value, i.e., when a concept is selected, the algorithm will test whether an attribute (e.g the individuals, and objects/data properties, etc.) is an instance or related to the selected concept (e.g. class), and concepts can only be specified for some pre-set attributes. For example, with the semantic-fuzzy miner application; one can test whether: For all **Persons** (i.e. Performer instances) does always (**condition check? -** exist some kind of milestones?) implies eventually (**class description:** Successful Learner). In other words, does any named **Person P:** hasCompleteMilestones **A** and **B** and **C** and **D**, where: **A** = DefineTopicArea, **B** = ReviewLiterature, **C** = AddressProblem, and **D** = DefendSolution, represents and points to the concepts within the domain ontologies.

QUANTITATIVE EVALUATION OF THE SEMANTIC FUZZY MINING APPROACH

In this section, the work presents how we quantitatively evaluate the accuracy and performance of the classification results by the semantic-based fuzzy mining approach.

Fore mostly, it is important to note that to quantitatively measure the results and outcomes of the process mining algorithms or techniques; it is essential that we must first focus on determining the level of accuracy of the classification results (i.e. the outcomes of the classifier over the given data sets) rather than focusing on the *seen* (or observed) process instances or behaviours. Moreover, the performance (quality) of the analysis of the classification process is perhaps useful to further predict good classifications for the *unseen* (unobserved) behaviours/patterns. Henceforth, given a dataset that consists of *N* instances, one can presumably note for each of the instances; what the actual class is, and what the predicted class is (often expressed as *confusion matrix*) (Van der Aalst, 2016; Van der Aalst, 2011).

According to Van der Aalst (2011), the confusion matrix considers a given set of data with only two sets of classes; Positive (+) and Negative (-) values, and are measured using some sort of performance formula for the classifiers as described in Table 2.

Table 2. Performance measures and formula for the Classifiers

Classifier Name	Formula
tp-rate	tp/p
fp-rate	fp/n
Error	$(fp + fn) / N$
Accuracy	$(tp + tn) / N$
Precision	tp/p'
Recall	tp/p
F1 Score	$(2 \times Precision \times Recall) / (Precision + Recall)$

As gathered in the table (Table 2):

- *tp-rate* (true positive rate) = *tp/p* also known as *hit rate* measures the proportion of positive instances that are indeed classified as positive.
- *fp-rate* (false positive rate) = *fp/n* also known as *false alarm rate* measures the proportion of negative instances wrongly classified as positive.
- *Error* = *(fp + fn)/N* is used to measure the proportion of instances misclassified.
- *Accuracy* = *(tp + tn)/N* measures the fraction of instances on the transverse of the confusion matrix, i.e, the proportion of instances correctly classified.
- *Precision* = *tp/p'* where *tp* is the number of traces that have been retrieved and also should have been retrieved, and *p'* the number of traces that have been retrieved based on some search query.
- *Recall* = *tp/p* where *tp* is as defined in *Precision* and *p* is the number of traces that should have been retrieved based on some search query.
- *F1 Score* = (2 x *precision* x *recall*) / (*precision* + *recall*) takes the harmonic mean of *precision* and *recall*. For instance, if either the *precision* or *recall* is really poor, then the *F1 Score* is close to or equals to 0. Whereas, on the other hand, if the *precision* and *recall* are really good, then the *F1 Score* is close to or equals to 1.

Indeed, *If* the following formula $N = tp + fn + fp + tn$ equals the total number of instances within the dataset, *Then* based on the definitive expression of the confusion matrix or measurement values, it becomes easy for one to determine the values of the class Positive (+) and Negative (-) as classified by making use of the classifier. For instance, the total number of actual positive instances, i.e., $p = tp + fn$ can perhaps be realized. Whereas, more so, the total number of instances that are actually negative, $n = tn + fp$ can also be determined. Likewise, If $p' = fp + tp$ refers to the total number of instances that are classified as positive by the classifier, Then $n' = fn + tn$ equally refers to the number of instances that are classified as negative by the classifier. To this end, the formulas as represented in Table 2 are construed.

Furthermore, according to Van der Aalst (2011), the number of *unseen* instances is potentially vast (if not infinite) and therefore an estimate needs to be computed on a test set which is commonly known as *cross-validation* (Van der Aalst, 2016). In theory, the cross-validation method is usually applied in settings where the dataset is split into a *training set* and a *test set*. In practice, *cross-validation* is one of the performance indicator methods that could be utilized to evaluate process mining techniques. Typically, to carry out the cross-validation process, the events log is split into a *training log* and a set of *test logs* in which the proposed mining approach has to learn process models from a major part of the logs (i.e. the training log) as well as the individual cases that form the event log (i.e. the test logs). As a result, the *training log* is utilized to discover the models, while the *test logs are* utilized to assess the fitness of the discovered models based on the discovered (unobserved) traces.

In general, the main idea of the cross-validation method is to quantitatively assess the fitness or performance of the learned models in relation to the test logs that contains the *actual behaviours* (i.e. fitting traces), as well as weigh up the quality of the learned models in relation to the test logs that contains *random behaviours* (i.e. artificially generated negative events). Theoretically, it is expected that the models score way better for the logs that contain the *actual behaviours* than the logs that contain the *random behaviours*. To this effect, the experimentations as carried out in this book (see: Chapter 7) and analysed here in this section measures to what extent the scoring of the discovered models, when encoded with semantics (formal domain knowledge) about the process elements (instances), helps to improve (enhance) the analysis of the process mining from the syntactic levels of analysis to a more conceptual-based one. Indeed, the main objective is to formally encode semantic knowledge to the discovered models in order to help identify the fitness (accuracy of classification) of the individual traces and analysis through semantic descriptions (assertions) and automated computing of the different process elements. In other words, determine the Positive (+) and Negative (-) values by the classifier.

Henceforth, to assess the performances of the semantic-based approach (i.e. Semantic-Fuzzy Miner) being able to correctly classify and analyse the individual traces within the models:

- given a trace (t) representing real process behaviour (i.e. *true positives* or allowed traces) or
- trace (t) representing a behaviour not related to the process (*true negatives* or *disallowed* traces) in the given sets of data.

The work conducted further experimentations on the results of the datasets in Carmona et al (2016) as described earlier in chapter 7. The available dataset stands for the same this study used for testing of the subject knowledge and practical application of the process mining in real-time (see: chapter 7). Typically, the characteristics of the datasets are explained in the objectives of the process discovery contest (Carmona, et al., 2016) that focuses on discovering worthwhile process models from a set of *training log* representing 10 different real-time business process executions, and sets of *test event logs* provided for evaluation of the employed process mining method. Typically, each of the test event logs represents part of the original model with a complete total of 20 traces in each log and are considered to have 10 traces which are capable of being replayed (*allowed*) and 10 traces which perhaps cannot be replayed (*disallowed*) by the model. Therefore, a wide variety of process mining problems are being represented.

In the method of this book (i.e. semantic-based fuzzy mining approach), the work has utilized the test events log with a complete total of 200 traces to validate the proposed method. Accordingly, the performance of the outcome of the experimentation and a cross-validation method was carried out in comparison of the semantic-fuzzy mining approach to the other existing benchmark algorithms that are used for process mining. This includes namely; Inductive Miner and Decomposition (Ghawi, 2016), DrFurby Classifier (Verbeek & Mannhardt, 2016), Heuristic Alpha+ Miner (Shteiner, et al., 2016), and Fuzzy-BPMN miner Okoye et al (2016 & 2017) that uses the same events log in Carmona et al (2016) to discover process models and provides replaying semantics for the individual traces that makes up the events log.

To do this, the work makes use of the Standard Percent of Correct Classification (PCC) (Baati, et al., 2017) formula to assess the performance of the classifiers. Thus, the standard Percent of Correct Classification (Baati, et al., 2017) for the *test logs* is defined as follows:

Log_PCC = (*number of correctly classified traces*) / (*total number of traces*) x 100

For example, for the *training_model_7* as shown in the following table (Table 3), the Standard Percent of Correct Classification (PCC) for the *test log* for the initial results as presented in chapter 7 (Fuzzy-BPMN mining approach) is determined as follows:

Training_Model_7 *(PCC)* = (19) / (20) x 100
    = 0.95 x 100
    = 95%

Likewise, the Standard Percent of Correct Classification (PCC) for the *training_model_7* as shown in the table (Table 3) for the Semantic-Fuzzy miner approach (chapter 7) is determined as follows:

Training_Model_7 *(PCC)* = (20) / (20) x 100
    = 1 x 100
    = 100%

In consequence, considering the discovered models and implementation results of the process mining approaches (see: chapter 7), the work represents in the following table (Table 3); the standard percent of correct classification (%PCC) for the initial results of the method (i.e. Fuzzy-BPMN miner and Semantic-Fuzzy miner). Perhaps, this is done by measuring the test logs and the associated training sets (models) as defined using the %PCC formula.

To this end, by using the logical formula and the results of the calculations as shown in the Table 3 (standard Percent of Correct Classification (%PCC)) (Baati, et al., 2017); the work further measures and analyse in Table 4 the performance of the semantic-fuzzy mining approach against the other existing benchmark algorithms (Ghawi, 2016; Verbeek & Mannhardt, 2016; Shteiner, et al., 2016) including the Fuzzy-BPMN miner Okoye et al (2016 & 2017) that are used to carry out real-time process mining and analysis. This is done in order to weigh up the overall impact of the proposed method and

Table 3. Standard Percent of Correct Classification (%PCC) for the test logs and training logs, i.e., classification results for the test logs against the discovered models respectively

	Fuzzy-BPMN Miner (%PCC)	*Semantic-Fuzzy Miner (%PCC)*
Training_Model_1	(20) / (20) x 100 = 1 x 100 = **100%**	(20) / (20) x 100 = 1 x 100 = **100%**
Training_Model_2	(16) / (20) x 100 = 0.80 x 100 = **80%**	(20) / (20) x 100 = 1 x 100 = **100%**
Training_Model_3	(12) / (20) x 100 = 0.60 x 100 = **60%**	(20) / (20) x 100 = 1 x 100 = **100%**
Training_Model_4	(17) / (20) x 100 = 0.85 x 100 = **85%**	(20) / (20) x 100 = 1 x 100 = **100%**
Training_Model_5	(20) / (20) x 100 = 1 x 100 = **100%**	(20) / (20) x 100 = 1 x 100 = **100%**
Training_Model_6	(11) / (20) x 100 = 0.55 x 100 = **55%**	(20) / (20) x 100 = 1 x 100 = **100%**
Training_Model_7	(19) / (20) x 100 = 0.95 x 100 = **95%**	(20) / (20) x 100 = 1 x 100 = **100%**
Training_Model_8	(17) / (20) x 100 = 0.85 x 100 = **85%**	(20) / (20) x 100 = 1 x 100 = **100%**
Training_Model_9	(20) / (20) x 100 = 1 x 100 = **100%**	(20) / (20) x 100 = 1 x 100 = **100%**
Training_Model_10	(19) / (20) x 100 = 0.95 x 100 = **95%**	(20) / (20) x 100 = 1 x 100 = **100%**

experimental results presented in this book. The outcome of the measurements and classifications results are as shown in the following table (Table 4), and represented in the following charts (Figures 1 to 3).

Indeed, as gathered in the table (Table 4) and the figures (Figure 1 to 3), the work observes that the semantic-based method (Semantic Fuzzy miner) considerably outperform respectively the Inductive miner (Ghawi, 2016) and iFuzzy-BPMN miner (Okoye et al, 2016 & 2017), although, the two algorithms Decomposition (Ghawi, 2016) and DrFurby (Verbeek & Mannhardt, 2016) stands for the state of the art classifiers amongst the existing process mining techniques particularly when compared to analysis (results/outcomes) of

Table 4. Evaluation results of the Semantic-Fuzzy miner and other benchmark process mining techniques

	Inductive Miner	Decomposition	DrFurby	Fuzzy-BPMN	Semantic-Fuzzy
Model_1	100	100	100	100	100
Model_2	100	100	100	80	100
Model_3	60	95	100	60	100
Model_4	100	100	100	85	100
Model_5	95	100	100	100	100
Model_6	85	95	100	55	100
Model_7	100	100	100	95	100
Model_8	75	70	95	85	100
Model_9	100	100	100	100	100
Model_10	100	100	100	95	100
Ave. Mean - PCC (%)	91.5	96	99.5	85.5	100
Sum of traces correctly classified	183	192	199	171	200

Figure 1. Chart showing the sum of correctly classified traces for the models (Model 1 to 10) broken down by the different techniques - using the standard Percent of Correct Classification PCC (%)

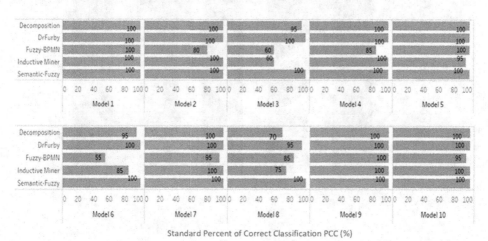

Standard Percent of Correct Classification PCC (%)

Figure 2. Average mean PCC (%) for the various methods

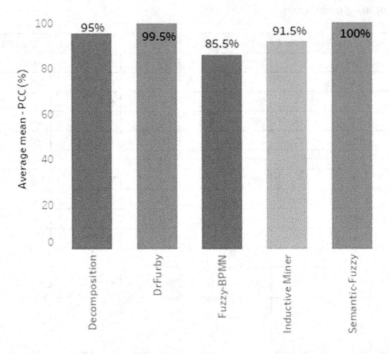

Figure 3. Total number of traces correctly classified by each method

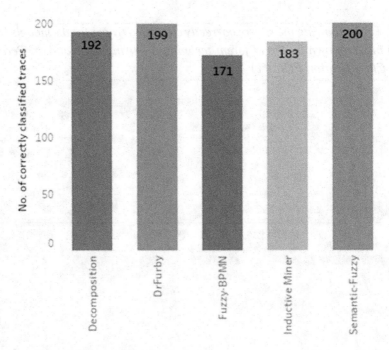

the different methods' classifications. Notably, the semantic-fuzzy mining approach has shown an error-free performance and accuracy when measured using the following classifier formulas (Van der Aalst, 2011) as follows:
Thus,

$$Error = (fp + fn)/N$$

where $fp = 0$ and $fn = 0$, such that,

$$Error = (0 + 0) / 200 = 0.$$

Accordingly, the method has shown an increased level of accuracy and performance through the formula:

$$Accuracy = (tp + tn)/N$$

where $tp = 100$ and $tn = 100$, such that:

$$Accuracy = (100 + 100) / 200 = 1.$$

In conclusion, going by the experimental results and the validation scores gathered from the above formulas; the precision and recall of the semantic-based method (semantic-fuzzy mining approach) including the resultant classifications measures are clearly efficient in comparison to the other standard methods which are used for the process mining and analysis.

CONCLUSION

Evidenced in the analysis of this book, the use of ontologies ($Ont \in Onts$) and assertion of the relations (R) between the concepts ($COnts$) defined in the ontologies are beneficial to aggregate tasks and compute formally the structure of the process models including the several abstraction levels of analysis (Gruber, 1995; Okoye, et al., 2016; Okoye, et al., 2017). Fundamentally, the idea is that for any semantic-based process mining approach; those aspects of aggregating the task (d'Amato, et al., 2008) or computing the class hierarchies (taxonomies) of the process models (Lehmann & Hitzler, 2010) should not only be designed to be *machine-readable* but must also focus on providing a system which is at the same time *machine-understandable*. Perhaps, this implies that an ample design and/or development of the machine-understandable systems (such as the semantic fuzzy miner) includes the provision of intelligent methods that are not just focused on retrieving information from the various process knowledge-bases they are used in, but also trails to provide some kind of means and/or (information) analysis that helps produce new knowledge about the systems which they are used to support. Moreover, this work notes that to benefit from the hybrid (intelligent) abilities of the resulting methods, the said systems has to be feed with process models which are already in a form that allows the computer to infer new facts (e.g. semantically annotated logs or the use of process description languages). Perhaps, this is done in order to explicitly manipulate or understand the underlying ontologies that make up the process models. Practically, the work illustrates the said method using the case study of the research learning process and data about the real-time business process from the IEEE CIS Task Force on Process Mining.

Functionally, the purpose of the semantic annotations that forms part of the construction block for the semantic fuzzy mining approach; is to seek the equivalence between *the concepts of the model* (i.e. the fuzzy models derived by applying the fuzzy miner algorithm on the events data logs) and the *concepts of the defined domain ontology*. Moreover, the fuzzy logic (Zadeh, 1999; Zadeh, 1965) has since been introduced as an extension of the Boolean logic that allows a proposal to be in another state as true or false (Dammak, et al., 2014) by enabling the modelling of uncertainty and imprecision (as earlier discussed in chapter 2) that often characterize the human representations of knowledge e.g about the captured datasets or models. Interestingly, we observe that by semantically integrating (de Giacomo, et al., 2018) the fuzzy models with concepts within a well-defined ontology, the resulting systems can make decisions as humans do. For instance, the learning questions and scenario described in chapters 5 and 6 which allows us to determine the different process instances within the learning model that are classified as successful learners or not.

Consequently, with such systems otherwise allied to the semantic-based process mining approach, the resulting methods proves to offer solutions that carry the characteristics of "intelligence" which are not only attributed to humans only but are consequently useful for solving domain-specific problems or limitations with the process mining. For instance, the work of Ceravolo et al (2016) notes that such limitations can be addressed through calibration of the process mining results based on some kind of Business Rules adopted by the said organizations (i.e domain-specific knowledge). In other words, integration of the results of the process mining with specific characteristics (semantics) of the domain processes in question (as entailed by the corresponding business rules or operational structure of the organization). Besides, such characteristics (properties) have been considered broadly as a specific feature of *Computational Intelligence* rather than just literally an area of *Artificial intelligence* applied for business process management purposes.

Currently, fuzzy logic has become mature and is being used in different areas of application within the information systems and communication technologies. For instance, as applied in this book to support the semantic-fuzzy mining approach. The intention of applying the concept in this book is particularly focused on using the fuzzy logic to represent imprecise and uncertain (complex) data that every now and then characterizes the existing business (operational) process. For example, the real-time business process data and problems described in Carmona et al (2016) which are also utilized for the purpose of the work done in this book (see: chapter 7). In short, this book has introduced the semantic-fuzzy miner as a tool which can be utilized to construct (or create) process models that are easy to understand, and yet, provides implicit as well as explicit information on the extensible sets of parameters (concepts) used to determine and analyse the derived process models at a more conceptual level (chapter 7). Essentially, this is done through a combination of the semantic labelling (annotation), representation (ontology), and reasoning (reasoner) aptitudes of the method. Moreover, the proposed framework (SPMaAF), semantically motivated algorithms, and the resultant semantic-fuzzy mining approach are important by establishing a direct connection between the discovered models and the actual low-level event logs information about the process elements applied to analyse the readily available datasets at different levels of abstraction. Thus, the term *conceptualization*.

Technically, as a collection of *concepts* and *predicates* (i.e. *ontology-based* system), the method has the ability to perform logical reasoning and bridge the underlying relations beneath the event logs and process models (e.g. discovered using the traditional process mining techniques) with *rich semantics*. In other words, whenever an *inference* (semantic reasoning) is made, a generalized associations of the process elements is created, and thus, provides consistency inference for those predicates by tuning the unlabelled (and unstructured) data associated with the fuzzy models into one (i.e. semantic fuzzy model) that have the best consistency by making use of the prior/underlying knowledge about the data.

Therefore, the main benefits of the semantic-based fuzzy mining approach as evaluated in this chapter of the book can be summarised in two forms;

- encoding knowledge about specific process domains or data, and
- conceptual reasoning and analysis of process models at a more abstraction level.

Indeed, the semantic-based fuzzy mining approach can be regarded as a fusion theory that is based on fuzzy logic and devoted to representing and analysing information in a qualitative and yet quantitative manner.

Moreover, this book has shown that it is possible to integrate the fuzzy models with other tools. For example, as represented in chapter 7, the work applies the combination of the Fuzzy-BPMN approach to construct process models with notational elements that are capable of describing the nesting of the individual activities (i.e. process instances) by using the event-based split and join gateways (AND, XOR, OR, etc.) Apparently, the integration of the process mining methods with semantic technologies in this book is as a result of the limitations that are generally related to the fuzzy models as discussed earlier in chapter 2; whereby, a lot of the time the fuzzy models appears to be relaxed in nature especially when compared with the semantics of other process modelling languages such as the Petri nets or BPMN. Thus, there are no explicit distinction possible between simple choice (i.e. OR split), parallel choice (i.e. AND split), or multiple choice (i.e. XOR split) with the fuzzy models. Moreover, the events gateways in the BPMN models are token-based semantics which can be used to replay a particular trace within the process models (Van der Aalst, 2011; Van der Aalst, 2016) and as such overcomes the noted limitations of the fuzzy models. Hence, the amalgamation and proposal of the Fuzzy-BPMN Miner introduced in this book. Besides, this book has also shown through the Semantic Fuzzy Miner and the evaluation outcomes presented in this chapter; that it is possible to improve the informative values of such type of models (i.e. fuzzy models) from the syntactic to a more conceptual level of analysis by carefully integrating and tuning the semantics metrics that those models lack.

REFERENCES

W3C. (2012). *Web Ontology Language (OWL)*. Oxford, UK: OWL Working Group.

Baati, K., Hamdani, T. M., Alimi, A. M., & Abraham, A. (2017). Decision quality enhancement in minimum-based possibilistic classification for numerical data. *Proceedings of the 8th International Conference on Soft Computing and Pattern Recognition (SoCPaR 2016)*, 634-643.

Bishop, B. (1999). WSML Reasoner. Boston, MA: IRIS Reasoner - SOA4All.

Carmona, J., de Leoni, M., Depair, B., & Jouck, T. (2016). *Process Discovery Contest @ BPM 2016*. Rio de Janeiro: IEEE CIS Task Force on Process Mining.

Ceravolo, P., Azzini, A., Damiani, E., Lazoi, M., Marra, M., & Corallo, A. (2016). Translating Process Mining Results into Intelligible Business Information. *Proceedings of the 11th International Knowledge Management in Organizations Conference on The changing face of Knowledge Management Impacting Society (KMO '16)*, 1–8. 10.1145/2925995.2925997

d'Amato, C., Fanizzi, N., & Esposito, F. (2008). Query answering and ontology population: An inductive approach. *Proceedings of the 5th Euro. Semantic Web Conference*, 288-302. 10.1007/978-3-540-68234-9_23

Dammak, S. M., Jedidi, A., & Bouaziz, R. (2014). Fuzzy semantic annotation of Web resources. *2014 World Symposium on Computer Applications & Research (WSCAR)*, 1-6.

de Giacomo, G. (2018). Using Ontologies for Semantic Data Integration. In S. Flesca, S. Greco, E. Masciari, & D. Saccà (Eds.), *A Comprehensive Guide Through the Italian Database Research Over the Last 25 Years. Studies in Big Data* (pp. 187–202). Cham: Springer. doi:10.1007/978-3-319-61893-7_11

de Medeiros, A., van der Aalst, W. M. P. & Pedrinaci, C. (2008). *Semantic Process Mining Tools: Core Building Blocks*. Galway, Ireland: ECIS.

Ghawi, R. (2016). Process Discovery using Inductive Miner and Decomposition. Rio de Janeiro: Technical Report Submission for the Process Discovery Contest @ BPM 2016, [1st Edition], IEEE Task Force on Process Mining.

Gruber, T. R. (1995). Toward principles for the design of ontologies used for knowledge sharing. *International Journal of Human-Computer Studies*, *43*(5), 907–928. doi:10.1006/ijhc.1995.1081

Horrocks, I. (2004). *SWRL: A Semantic Web Rule Language Combining OWL and RuleML*. Network Inference, Canada and Stanford University: W3C Member Submission - 2004 National Research Council of Canada, Network Inference, and Stanford University.

Horrocks, I., Patel-Schneider, P. F., McGuinness, D. L., & Welty, C. A. (2007). Owl: a description logic based ontology language for the semantic web. In *The Description Logic Handbook: Theory, Implementation, and Applications* (2nd ed., pp. 458–486). New York, NY: Cambridge University Press. doi:10.1017/CBO9780511711787.016

Lehmann, J. & Hitzler, P. (2010). Concept learning in description logics using refinement operators. *Machine Learning, 78*(1-2), 203-250.

Lisi, F. (2008). Building Rules on Top of Ontologies for the Semantic Web with Inductive Logic Programming. *Theory and Practice of Logic Programming, 8*(3), 271–300. doi:10.1017/S1471068407003195

Okoye, K., Naeem, U., & Islam, S. (2017). Semantic Fuzzy Mining: Enhancement of process models and event logs analysis from Syntactic to Conceptual Level. *International Journal of Hybrid Intelligent Systems, 14*(1-2), 67–98. doi:10.3233/HIS-170243

Okoye, K., Naeem, U., Islam, S., Tawil, A. R. H., & Lamine, E. (2017). Process Models Discovery and Traces Classification: A Fuzzy-BPMN Mining Approach. *Journal of International Technology and Information Management, 26*(4), 1-50.

Okoye, K., Tawil, A. R. H., Naeem, U., & Lamine, E. (2016). A Semantic Reasoning Method Towards Ontological Model for Automated Learning Analysis. *Proceedings of NaBIC Conference*, 49-60. 10.1007/978-3-319-27400-3_5

Okoye, K., Tawil, A. R. H., Naeem, U., & Lamine, E. (2016). Fuzzy-BPMN miner approach - Process Discovery Contest @ BPM 2016. Rio de Janeiro: Technical Report Submission, IEEE CIS Task Force on Process Mining discovery contest [1st Edition] in BPI workshop at BPM 2016 Conference.

Shteiner, M., Bodaker, L., & Senderovich, A. (2016). Heuristic Alpha+ Miner (HAM): Process Discovery Contest 2016. Rio de Janeiro: Technical Report Submission for the Process Discovery Contest @ BPM 2016, [1st Edition], IEEE Task Force on Process Mining.

Sirin, E., & Parsia, B. (2004). Pellet: An owl dl reasoner. *Proceedings of the 2004 International Workshop on Description Logics (DL2004)*, 104.

Sure, Y., & Domingue, J. (Eds.). (2006). Lecture Notes in Computer Science: Vol. 4011. *The Semantic Web: Research and Applications. ESWC.* Berlin: Springer.

Van der Aalst, W. M. P. (2011). *Process Mining: Discovery, Conformance and Enhancement of Business Processes* (1st ed.). Berlin: Springer. doi:10.1007/978-3-642-19345-3

Van der Aalst, W. M. P. (2016). *Process Mining: Data Science in Action* (2nd ed.). Berlin: Springer-Verlag Berlin Heildelberg. doi:10.1007/978-3-662-49851-4

Verbeek, E., & Mannhardt, F. (2016). DrFurby Classifier: Process Discovery Contest @ BPM 2016. Rio de Janeiro: Technical Report Submission for the Process Discovery Contest @ BPM 2016, [1st Edition], IEEE Task Force on Process Mining.

Zadeh, L. (1965). Fuzzy sets., Information Science. *Information and Control*, *8*(3), 338–353. doi:10.1016/S0019-9958(65)90241-X

Zadeh, L. A. (1999). Fuzzy sets as a basis for a theory of possibility. *Fuzzy Sets and Systems*, *100*(1), 9–34. doi:10.1016/S0165-0114(99)80004-9

Conclusion

ACHIEVEMENTS OF THIS BOOK

First and foremost, the targeted goal of this book is to identify challenges with existing process mining techniques and their influence towards the provision of suitable and effective models for an abstract representation of the different process domains. On the one hand, the resultant method (a semantic-based process mining approach) proves to allow for an abstraction levels of analysis through integration of the main (semantic) technologies (annotation, ontologies, and reasoner). On the other hand, the series of analysis carried out in this book tends to support the semantically motivated information (data) processing and conceptual analysis. This is done by introducing the semantic-based approach that trails to resolve some of the challenges related to the process mining technique. Perhaps, the proposed method entails the process of collection and transformation of the readily available datasets (i.e. event logs) about any given process domain for effective process models discovery and analysis. This is achieved through the method for semantical preparation (annotation) and representation (ontologies) of the extracted models for further analysis at a more conceptual level (semantic reasoning) and the capability of describing the various relationships that exist between the process elements. In turn, the quality of the system performance and the classification results are improved based on the outcome of the experiments and accuracy of results, respectively.

Fundamentally, this book uses the case study of the learning process domain and data about a real-time business process (IEEE CIS Task Force on Process Mining) (see: chapter 5 to 7) to do the following:

- extract data from the different process domains to show how we semantically synchronize the events log formats for process mining.

- semantically prepare the available datasets and models through an ontology-driven search for explorative analysis of the learning process activities and/or executions.
- transform the input datasets into mining executable formats to support the discovery of valuable process models through the proposed method for annotation of the unlabelled learning activities and sequence workflows using ontology schema/vocabularies.
- enhancement and/or extension of the real-time processes through further semantic analysis of the discovered models.

❖ provide an effective method for accurate classification of the different process instances (observed traces) in the models, and useful strategies towards the development of process mining algorithms that are intelligent with a high level of semantic reasoning capabilities.

❖ show the importance of the semantic-based process mining to augment information values of the captured datasets and process domains (e.g. case study of the learning process).

In essence, the focus of this book is on ascertaining by the series of validation experiments; how the process mining technique and the classification process (i.e. the individual trace or process instances) can be enriched through the proposed method for semantic-based (conceptual) analysis and representations of the derived models. Consequently, the main components realized in this book include the semantic-based process mining and analysis framework (SPMaAF), sets of semantically motivated algorithms, and the semantic fuzzy mining approach introduced in this book.

For all intents and purposes, this book leverages the semantic technologies (such as the ontologies) to enhance the outcome of the process mining and analysis from the syntactic to a more conceptual level. Technically, the book makes use of the metadata (semantics) descriptions and semantic reasoning to connect and link to concepts that are well-defined within the ontologies. Perhaps, the semantic reasoning is supported due to formal definitions and/or structural compositions of the ontological concepts (taxonomies) and assertion of the different relationships (process descriptions) that exist between the process elements in the derived models. Moreover, the SPMaAF method makes use of the semantics of the sets of activities in the models to generate rules or facts relating to the different activities in order to automatically discover hidden traces (i.e. unobserved behaviours) and to enhance the process models. This is achieved through the technique for annotation and representation of the different process elements that can be found within the process model or knowledge-base.

Practically, the work introduces the semantic-based fuzzy mining approach as means towards discovering and enrichment of the sets of recurrent behaviours/patterns that can be found within the process domains (Okoye et al, 2018). Moreover, the main aim is to determine the attributes the process elements share amongst themselves, or that distinguishes a particular set of entities (process instance) from another. In short, the drive for the development of the semantic-based approach is: by pointing to references (i.e. concepts - classes, individuals, objects/datatypes properties or assertions/annotations) in the ontologies (Okoye et al, 2020) and application of semantic reasoning (Okoye et al, 2016), it becomes easy to refer (through the classification method) (Okoye et al, 2017) to particular cases or events within the available datasets and discovered process models. The book also explains how the semantic fuzzy mining approach is used to address/determine the presence of different patterns within the derived models. Besides, the purpose for developing the semantic fuzzy mining approach is particularly focused on using the fuzzy logic to represent the imprecise and uncertain (complex) data about the domain processes, and then consequently present the resultant models in a format that allows one to analyse the available data based on concepts rather than the tags or labels in the events logs about the processes in question. For instance, the work describes the process of determining the traces within the discovered models (see: chapter 7) that are fitting (i.e. true positives) or not fitting (i.e. true negatives) the original model. This is owing to the fact that this book leverages the fuzzy logic which permits a proposal to be in another state as true or false by using a classifier (reasoner) to perform the automated reasoning or computing. Thereby, allowing us to determine through the classification process; the presence of different patterns that can be found within the discovered models. For example, through the classification process, we determine the total number of traces that can be replayed (fitting) or cannot be replayed (non-fitting) within the model.

Theoretically, the unabridged notion of the proposed semantic fuzzy mining approach, design framework, sets of algorithms, and experimental results proves that the semantic concepts (i.e. annotation, ontology, and reasoning) can be layered on top of existing information asset (e.g. process models, event data logs, etc) to provide a more accurate and intuitive way of analysing the real-time processes that is capable of providing real-world answers (insights) that can be easily grasp by the process analysts/owners. In addition, the work qualitatively validates the method using the case study of the learning process (see: chapters 6 and 7), and also quantitatively assesses the reliability and accuracy of the classification results using the real-time business process data from the IEEE CIS Task Force on Process Mining (see: chapter 7).

In general, the results and outcome of this book can be easily adopted or applied by the process owners, process analysts, IT experts and Software developers in understanding/analysing their everyday processes at a more abstraction level especially for improved decision-making purposes at large. Moreover, the conceptual method of analysis proves to be more effective as opposed to the traditional process mining frameworks which do not consider the semantic aspects of information that are contained in the events log. Henceforth, the proposed framework (SPMaAF) can be applied to mine and/or analyse the events data log about any given process domain (e.g. the business process, learning process, etc.) independent of the chosen application development or implementation platform. In other words, the SPMaAF framework and the resultant sets of algorithms described in this book can be implemented (or applied) in any given domain of interest. perhaps, be it within the same organization that uses the different types of models or similar operational processes applied to a different sector.

10.2 Impact of the SPMaAF Method and Achievement.

Clearly, the main implications and/or achievement of this book are summarized as follows:

❖ Firstly, the work makes use of the fundamental concepts of the semantic-based process mining approach to provide formal structures on how to perform and represent the process mining results in a more intuitive, accurate, easy, and functional way. For example, the method is applied in order to abstract key information that can be used to envisage the relationships between the various process instances. In principle, we assume that this work provides a semantic rule-based approach that proves useful towards efficient mining of useful patterns or models from the event logs.

❖ Secondly, this work provides a process mining technique that is able to induce new knowledge based on previously unobserved behaviours. Moreover, the method can be used by the process owners, process analysts or IT experts to perform information retrieval and query answering in a more efficient, yet effective way compared to the other standard logical procedures for process mining. This is owing to the method's ability to accurately classify the model to predict behaviours of unobserved instances or individual traces within the process knowledge-base. In other words, the work introduces a semantic-based process mining approach that exhibits a high level of accuracy during its classification process and as such do not make critical mistakes due to the formal integration of semantic knowledge to the system. Moreover, the method can be exploited to predict and/or suggest missing information about the various process elements especially when completing the large ontology-based systems. Perhaps, this is as a result of the predictive accuracy of the classifications process and error-free analysis.

❖ Thirdly, this book introduces the semantic-based process mining application (Semantic-Fuzzy Miner) as a way of practically showing and realizing its main contribution to the current literature. This is as a result of the proposed design framework (SPMaAF) that highly influence and support the development of process mining algorithms and applications that exhibits a high level of semantic reasoning aptitudes.

Overall, the main purpose for designing the SPMaAF framework, the sets of semantically motivated process mining algorithms, and the semantic *fuzzy mining approach*; is to extract, semantically prepare, and transform events log about the given domain processes into minable executable formats that allow for a more abstract analysis of the captured data and derived models through the conceptualization method. Practically, the work applies the case studies examples described in this book (see: chapter 5) to illustrate the technical application of the semantic-based process mining approach. Clearly, the purpose for developing such an intelligent system (semantic-based) is to perform a more conceptualized analysis of the available datasets and models that are capable of providing real-world answers that are closer to human understanding (machine-understandable systems). For instance, the learning questions described in chapter 5 and 6 which this book addresses in order to determine the *successful* and *uncomplete* learners within the learning knowledge base.

Finally, in addition to the stated achievements of this book summarized earlier, I believe this book has presented and comprehensively describe the main construction blocks or components of any semantic-based process mining approach (i.e. semantic annotation, ontologies, and reasoner). Eventually, this work assumes that when those essential elements are considered or integrated into the process mining framework (such as the SPMaAF framework) (see chapter 3); not only will the developers/analysts achieve a method that is capable of analysing the different datasets or models at a more conceptual levels, but in turn must have provided a machine-understandable system. Nonetheless, this work did not only illustrate how it has integrated the main building blocks (semantic annotation, ontology, and reasoner) to support the development and implementation of the semantic-based process mining approach (see: chapters 4 and 5). But we also empirically evaluate and looks at the level of influence and reasoning by the system (see: chapters 6 to 8).

To conclude the work in this book, we summarize the main purpose of integrating the semantic technologies with the process mining techniques. Indeed, the process mining presents itself as not just the bridge between the data mining and business process management field but also serves as a method that can be leveraged to address the gap between the real-time business processes and information technology. According to Van der Aalst (2016), the unprecedented presence of the big data and the associated opportunities it brings has paved the way to the manner in which the society is being governed today especially in terms of how we do business, conduct research, and even socialize. For example, the astonishing capabilities of the big data notion as it concerns the process mining field means a greater modern information and communication technologies infrastructures and/or responsibilities such as transparency, accuracy, confidentiality, and fairness within the business processes in reality. Perhaps, it must become the responsibility of the process analysts/owners to ensure the ample implementation or application of the aforementioned infrastructures, and to maximize the opportunities that are being offered through the combination of the semantic technologies and process mining as proposed in this book.

LIMITATIONS AND FUTURE WORK

The study carried out in this book has identified and discussed the problems with current tools and methods that are used for process mining. This book also studies how to resolve the different challenges particularly as it concerns the semantics aspects that the process mining techniques lack. For this reason, this book has proposed a process mining approach that proves adequate and efficient for semantical analysis of the event logs and models. However, whilst the author believes that the proposed methods are practically suitable for mining any given process at a more conceptual level, there could also exist a number of limitations and threats to validity. For instance, whereas this book has introduced a set of descriptive framework and/or conceptual method of analysis to resolve the sets of identified problems and question that motivates the writing of this book; there could be potentially many ways to address those problems, or even, bigger areas that have not been yet addressed. This is owing to the fact that the semantic process mining is a new area within the process mining field, and there are not too many tools or algorithms that support such an approach currently in the literature. Therefore, we assume that this work is only an incentive and methodological road map to more robust and intensive research studies to come within the context of the semantic-based process mining.

Furthermore, the technique for semantically annotating and analysing the various domain processes that this book introduces; is one of the main important contributions of this book. Moreover, the method is capable of extracting conceptual information from the event logs and the resultant process models. Nonetheless, the correlation and integration of the main building blocks (i.e. annotated logs/models, ontology, and reasoner) that underlies the proposed method presumes that the work has presented a semantic-based process mining approach which can possibly be further re-introduced or extended in future works in a more resourceful way.

Perhaps, an additional limitation of the semantic-based approach as described in this book is that it appears to be a fusion theory which characteristically integrates the fuzzy model with other tools. However, we note that in many settings, the fuzzy models have proven to be ambiguous and characteristically contains a vast number of arc nodes which are disjointed via impounded nodes that are primitive in nature. Therefore, with the process models (fuzzy models) it may not be practically probable to extract a distinctive level of meaningful information about the process elements. Although, this work has shown that it is possible to improve the information values of such type of models to some greater extent by carefully integrating and tuning the semantics metrics that those models lack. Nevertheless, the process still appears to be a cumbersome task and does not guarantee or carry some form of threats to the validity of the resultant outcomes.

Moreover, another threat to the validity of this study is that there are no currently tools capable of directly converting the fuzzy models into some other process modelling formats or notation. In consequence, the work leverages a varied range of events log conversion in order to achieve the different viewpoints about the process domains. Actually, future works could focus on extending the method (fuzzy models) through the provision of tools capable of automatically integrating the aforementioned features or metrics with the fuzzy models to support their analysis at a more abstraction level, and better still, guarantee the accuracy of the results and/or re-modelling of the siad processes. Interestingly, this work has shown that a way to resolve those problems is to provide the option for specifying semantics which in turn is capable of allowing for a value-added (well-structured) and precise format for the models.

Finally, the experiments and research conducted during the time of writing this book reveals that there is a lot of opportunities for future works especially as it concerns the adoption and/or extension of the proposed method of this book. Notably, a worthwhile extension will be to complement the method with a platform for completely automatic discovering and/or integration of the semantic information within the process models. Moreover, the semantic-based approach presented in this book appears to be one of the many methods for process and information management/processing in the current literature that can be utilized to analyse event logs, and as a result, derive meaningful models that can be used to describe the different process domains. Obviously, there are several directions towards which the outcomes and proposals of this book can be improved or further extended in the future. Future works can adopt the proposed approach (e.g. the semantic fuzzy miner) to analyse data extracts from any domain of interest or settings, including refinement of the realized process mining algorithms and framework that has already been developed in this book. For instance, future extensions may include a more pro-active technique for annotation of the events log and models, or higher technical description and application of the ontological schemas, in addition to provision of added features or functionalities to support the logical reasoning capabilities of the semantic process mining methods that have already been defined in this book.

To conclude the directions or road map for future extensions of this book; there are potentially a number of worthwhile areas to pursue in the future. For example, one of the future extensions could be to expound on the method to include and spread out to diverse organizations or business owners in their current operational systems or settings. Perhaps, this may also include the development of patent softwares or authoring tools that augments the stated achievements of this book.

REFERENCES

Okoye, K. (2018). Semantic-based Model Analysis towards Enhancing Information Values of Process Mining: Case Study of Learning Process Domain. *Proceedings of SoCPaR 2016 Conference*, 622-633. 10.1007/978-3-319-60618-7_61

Okoye, K., Islam, S., & Naeem, U. & Sharif, S. (2020). Semantic-based Process Mining Technique for Annotation and Modelling of Domain Processes. *International Journal of Innovative Computing, Information, & Control*.

Okoye, K., Naeem, U., & Islam, S. (2017). Semantic Fuzzy Mining: Enhancement of process models and event logs analysis from Syntactic to Conceptual Level. *International Journal of Hybrid Intelligent Systems*, *14*(1-2), 67–98. doi:10.3233/HIS-170243

Okoye, K., Tawil, A. R. H., Naeem, U., & Lamine, E. (2016). A Semantic Reasoning Method Towards Ontological Model for Automated Learning Analysis. *Proceedings of NaBIC Conference*, 49-60. 10.1007/978-3-319-27400-3_5

Van der Aalst, W. M. P. (2016). *Process Mining: Data Science in Action* (2nd ed.). Berlin: Springer-Verlag. doi:10.1007/978-3-662-49851-4

Index

Ensure Quality Research is Introduced to the Academic Community

Become an IGI Global Reviewer for Authored Book Projects

Premier Reference Source

Emerging GIS Applications for Emergency and Disaster Management

Premier Reference Source

Managerial Strategies and Green Solutions for Project Sustainability

Premier Reference Source

Comparative Approaches to Using R and Python for Statistical Data Analysis

Premier Reference Source

Solutions for High-Touch Communications in a High-Tech World

The overall success of an authored book project is dependent on quality and timely reviews.

In this competitive age of scholarly publishing, constructive and timely feedback significantly expedites the turnaround time of manuscripts from submission to acceptance, allowing the publication and discovery of forward-thinking research at a much more expeditious rate. Several IGI Global authored book projects are currently seeking highly-qualified experts in the field to fill vacancies on their respective editorial review boards:

Applications and Inquiries may be sent to:
development@igi-global.com

Applicants must have a doctorate (or an equivalent degree) as well as publishing and reviewing experience. Reviewers are asked to complete the open-ended evaluation questions with as much detail as possible in a timely, collegial, and constructive manner. All reviewers' tenures run for one-year terms on the editorial review boards and are expected to complete at least three reviews per term. Upon successful completion of this term, reviewers can be considered for an additional term.

If you have a colleague that may be interested in this opportunity, we encourage you to share this information with them.

Printed in the United States
By Bookmasters